# Leading Schools During Crisis

## What School Administrators Must Know

MATTHEW J. PEPPER,
TIM D. LONDON,
MIKE L. DISHMAN, AND
JESSICA L. LEWIS

Published in partnership with the
American Association of School Administrators

ROWMAN & LITTLEFIELD EDUCATION
A Division of
ROWMAN & LITTLEFIELD PUBLISHERS, INC.
*Lanham* • *New York* • *Toronto* • *Plymouth, UK*

Published in partnership with the American Association of School Administrators

Published by Rowman & Littlefield Education
A division of Rowman & Littlefield Publishers, Inc.
A wholly owned subsidiary of The Rowman & Littlefield Publishing Group, Inc.
4501 Forbes Boulevard, Suite 200, Lanham, Maryland 20706
www.rowmaneducation.com

Estover Road, Plymouth PL6 7PY, United Kingdom

British Library Cataloguing in Publication Information Available

**Library of Congress Cataloging-in-Publication Data**
Leading schools during crisis : what school administrators must know / Matthew J. Pepper . . . [et al.].
    p. cm.
  "Published in partnership with the American Association of School Administrators."
  ISBN 978-1-60709-343-5 (cloth : alk. paper) — ISBN 978-1-60709-344-2 (pbk. : alk. paper)
  — ISBN 978-1-60709-345-9 (electronic)
  1. School crisis management—United States—Case studies. I. Pepper, Matthew J., 1977– II.
American Association of School Administrators.
  LB2866.5.L43 2010
  371.2'07—dc22                                                                2009029552

∞™ The paper used in this publication meets the minimum requirements of American National
Standard for Information Sciences—Permanence of Paper for Printed Library Materials, ANSI/NISO
Z39.48-1992.

Printed in the United States of America

# Contents

### Internal-Unpredictable

### Internal-Predictable

### External-Predictable

# Foreword

It is difficult for a school to shelter itself from the threat of crisis. Some schools may enjoy relatively long periods of time without having to confront a crisis, but no school is immune. As I write this foreword in the winter of 2009, the United States as a nation is confronting a financial crisis of unknown, but clearly momentous, proportions. Every institution of our society is being challenged, and the depths of those challenges remain to be seen. K–12 schools are no exception. As budget shortfalls mount, every school leader will be challenged to keep their school effective. Schools are in for hard times. How will school leaders manage these crises? I predict that school leaders who study this volume will be more successful than those who don't.

*Leading Schools During Crisis* is written for practicing or aspiring education leaders—school leaders, superintendents, and school board members. The authors offer a simple but useful typology for organizing the cases, applying it as a lens to twelve school crises faced by school leaders. The authors' approach is analytic yet pragmatic, and the lessons to be learned are timely and powerful. They culminate in an ultimate message that an ounce of preparedness is worth a pound of response. In the dozen cases examined, each school administrator successfully managing a crisis was ready—even for the unpredicted. Forecasting and minimizing the unpredictable is a proven strategy to employ in dealing with crisis. Toward that end, this book should go a long way.

The book offers the first theoretical definition of what constitutes crisis in a school environment, recognizing that "crisis" is often overused in education. Admittedly, what seems like a crisis to some may not be to others; however, each of the cases considered is clearly an example of a major threat to a school's functioning. School leaders must be able to manage crises so that their school continues to focus on the core mission of student achievement. The twelve cases describe leaders who manage to accomplish exactly that. In their successes are powerful lessons from which the reader will profit.

Reflecting upon the principles for effective crisis management in schools, I could not but note the similarities between these six principles and the effective-schools "formula" put forward by Wilbur Bookover, Ron Edmunds, and Larry Lezotte at Michigan State University in the 1970s. An effective school begins with clear and shared goals. An effective school has a strong leader and, certainly, one who uses all six principles as his or her road map.

Perhaps not surprisingly, the authors find that a school leader that successfully deals with a crisis has already built a strong school with established routines and an internal professional community, where respect is common both among and between teachers, students, administrators, and a community beyond the school.

Another principle is to stay focused. The veteran administrators in the twelve cases were not distracted, nor were their efforts diffused by the challenges of the crisis. Perhaps because they had already made substantial progress toward building a strong school with emerging or already robust internal and external communities and because of their commitment to the core mission of schooling, they were able to stay focused even in the face of potential disaster.

The fourth principle is effective communication. Successful leaders in any sector know that effective communication is key. Unfortunately, as the cases illustrate, effective communication is not easy, and it cannot begin amid a response to a crisis. No matter how good you are as a leader and no matter how effective your organization, communication can be improved. I hazard to say that building a strong school with strong internal and external communities would be impossible without effective communication.

Principles five and six demonstrate that school administrators who deal effectively with crisis are both resourceful and steadfast. Like communication, these are attributes of successful administrators whether or not they are facing crisis, but they are even more important in the face of crisis.

The book ends exactly where it should. In crisis, there are problems that must be confronted, but there are also opportunities to bring your school to a whole new level of effective functioning. Change requires leverage and crisis demands change. The case studies move the reader from general principles to practical solutions and from those practical solutions back to the principles. In this way, the authors accomplish the "Holy Grail" of connecting research and practice.

A. Porter
February 2, 2009

*Andrew Porter is the George and Diane Weiss Professor of Education and Dean of the Graduate School of Education, University of Pennsylvania. Previously, he served as the Patricia and Rhodes Hart Professor of Leadership, Policy, and Organization at Peabody College of Vanderbilt University. Dr. Porter is also past president of the American Educational Research Association.*

# Preface

## Leading Schools During Crisis

*Operating a large, complex, and often aging facility with inadequate support.*

*Overseeing a multi-million-dollar budget subjected to rigorous and frequent audits.*

*Fostering the professionalism, collegiality, and personal needs of numerous adults in a high-stress environment, with limited control of salaries, hiring, and firing.*

*Maintaining curricular rigor in a high-stakes accountability environment.*

*Being ultimately responsible for the education of hundreds, if not thousands, of students with increasingly complex instructional demands.*

*Welcome to educational leadership.*

The demands on school leaders are substantial. In the twenty-first century, school leaders are expected to lead complex organizations, be experts in fields ranging from finance to instruction to special education, and deftly handle the needs and concerns of parents, teachers, staff, students, the district office, and the wider community. In short, school leaders may find themselves managing a multi-million-dollar facility with a hundred or more staff while leading human learning and development for thousands of students. Leaders are expected to achieve these goals in a highly regulated industry with widely varying quality and quantity of training and support.

Given the extraordinary complexity of the organizations school leaders serve, each day brings a new set of problems and challenges to a principal's doorstep. Usually, the scope of these challenges will be manageable. Candidate interviews bring in new hires, special education meetings determine appropriate instructional interventions for students, and community meetings communicate policy changes to school stakeholders.

However, the unfortunate reality for school leaders is that more substantial problems occasionally surpass these less exceptional mishaps—events so potentially damaging to a school's core values and foundational practices that they rise to the level of a *crisis*. As with any major school issue, the successful management of a crisis depends on the preparation and involvement of a school's leader. We hope that the lessons contained within this book help school leaders prevent the onset of crisis, lead a school in the midst of a crisis, and recover from the crisis.

The "modern" systematic study of crisis preparation, management, and response grew from the study of Johnson and Johnson's response to cyanide being found in Tylenol in 1982.[1] Since then, significant study has been devoted to the consideration of crises in business and management. However, few studies have considered crises in the context of public education. This work synthesizes and applies crisis literature in the American school context, proposing—for the first time—a definition of crisis in education. It also presents a theoretical lens through which subsequent case studies on crisis events in the education sector can be more deeply understood.

This theoretical framework is overlaid onto twelve case studies, following past and present school leaders enduring crises in their own schools. Each case study offers a detailed description of the circumstances prior to the crisis, the origins of the crisis, leadership in the midst of crisis, and recovery efforts and organizational learning. The individuals profiled understand that learning occurs by examining both appropriate and imperfect actions. This is not a book about "superheroes," but rather veterans whose experiences offer opportunities for learning.

The case studies presented in this book serve as learning tools for current and aspiring leaders—they are not intended as step-by-step instructions for individuals experiencing similar challenges to the profiled leaders. While an educational leader facing a similar crisis profiled in this book may not follow the exact methods discussed in a particular case study, he or she will recognize similarities to his or her organizational resources and constraints, implementing similar strategies to the extent that the experiences of the interviewees resonate with him or her. Most importantly perhaps, these case studies are intended to assist the reader to recognize within his or her school community the capacity to overcome crisis. Toward this goal, each chapter ends with a number of reflective questions to help the reader apply the lessons of the case study to his or her leadership context.

The book concludes by synthesizing the common lessons learned from the case studies, exploring the following six primary principles for leadership during crisis:

Principle 1: Respond to a Crisis Before It Becomes One

Principle 2: Identify Truly Immediate Priorities

Principle 3: Let Time, Efforts, and Resources Flow in Proportion to Your Prioritization

Principle 4: Communicate, Communicate, Communicate

Principle 5: Be Flexible

Principle 6: Do Not Personally Succumb to the Crisis

The appendix then provides a set of global questions and exercises that school leaders can use to reflect on their own school's preparation and capacity to overcome crisis.

The theory presented in chapter 1 and applied through the twelve case studies is designed to be complementary. However, the authors recognize that not all readers are interested in a detailed discussion of theory in chapter 1. Readers wanting a less complete coverage of theory are encouraged to focus on chapter 1's section 4 (The Dimensions of School Crisis) and figure 1.1 (Model of Leading Schools During Crisis), using their time to review case studies of interest and the concluding chapter. Ultimately, the authors hope this book offers current and aspiring school leaders the tools and reflective opportunity to better prepare themselves and their school communities to avoid crises. If they cannot be avoided it is the authors' hope that school leaders during crisis will, in the words of William Faulkner (1950), "not merely endure . . . but prevail."[2]

# Acknowledgments

Writing this book has been exceptionally challenging and rewarding. We are proud of what we have produced, but we are also very cognizant that we could not have completed this project without the guidance, help, and support of many people. Tom Koerner at Rowman & Littlefield Education originally approved and served as a sounding board for this project, and Professor Joseph Murphy helped shape our original idea into a working model. Their assistance is greatly appreciated.

As we progressed, we received helpful feedback on the book's content and layout from Dave Laurance, Marisa Houghland, and numerous educators and family members. The final product is significantly improved through their insights. We also benefitted from graphic design assistance from Kathryn McBurney and Emily Lytle. The case study on P.S. 234 was bolstered with content from interviews originally conducted by Linnae Hamilton of Mighty Media, Inc. We also thank our copyeditor, Laura Dewey, for the improvements she made.

While finalizing the content, the authors received wonderful input from our reviewers, including Gene Hollenberg, director of High School Programs, South Bend Community School Corporation, Anna Switzer, former principal of P.S. 234, New York City Schools, and Molly Howard, 2008 National High School Principal of the Year. Additionally, the AASA Publication Review Board provided valuable and thoughtful recommendations, particularly on the design of the reflective questions closing each case study. Finally, a special thanks to Dr. Andrew Porter, George and Diane Weiss Professor of Education and Dean of the Graduate School of Education, University of Pennsylvania, for agreeing to write the book's foreword—we could not ask for a better endorsement of this work.

Our families and friends have been gracious and understanding throughout two years of evenings and weekends dedicated to the book's production. Our "significant others" deserve particular gratitude—thank you to Traci, Hi, and Tracy.

And finally, we deeply acknowledge the time, effort, and experiences of the individuals who consented to having their experiences included in this work. These include (in order of their appearance):

Anna Switzer, former principal of P.S. 234, New York City, New York

Dr. Vanessa Eugene, principal of G.W. Carver High School for the Arts, New Orleans, Louisiana

Bryan Krause, former principal of Platte Canyon High School, Bailey, Colorado

Sharon Birnkrant, principal of H.W. Smith K–8 School, Syracuse, New York

Craig Martin, assistant principal of H.W. Smith K–8 School, Syracuse, New York

Laureen Lane, assistant principal of H.W. Smith K–8 School, Syracuse, New York

Dr. Sallie Pinkston, principal of James Weldon Johnson Elementary School, Chicago, Illinois

Marco Franco, principal of Sobrante Park Elementary School, Oakland, California

Santo Nicotera, former assistant director of the Reform Initiative, Manual High School, Denver, Colorado

ACKNOWLEDGMENTS                                                        xix

Dr. Nancy Sutton, former principal of Manual High School, Denver, Colorado

Jeremy Kane, school director, LEAD Academy Charter School, Nashville, Tennessee

William Grimm, former principal, Franklin Career Academy, Franklin, New Hampshire

Dr. Noris Price, associate superintendent, Clarke County School District, Athens, Georgia

Barry Fried, principal, John Dewey High School, Brooklyn, New York

Your dedication to your students, your staff, and your community serves as the inspiration for this book. Your willingness to share your learning experiences with others made this book possible.

# 1

# Understanding Leadership During Crisis

## Moving from Common Notions of Crisis Toward a School Context

Educational leaders often encounter dilemmas of significance, whether financial or human resource constraints, unmotivated or disengaged students or parents, or seemingly unrealistic accountability measures. What is less prevalent, but potentially catastrophic to school leaders, is encountering a true *crisis* within their schools. Such critical circumstances not only undermine a school's well-being (and sometimes its very existence), but threaten to derail its core function of teaching and learning. It is these moments of crisis that this book addresses, not merely recounting stories of significant achievement, but providing a learning tool for current and future education leaders.

While every school's situation is unique, schools in crisis share certain commonalities from which lessons can be drawn. To fully appreciate these lessons, any meaningful study of school leaders' encounters with crises should be grounded in a thorough, multidisciplinary review of relevant research and theory. Unfortunately, there is limited research on crises in the field of education, and virtually all of it is limited to school violence, which, while catastrophic, is only *one type* of school crisis.

By contrast, the field of management has developed an extensive literature focused on the preparation for, and response to, multiple types of crises within organizations. While a school operates under a different set of assumptions, goals, and constraints than most for-profit and nonprofit businesses, components of this literature are certainly applicable to the educational environment.

1

The goal of this chapter is to modify the organizational lessons drawn from management literature, applying them to the context of twenty-first-century education. Its secondary purpose is to establish the theoretical framework facilitating a more robust learning experience from the case studies in succeeding chapters.

Section 1 of this chapter provides an overview of the organizational and management approach to crisis. Section 2 discusses how the organizational contexts of service industries, in which K–12 schools fall, increase the probability of a crisis. Section 3 proposes a definition of crises within schools. Section 4 provides a two-dimensional typology of educational crises, further framing the case studies in the book. Section 5 closes the chapter by investigating the essential role of leadership during crisis.

## SECTION 1: CRISIS MANAGEMENT FROM A BUSINESS PERSPECTIVE

Since the Tylenol poisoning crisis of 1982, crisis management and response has been a "hot" topic in business literature. The current economic crisis (as of this writing) is providing additional opportunities for management experts to consider and refine the study of organizational crisis, with such business stalwarts as *Harvard Business Review* and *Fortune* magazine promising to help readers "capitalize" on crisis. Crisis analyses frequently concentrate on a particular theme, such as the importance of training public relations staff to communicate quickly and honestly, or the pre-crisis preparation of a particular business and how it minimized the impact of a crisis.[1] However, some critics of current crisis research believe the scholarship on crises has been somewhat disjointed. They suggest it is difficult for a true definition of crisis and response to emerge as crisis analyses are so dependent upon the context in which they occur—how can, for example, a business crisis arising from international price controls inform how a hospital emergency room handles triage?[2]

Researchers have attempted to bring order to the process by categorizing crises. Mitroff, for example, utilizes seven broad categories: economic, natural disaster, informational, physical, human resource, psychopathic acts, and reputation-related.[3] Other scholars have described crises along a number of dimensions, including their type, intensity, scope, frequency of reoccurrence, and duration. Each dimension is then explored, such as the duration of a crisis, or the length of time the initial and secondary effects of a crisis affect an organization.[4] At times, the varying conceptions of how to best identify and respond to a crisis have led to disagreement about the ultimate question—what, exactly, is a crisis? Current crisis research proposes an assortment of definitions, including:

- A disruption that physically affects a system as a whole and threatens its basic assumptions, its subjective sense of self, and its existential core.[5]
- A major occurrence with a potentially negative outcome affecting an organization, company, or industry, as well as its publics, products, services, or good name.[6]
- A low-probability, high-impact event that threatens the viability of the organization and is characterized by ambiguity of cause, effect, and means of resolution as well as by a belief that decisions must be made swiftly.[7]
- An extraordinary condition that is disruptive and damaging to the existing operating state of an organization.[8]
- A serious threat to the basic structure or fundamental values and norms of a system, which under time pressure and highly uncertain circumstances necessitates making vital decisions.[9]

These definitions were developed to broadly apply to organizational environments, though, as a result, they suffer from their generalized nature. The contexts of K–12 American education provide a unique set of organizational pressures and constraints, and we believe any definition of a "crisis" in schools must be specific to this unique context.

## SECTION 2: THE CONTEXT OF TWENTY-FIRST-CENTURY SCHOOLS

Denis Smith, a researcher whose work has focused on crisis, contends that the service sector (which includes education) is distinctly vulnerable to crises. Smith observes that human-driven and -dependent service organizations are (1) shaped by the cultural and organizational dynamics of internal stakeholders and surrounding communities, (2) labor intensive, (3) continuously engaged with consumer groups, and (4) often increasing in scale of operation over time.[10]

These characteristics strongly correspond with K–12 education. Perhaps even more than other service organizations, schools depend almost entirely upon "human" resources—with their attendant variability and inconsistency— for the complex work of educating students. Moreover, unlike other types of service organizations in the last two decades, education has been minimally impacted by technology, and it is unlikely that technology will ever supplant the human element required in teaching students.[11] The extensive human element in American schools is not a challenge simply because so many people are involved. The growing diversity of communities and the ever-evolving expectations of schools make high-quality, consistent education a more daunting task.

Unlike a traditional "bottom line" business orientation, stakeholders in public education are motivated by a unique balance of intrinsic and extrinsic incentives rarely seen outside education. Extending this, many educators, policymakers, and advocates widely disagree on the purpose of schooling, and even what constitutes a "good" school. One of the few commonalities in crisis research is that organizational systems built almost entirely around humans (and particularly humans lacking a common unifying vision or purpose) create an environment ripe for crisis.

Further contributing to the complexity of addressing crises in schools is the nature of school governance, which has been described as a "fragmented, complex, multi-layered educational policy system" with control of various aspects dispersed between the district, state, and federal levels.[12] Unlike business organizations that constantly emphasize market adaptability, schools continue to epitomize slow-changing and reactive organizations. As a result, the political structures surrounding the education system often have overlapping authority and misaligned accountability.

Within this immensely complicated organizational structure, schools must contend with the cultural dynamics of its internal stakeholders (e.g., students, families, teachers) as well as its external ones (e.g., policymakers, business leaders), including such issues of immigration, mainstreaming/inclusion, and encroaching federalism. In concert, these forces create unclear—and potentially contradictory—lines of authority, strain organizational stability, and create many potential sources of crisis and limitations on crisis planning and response.[13]

Ultimately, schools are not business organizations, and their highly regulated and politically sensitive organizational structures are far more convoluted than clear. Therefore, schools require a crisis theory addressing the unique environment in which they exist.

## SECTION 3: MOVING FROM COMMON NOTIONS OF CRISIS TO A SCHOOL CONTEXT

Building on existing crisis literature and the operational content of schools, this section suggests a definition of the term *crisis* within schools. This is a difficult task owing to the trend by media to label virtually every problem occurring in schools as a "crisis." Instructively, a set of interviews with nine principals showed significant disagreement even among career-educators on when a situation evolves from a problem into a crisis.[14] While an educational leader will be confronted with numerous challenges during his or her career, the focus of this book is solely on those critical events moving *beyond* a challenging circumstance— that is, on events of crisis.

Unfortunately, existing perceptions on crises within schools often take one of two flawed approaches. The first, seen primarily in the popular press, considers schools to be in a permanent state of crisis, with dire predictions for society due to schools' failings. This is hardly new—as William Boyd and Robert Crowson noted in 1981 (two years before the publication of *A Nation at Risk*), the history of American schooling is an unbroken movement from one perceived "crisis" to another.[15] The most current manifestation—the performance "crisis"—presents low-achieving students, incompetent teachers, disinterested parents, and international comparisons showing a U.S. educational ranking well below average.

It could certainly be argued that the national "failure" of American high school students to score as highly on international mathematics examinations as their Korean counterparts is a challenge; however, it is unlikely to lead to a particular school's being unable to continue operation, and thus not a *school* crisis. While there are similarly authentic challenges in schools across the country, such general statements are primarily intended to bring attention to a subject (or sell magazines) and do not contribute to a true awareness of *crisis*.

This misperception and over-identification has devolved to the school site, leading to school leaders' labeling *every* problem as a crisis. This is the middle school leader constantly rushing through the hallways during his entire day, proverbially putting out fires, the high school principal addressing a booster club revolt over dissatisfaction with coaching decisions, or an elementary school principal discovering that a second grader who was supposed to be in an after-school program got on the school bus and was dropped off at an empty home. While such events are certainly *challenges*, the preponderance of problems a leader will encounter during his or her career will be just that—problems. For this work, the distinction between a crisis and a problem is determinably important.

These misidentifications of challenges as crises can have significant effects. As our model suggests, perhaps the best way to avoid a crisis is early identification of crisis indicators and appropriate response; mislabeling virtually every problem occurring in public schools as a "crisis" results in a numbing, "crying wolf" effect. It becomes difficult for school stakeholders to perceive and respond to *actual* crises because they have become desensitized by application of the term to non-crisis events.

The second flaw of the present treatment of crises within education is diametrically opposed to the first—it is the limitation of crisis to severe acts of violence, natural disasters, or other threats to the physical well-being of a school's students, staff, or facilities.[16] Physical safety is an obviously crucial issue, but this narrow conception overlooks the other crises that threaten the core foundation of schools. Loss of financial capacity, dramatically shifting student enrollments, or severe high-stakes accountability sanctions pose just as real a threat to the viability of a school as arson or a shooting incident. By utilizing theory from existing crisis literature, this book distinguishes crises from challenges, contemporaneously broadening the scope of crises beyond the common "threat to student safety" approach.

We propose a three-part, unified theory of crisis within education. The first of these—*a school crisis is an event or series of events that threaten a school's core values or foundational practices*—prevents the over-identification of every problem as a crisis. The second—*a school crisis is obvious in its manifestation, but born from complex and often unclear or uncontainable circumstances*—recognizes that the origins of school crises may arise from multifaceted sources. The third—*a school crisis necessitates urgent decision-making*—incorporates the decision-making required to address the crisis, often without sufficient information or resources. These three definitional components are further explored below.

**1) A School Crisis is an Event or Series of Events That Threaten a School's Core Values or Foundational Practices.**

A crisis threatens the core foundation of a school's being, not peripheral features of the school's operation. This distinguishes crisis events from the more common problems faced by school leaders. Existing school organizations can readily handle challenges that do not rise to the level of crises. While challenging, schools have evolved structures, roles, policies, standardized forms of communication, and formalized relations to sustain themselves through problems.[17] By contrast, crisis events *overwhelm* these structures, which are not designed to address them, and even the best-formulated strategies cannot wholly prevent or contain them.

A teacher habitually calling in sick may present a logistical challenge, but a school annually replacing 60 percent of its teaching staff is a crisis. A decline in yearly performance on state standardized tests among a single student subgroup is a problem, but failing to meet "adequate yearly progress" for the fifth consecutive school year and facing closure or "restructuring" is a crisis. What unites crises—and distinguishes them from challenges—is the extent to which crises threaten the core foundations of the school. While crisis events may dismantle the core operation of schools with great speed or slowly erode it, the end result is the same—the school cannot continue its foundational practices of teaching and learning.

This element of a school crisis requires identification of a school's "core values" and foundational practices. These include underlying assumptions guiding a school's policies, actions, interactions, and inactions. It is the school's "culture," value system, pervading professional practice, all reinforced and replicated by faculty, parents, and students. It is, quite simply, how the majority of stakeholders would describe their school if asked to do so. As seen in chapter 13, John Dewey High School's belief in an autonomous, intellectually driven student body is an example of a school's core value, as was Woodland Elementary School's focus on pervasive parental involvement (see chapter 12).

The applications of a school's core values are its foundational practices, or the daily organizational and behavioral manifestations of a school's core values. These may include innovative instructional models, a professional learning community, or a very supportive set of parent-teacher relationships. Simply put, the core values of a school are its belief system, and the foundational practices of a school are the routines that implement this belief system.

**2) A School Crisis Is Obvious in Its Manifestation but Born from Complex and Often Unclear or Uncontainable Circumstances.**

The second element of a school crisis is that while the crisis—after starting—is a clear threat to the school, it often results from a multitude of unanticipated and unforeseen factors. It is often only in hindsight that the root from which the crisis grew *may* become apparent. These circumstances may include politics, faculty demands, diverse community needs, and other external pressures. Schools must meet local, state, and federal expectations while constrained by the varying needs of staff, students, and their communities.

These overlapping pressures ensure that schools are continually threatened through a multitude of pathways, and that problems often have complex origins. A school might be immediately challenged by an influx of new and very different students (see Manual High School, chapter 9); however, the root of this problem is a controversial zoning change made by the school board motivated by a variety of inputs, including racial animosity, the future political ambitions of board members, and a business community concerned about a city's image. A gunman taking students hostage in a school classroom is clearly a crisis; however, his motivations for choosing this particular school and this specific classroom are not (see Platte Canyon High School, chapter 4).

The twelve case studies presented within this book are a reflection of the complexity of forces that interact with schools. Among the crises profiled are ones immediately based upon accountability pressures, demographic changes, teacher turnover, and the challenges of integrating an immigrant community. All of these individual, immediate pressures, however, have attached to them a complex, underlying set of organizational, legal, and political constraints that shape their manifestation.

### 3) A School Crisis Necessitates Urgent Decision-Making.

The final element of a crisis stems from the severity of potential consequences for a school's core foundation if a leader's response is deficient. The tremendous pressures involved in facing a crisis necessitate quick and decisive leadership, even when acting with imperfect information and under high-stakes circumstances. A crisis does not pause to permit empanelling a task force or building intergovernmental agency relationships facilitating crisis response. Unfortunately, the common response to crises is often a compilation of panic, uncertainty, defeatism, and melodrama. Instead, knowledge should be gathered quickly and distilled efficiently, and attacking the true source of the crisis should occur with determination and resolve. For example, nothing in Anna Switzer's professional training or experience prepared her to face the challenges of evacuating an elementary school amid the collapse of the World Trade Center.

## SECTION 4: THE DIMENSIONS OF SCHOOL CRISES

As crises are as unique as the school context in which they occur, no school crisis is identical. However, the crises examined in this book have been grouped in table 1.1 by common dimensions, permitting school leaders facing a potential or current crisis to identify the *origins* of their crisis and to compare their response to that of successful school leaders handling similar crises.

The first dimension—Internal or External—classifies the crisis's epicenter, identifying whether the crisis originates from a point internal or external to the immediate school community. A school's immediate community includes students, their families, teachers, and community groups dedicated primarily to the school (like a PTA or PTO). It excludes the broader policy and bureaucratic entities that may have a significant impact on the school but are outside a principal's immediate influence. These external sources of crisis may include a force with an agenda and constraints broader than the school community (such as a federal educational policy mandate), or may be acts wholly outside the school's control (such as a natural disaster or terrorist attack).

The second dimension identifies the extent to which crises can or should be foreseen by the school leader. Predictable crises are those in which an

**Table 1.1.  Origins of Crisis**

|  | PREDICTABLE | UNPREDICTABLE |
|---|---|---|
| | *Internal-Predictable Crises* | *Internal-Unpredictable Crises* |
| **INTERNAL** | 1. Major facility problems/construction<br>2. Faculty (strike, significant teacher turnover)<br>3. Leadership retirement | 1. Student violence<br>2. Student walk-out, text message threat<br>3. Sudden demographic transitions |
| | *External-Predictable Crises* | *External-Unpredictable Crises* |
| **EXTERNAL** | 1. Community economic<br>2. Immigrant influx<br>3. Massive budgetary cuts<br>4. Demographic zoning shifts<br>5. Accountability (NCLB takeover) | 1. Political (terrorism, war)<br>2. Public relations (sexual scandal, financial impropriety)<br>3. Natural disasters (earthquake, tsunami) |

*Adapted from Snyder, et al. (2006) ***

*Snyder, P. et al. (2006). Ethical responsibility: A strategic approach to organizational crisis. *Journal of Business Ethics, 63*, 371–83.

astute school leader would recognize the existence of early warning signs foretelling the impending arrival of a crisis. Such early warning signs allow for some preparation and mitigation of a crisis. An Unpredictable crisis, by contrast, is one lacking any warning indicators and one that no school leader could anticipate—such as the terrorist attack of 9/11 (see P.S. 234, chapter 2). However, as Norman Augustine notes, "Lacking control over the origin of a problem does not exempt you from living with its consequences."[18]

These two dimensions create four categories into which school crises fall. An Internal-Predictable crisis originates within a school and is associated with early warning signs, such as dissatisfaction among faculty (which may lead to a teacher strike) or dramatic restructuring of a school's leadership team (leading to a change in the school's culture). External-Unpredictable crises, such as a terrorist attack or natural disaster, arise without forewarning and may find the school completely unprepared to respond—owing both to the external locus of the event and its unexpected nature.[19]

Appropriately identifying crises may facilitate response—for example, school leaders facing Internal-Predictable crises generally have much greater ability to anticipate and authority to handle these crisis events than those arising from events beyond the school. Readers will immediately note that a disproportionate number of crises in this book arise from external sources, perhaps owing to the complex factors that constantly influence schools or because potential Internal crises are easier to avoid. The twelve crises considered in this book are categorized as in table 1.2.

**Table 1.2.   Twelve Case Studies: Leading Schools During Crisis**

|  | PREDICTABLE | UNPREDICTABLE |
|---|---|---|
| **INTERNAL** | *Internal-Predictable Crises* | *Internal-Unpredictable Crises* |
|  | Chapter 7: Permanent Teacher Turnover | Chapter 5: Systemic Grade Fraud<br>Chapter 6: Challenges of an ELL Population |
|  | *External-Predictable Crises* | *External-Unpredictable Crises* |
| **EXTERNAL** | Chapter 8: Accountability (NCLB)<br>Chapter 9: Demographic Transition<br>Chapter 10: Charter School Start-Up<br>Chapter 11: Charter School Finances<br>Chapter 12: Elementary School Zoning Changes<br>Chapter 13: High School Zoning Changes | Chapter 2: School at Ground Zero, 9/11<br>Chapter 3: High School after Hurricane Katrina<br>Chapter 4: School Violence |

## SECTION 5: LEADING SCHOOLS DURING CRISIS

When making high-stakes decisions during a volatile time in an organization, great responsibility falls on a leader to understand why a crisis emerges, how it will progress, and how to best resolve it.* Given the significance such a moment has for a leader, we introduce a model for leadership throughout the life cycle of a crisis. This model, presented in figure 1.1, brings together ideas about the evolution of crises and the strategies a leader should employ during its life cycle. This model—along with other important considerations of leadership during crisis—is explored through the remainder of this chapter.

Figure 1.1 categorizes crises using a two-dimensional typology, noting both the center of gravity and predictability of a crisis; however, where the life cycle of a crisis noticeably differs is along the Predictable-Unpredictable axis. By definition, the emergence of a Predictable crisis is preceded by early warning signs, such as testing data, research, or feedback from members of the school

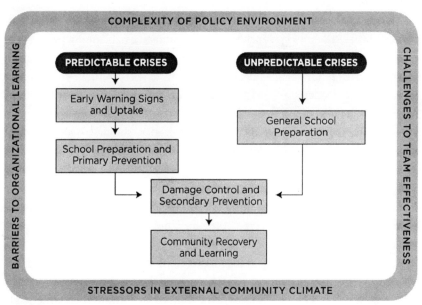

FIGURE 1.1.
Crisis Leadership Model

---

*"Leadership" is conceptualized singularly through this book—embodied as a school principal—however, the authors recognize that some schools are led by a collaborative team, with teacher leaders, counselors, and assistant principals each contributing in ways described in this chapter.

or the outside community. These "early warning" signs are of value only to the extent that a school leader has a systematic process to gather feedback from data sources and stakeholders.[20]

Crisis-astute school leaders have multiple uptake systems in place—formative, summative, and through strategic relationships inside and outside the immediate school community—warning leaders of the variety of crises to which they are vulnerable. The more cultivated and widespread the information uptake measures, the greater a leader's likelihood of detecting the onset of a crisis.

Immediately following detection of the signs of a Predictable crisis, a leader should employ primary prevention strategies, thereby strengthening an organization's resilience and hopefully preventing a crisis from developing (or at the very least, minimizing its damage).[21] The steps utilized will be context-specific and may include additional professional development, meetings with district leadership, parent communication, and/or curricular or scheduling modifications.

During the "school preparation" and "primary prevention" phases of Predictable crises, a school leader should begin strategically planning methods to respond to a crisis. As Harvard Business School professor Abraham Zaleznik asserts, "When it ain't broke may be the only time you can fix it."[22] These two phases require leaders to forecast the best way to respond to potential crises by predicting how the crisis may develop and what the probable consequences are of its occurrence. During this discussion, leaders should involve multiple stakeholders, formulating probable responses and identifying available resources. Ideally, these "pre-crisis" discussions will increase awareness among stakeholders for potential signs of crisis.

Whereas in a Predictable crisis a school leader can identify early warning signs and prepare for the specific crisis, an Unpredictable crisis—by its very nature—does not present such opportunities. A leader facing an Unpredictable crisis may know nothing of the forthcoming threat (such as 9/11 or Hurricane Katrina; see chapters 2 and 3). Despite this, organizational strength remains the best predictor for whether an organization will successfully surmount a crisis. In reflecting upon the success of her faculty and staff in handling the crisis that occurred at their school a few blocks from "Ground Zero" on 9/11, P.S. 234 principal Anna Switzer remarked, "You can only be the school on the day of the crisis that you were the day before a crisis."

Successful responses to Unpredictable crises turn on the degree to which the school community has built trusting, empowering relationships between the principal, teachers, parents, and the larger community; the degree to which the school has practiced or experienced a similar crisis; and whether the school's leader has leverage to ensure adequate district attention and resources during the crisis.

One of the most important components of general school preparation is forecasting and practicing organizational response to a potential crisis. For school violence incidents, this might include annually practicing a school-wide lockdown and building a relationship between school resource officers and students.[23] Overall, honest conversations regarding the mission of the school, opportunities for distributive leadership, and active outreach projects can be utilized by leaders to strengthen their school's resiliency in preparation for an Unpredictable crisis.

After the preparation and prevention phases, the cycle for both Predictable and Unpredictable crises converges at the phase of damage control (often called "secondary prevention").[24] This is the phase in which the crisis occurs, and a school attempts to restrain the intensity and scope of its damaging impact. Crisis scholars have found that damage can be limited when the responsibility for containment is distributed throughout multiple levels of an organization rather than isolated at the top of the organizational hierarchy.[25]

Depending upon the nature of the crisis, a leader might consider how to best utilize the power of external communication networks during and after crisis.[26] At LEAD Academy (see chapter 10), Jeremy Kane made extensive use of media contacts to bring public attention to what he believed was intentional bureaucratic "sandbagging" to prevent LEAD Academy from opening. By contrast, in Platte Canyon, Bryan Krause saw the media as adversarial and sought to protect his students and their families from media intrusion into their private grief (see chapter 4).

Communication can be handled in many ways, including traditional press briefings, meetings, newsletters, and nontraditional vehicles (websites, blogs, and "calling trees"). When utilized, communication should be aimed at addressing both those immediately impacted and those who have an indirect relationship with the school or crisis. While many school leaders may have the instinctual reaction to avoid media coverage, the media can be a powerful tool to ensure that the school's version of a particular story is heard, limiting potential misinformation. In crises of higher magnitudes, the media is guaranteed to be involved, so the challenge becomes using the media as an effective partner in damage control.

The final phase of a crisis's life cycle is recovery and learning. This phase should not be viewed as simply a time of recuperation and picking up the pieces but, more importantly, a time for learning and reevaluation.[27] The recovery and learning process—if successful—should help the school community derive some positive meaning from the crisis, decreasing the likelihood of the crisis repeating.[28] It is also during these periods filled with anger, confusion, anxiety, and uncertainty that great opportunities exist for healing and growth. Increasing one's community support can be a positive, unexpected consequence of a school crisis. Many of the leaders profiled in the following case studies describe a remarkable and enduring bond formed between themselves and school stakeholders through the recovery from a crisis.

Importantly, school crises do not occur in isolation but are constantly entangled with external forces so prevalent in public education. The four forces literally and figuratively framing a crisis's life cycle are barriers to organizational learning, impediments to team effectiveness, complexity of policy environment, and stressors in external community climate. Impediments to organizational learning in schools can include the rigidity of core beliefs and assumptions, little collaboration or participation within the school or with its community, and a lack of a unified vision or culture.[29] Additionally, the oft-described "egg-crate" structure of schooling, the lack of time, and shifting organizational expectations may prevent the teamwork necessary for successful crisis resolution.[30] Finally, schools must abide by a wide array of overlapping and sometimes contradictory federal, state, and local laws (complexity of policy environment) while satisfying a broad community of stakeholders (stressors in external community climate). These four constant pressures create the context in which a crisis will operate, and they will therefore interact and influence it throughout its life cycle.

The life cycle of a crisis illustrated in figure 1.1 provides a general reference for school leaders when encountering a crisis. These principles cannot provide the school-specific nuances so important to successfully leading a school in crisis. Accordingly, the remainder of this book will present a series of case studies that offer real-life examples of school leaders in crisis. Each case study closes with reflective questions in order to apply its lessons to the reader's leadership context. Through these case studies, the details of crisis leadership become more evident and provide greater clarity about how to successfully navigate the breadth of crises that can readily arise within the field of education.

# EXTERNAL-UNPREDICTABLE

**2**

# "The Birds Were on Fire"

## *How Manhattan's P.S. 234 Functioned on 9/11*

**OVERVIEW**

The attacks of September 11, 2001, transformed America as certainly as those of December 7, 1941. While this event impacted the entire nation, New York City felt it most directly. The $30 billion in property damages was staggering, but the psychological cost to the adults and children of New York City living through the events of that day defy ready calculation. One individual at the epicenter of this ordeal—a person with the responsibility of protecting not only herself, but the staff and hundreds of young students of an entire elementary school—was Anna Switzer, principal of New York Public School 234. Significantly, P.S. 234 is approximately four hundred yards away from what is now known as "Ground Zero."

Leading her staff and students to physical safety was only the first part of Principal Switzer's journey. The attacks rendered the buildings of P.S. 234 unusable for six months. When classes resumed three days after the attack, they were initially held in another school that was already at full capacity. Teachers and students struggled with the new classroom density, and Principal Switzer strove to be an effective leader from her new, displaced position. After three weeks, P.S. 234 moved to another temporary location where they could again begin to address the emotional and psychological challenges resulting from the attacks. On February 4, 2003, P.S. 234 returned to its original home. The attacks of 9/11 occurred within a few hours, but the devastating effects impacted the staff and families of P.S. 234 for years afterward.

This case study is a prototype External-Unpredictable crisis—there is no way that Principal Switzer could have specifically anticipated and prepared for the terrorist attacks of September 11. However, Switzer's crisis involved much more than surviving a terrorist attack and losing a school building. In the immediate moment of crisis, she was quickly forced to devise a plan to evacuate the building, communicate with the district office and parents, make crucial decisions with imperfect information amid uncertainty and chaos, and ensure a safe transfer of elementary-age students to another school. In the following months, the crisis compelled her to relocate and restart the school several times, develop a support system for posttraumatic mental health issues, and meet both the academic and social needs of students and families.

**CASE NARRATIVE**

On September 10, 2001, the thirty-seven teachers of New York's P.S. 234 served 620 students in grades pre-kindergarten through fifth grade. Located in lower Manhattan in the Battery Park City neighborhood, the school is four hundred yards from Ground Zero. Principal Anna Switzer describes her school as "a pretty middle-class [to] upper-middle-class community, and a middle-class teaching staff, and [had] a lot of things in place . . . we did have a lot of resources." Overall, 72 percent of students were white, 12 percent were Asian/Pacific Islander, 11 percent were black, and 6 percent were Hispanic. Of those students, approximately 10 percent qualified for free or reduced-price meal services.[1]

Demographically, P.S. 234 was an anomaly in the New York City public school system, whose 1.1 million students and 1,400 schools are more representative of the city's diversity—39 percent Hispanic, 32 percent black, 14 percent white, 13 percent Asian/Pacific Islander/Filipino, and 2 percent from other racial groups. Supporting the nation's largest school district requires a bureaucracy split into forty-two districts and an annual operating budget of close to $17 billion.[2]

The principal of P.S. 234 for ten years as of 2001, Anna Switzer helped to build a school culture valuing input from parents and staff—"a system that worked [both] top-down and up-from-the-bottom"—focusing on remaining positive and ensuring the school did "not [have] an atmosphere where it was considered culturally acceptable to be truly negative about students." The relationship between the school administrators and staff was also strong, built on ten years of mutual trust and respect. In describing her relationship with her teachers, she says that

> it was a combination of consensual decision making, but with very strong leadership. I never went into a staff meeting where I didn't have an agenda, and I never came out of a staff meeting where the decisions we made were exactly what I [had] anticipated. With staff input, there was always a better solution than I had thought of on my own. I had a very smart staff, and it was a safe place to voice your opinion . . . it was a very strong culture—the culture . . . [was] about working hard for kids and learning, and feeling that you were very privileged to work in this school.

Teachers were expected to work together and, because they had almost all been hired by Principal Switzer, all shared a common vision of what good teaching and learning looked like.

> We did so much work around cooperative teaching, and we did so much collaboration around thematic curriculum—a whole grade would study something for six months at a time. The whole grade would have to develop the theme, create a course outline and develop a curriculum, develop a day-by-day plan; people would take different responsibilities, so people were very used to working together. And the golden rule was you weren't really allowed to say "no" to a staff member if they needed help—you really were expected to help each other, and support each other as teachers and learners.

P.S. 234 focused on maintaining high standards within the classroom. Principal Switzer states that she wanted "to see smoke coming out of the kids' ears." This rigorous focus extended throughout the student body, even to the twenty-five to thirty disabled kids who were provided full inclusion in the school. As a result of this common culture and commitment, P.S. 234 was academically high performing.

This high-functioning school community faced an unprecedented challenge on the day that two planes were intentionally flown into the Twin Towers. The nature and scope of the attack immediately rendered the school's safety and evacuation plan obsolete. With no advance warning of the event, few sources of reliable information during the attack, virtually no access to resources beyond the school, and seemingly total chaos by 10 A.M., decisions had to be made quickly and with a minimum of information upon which to base them.

## CRISIS DESCRIPTION

On the morning of September 11, 2001, nineteen hijackers boarded planes in Boston, Newark, and Washington, D.C. Their plan was the result of five years of planning by the Al-Qaeda Islamist movement, intending to use two loaded passenger planes as weapons targeting the World Trade Center in lower Manhattan and two at targets in Washington, D.C. By noon, 2,603 New Yorkers were killed as a result of the crashing of United Airlines Flight 11 and American Airlines Flight 175 directly into the 110-story Twin Towers.

Principal Switzer remembers the beginning of September 11, 2001, as "the most beautiful day." It was the fourth day of the school year. Second-grade teacher Laura Siskind recalls that it was "the first day that we were going to do math."[3]

When the first plane struck the World Trade Center towers at approximately 8:47 A.M., the sight was plainly visible from the P.S. 234 building. Watching the first plane strike one of the towers of the World Trade Center, Switzer initially perceived it as a tragic accident, thinking what a "terrible thing for the people in the building." She consulted with the district office and advised her staff to continue their school day while awaiting further information. Things dramatically changed, however, approximately fifteen minutes later, at 9:02 A.M., "right when the second plane crashed—that's when we knew that it wasn't an accident." It became clear to Switzer that the school was in danger. She immediately began communicating with her staff, but decision-making was hindered by incomplete and contradictory information. She states,

> I was on the PA—and the PA didn't always work—giving directions, consulting a little bit, but mostly trying to make decisions. . . . So everybody in the building was working together, and looking to me for what we were going to do next . . . and I wasn't that sure.

Switzer describes the situation as chaotic and extremely stressful. Additionally, a parent—who was also a policeman—arrived at the school and began disseminating erroneous information to parents, faculty, and staff:

They had bombed the White House, that they had bombed the Pentagon, they were fighting in the streets—he really said this stuff to us. I was trying to figure out what the hell to do, and I really just wanted to get rid of him. Because he's spreading this panic, and making this decision-making very hard.

She immediately allowed any parents remaining in the building to take their children and leave. She then began moving children and faculty to what she regarded as "safer" parts of the building—first to the cafeteria, then to the gymnasium, and ultimately into the basement. Upon the move to the basement, the school's librarian characterized the mood as one of concern—"there wasn't a panic, but there was an intensity that was growing."[4]

Throughout, Switzer relied upon the faculty and parents of the school. Her new PTA president—a former Marine colonel—stood at the door of the gymnasium, maintaining order and ensuring that parents gained their composure before entering the gymnasium and encountering students. Switzer describes similar clear thinking by faculty.

They mobilized right away, for example, by shutting all their blinds. They immediately got the kids calm, started singing songs, started reading stories, getting them together. Parents started coming in and taking kids home. . . . And again, these were extraordinary teachers, they knew how to keep their kids calm, and they had taught their kids to be orderly, to help each other, to trust their teachers. . . . There were an awfully lot of smart people that day who just were at their dedicated, remarkable . . . best.

The district office, which was geographically and situationally removed from the crisis in lower Manhattan, insisted that Principal Switzer follow established procedures, which had the school evacuating to a nearby high school. Switzer did not believe this was a viable option amid the chaotic emergency response. She found herself breaking other rules because of the extraordinary circumstances four blocks away, stating,

Supposedly only parents can sign a student out. Well, if a neighbor came, and she was taking her kid, and wanted to take another kid, that kid was going.

Approximately an hour later, at 9:59 A.M., the South Tower collapsed. "When the building [South Tower] went down, it was a decisive moment—'OK, let's get out of here.'" Remaining in the building no longer seemed to be an option. Switzer made the decision to take the remaining seventy-five to one hundred students whose parents had not yet picked them up to P.S. 41, a school 2½ miles north.

> When the [South Tower] fell down . . . we had all the kids in the basement, and we took them up from the basement, put them in the hallway [in lines], opened the doors, and started to run out. At which point, about 90 percent of us were out—I wasn't out—all the kids were out, but there were a few adults that weren't out.

Lacking school buses or police escort for the evacuation, teachers found themselves clinging to the hands of students and running north to safety. At this point, with most of the remaining students and staff fleeing on foot, the North Tower collapsed with the force amplitude of a small earthquake. Amid the evacuation, Switzer recalls,

> And the second building collapses. And the day turns to night. I mean, literally, the day turns to night. At that point, there are a couple of firemen, and they show up suddenly, and they pushed the rest of us back into the building. You really couldn't run out at that point. That was the worst moment . . . those of us who were left in the building had no idea what had happened to those who had run ahead, and the 90 percent who had run ahead had no idea what happened to those of us who were still in the building.

The collapse of the second building created a hazy cloud around the evacuees, but the dispersed group followed the sound of one of the school's support staff's ever-present playground whistle. The staff's ability to continue to function at a high level contributed to the miracle of no injuries or deaths amid the falling debris of the Towers. As Switzer recalls,

> I got to P.S. 41 probably forty minutes after everybody else but, by that time, the staff who had gotten there before me—and Lucille [P.S. 234's secretary] had grabbed the previous year's emergency cards—they were on the phone calling parents. They already had a sign-out system for people showing up to pick up their kids . . . this was a well-oiled machine.

With students and staff safely evacuated to a secure building, parents began to pick up students. Switzer turned to making provisions for the students whose parents had not arrived. Switzer contacted the district office for guidance, but it appeared to her that the central administration still failed to appreciate the situation:

> Now it's getting to be five or six o'clock, and we have a few kids that nobody has picked up. So we called the district office, and talked to our person in charge . . . and we say to him, "we have three kids left and teachers want to take them home." And he has a fit, "you can't take those kids home—what would Burt Sacks say?" Burt Sacks was somebody in charge of operations for the entire board of education—every memo we ever got at the school we got from Burt Sacks. He's like this giant ogre who's going to kill you if you make a mistake. This was the theme . . . all that afternoon: "What would Burt Sacks say?" And in the end [taking students home] is what the teachers did.

On September 12, 2001, the immediate threat to the physical safety of faculty and staff of P.S. 234 had passed; however, the school building was unusable and the neighborhood served by the school was uninhabitable. The students, staff, and families of P.S. 234 began a long and difficult process of finding a "home" again.

The immediate priority for Principal Switzer was her staff, which convened the very next day at the district office. The staff had the help of child psychologist Bruce Arnold, whom the PTA had funded for several years to work with teachers and parents. Arnold believed that the staff needed to be helped through their experience before they could turn to helping their returning students. Additionally, he believed familiarity with students ideally situated the school's faculty to assist students. Under Arnold's guidance, the faculty spent the first day

> just telling our stories—they were pretty amazing stories. . . . That was probably one of the best things that we did because we became closer. We heard how upsetting it was for a lot of people, and what they had gone through, and it just brought everybody closer together.

After reconnecting and sharing experiences, the faculty prepared to resume school. With the P.S. 234 building now serving as a base for rescue workers and firefighters, classes resumed in an existing school. The lack of space created difficulties, but the pace at which students returned suggests the healing power of returning to one's community. Principal Switzer states,

> All of our kids came back so fast. The parents really trusted us, they trusted the school. They were out of their homes, they were out of their neighborhood; the one constant was the school, which really didn't exist anymore except as a community of people. So we opened the gates to the school yard to P.S. 41, and there are hundreds of people waiting outside who wanted to come to school, with three classes in each room. It was affirming at first, but that was the most stressful time—we were really on top of each other.

Switzer and other school stakeholders wanted their own building, returning to the pre-9/11 identity of their school as an independent culture—if not one within the original building. P.S. 234 parents and faculty suggested moving to an abandoned parochial school. Switzer remembers fighting a district office plan to divide their school, characterizing her behavior as that of a "protective mother":

> We had to fight to get out of P.S. 41, and get St. Bernard's, this old, abandoned, parochial school. . . . So I'm on the street, and I get a call on my cell phone and it's Burt Sacks . . . and he says, "We have a plan. What we're going to do is divide your school up—we're going to put all of 89 [a very small school], and your lower grades in St. Bernard's." And I thought that I was going to have a stroke. I started screaming at this guy, and he was a real big shot. But certain things are visceral, and certain things you just thought you had to do because you had to protect. . . . I said, "we are not splitting up our school." And I really screamed at him—I don't know if anyone had ever screamed at him like that. We became very good friends after that, and he didn't split up the school.

The temporary move to St. Bernard's allowed for the school to more completely return to its singular identity. Switzer compares the move to St. Bernard to an "old-fashioned barn-raising." Hundreds of hours of work were donated by parents and community members as scores of parent volunteers cleaned the building, put together the new furniture, spent hours painting, and assisted the NYC school district employees working on the building. Principal Switzer states that the school's staff also began contacting the few students who had not returned to encourage them to "come back home."

The "return to normalcy" also allowed teachers to begin guiding students through an important healing process. Initially, students drew pictures of flying planes and people falling out of buildings. With guidance and training from the school psychologist, teachers began helping students learn how to understand their feelings, express them, and move beyond them. Some of the school's curricula was designed around this healing process. Principal Switzer states that the teachers were prescient at picking "what was the next thing on kids' minds, and—remembering that they were teachers," turning it into a learning exercise. Teachers "ha[d] the students write something, but write for an audience, then edit it, revise it, change it, and illustrate it."

Increasingly, there was little conversation about returning to the original building, as "the firemen were in there using it . . . sleeping [there], and it was completely trashed. But the real issue was the air quality downtown—and at what point the school would be clean enough, and at what point the air would be safe enough." As cleanup continued and confidence in a return grew, the question of returning to their original school switched from "if" to "when." Facilitating that discussion was the final significant challenge of the crisis. Principal Switzer explains:

> Emotionally, we found this wonderful little haven—St. Bernard's—we killed ourselves getting it ready, but then actually it was a lovely place, and we came to love it. And it was like our safe haven, and then we really didn't want to leave it. There were two things I did that were really good on that score. One was that when it was time to leave, I was able to talk to the parents about the fact that "we love it here, but it is time to go home." But more important than that, I had a meeting with the staff about helping convince the parents that it was time to go back and it was the only time that I had a meeting where everybody was saying different things and it was not really coherent. And I remember leading that, and finally saying, "You have to decide on three key points when you get up at the parent meeting tomorrow. And everybody has to stress those three points." And then we came to a consensus about what those three points were. And if you read the communications after that, the parents say, "well, the teachers were all saying the same thing."

On February 4, 2002, the school community returned to their original home at the corner of Greenwich and Chambers.

Considering the violent events of September 11, it is incredible that all P.S. 234 students and staff emerged without serious physical injury. The immediate crisis, however, created a much longer-term crisis for the community of P.S. 234. After getting everyone safely out of the building, the school began a search for a more permanent home while carrying out a painstaking process of mental and emotional recovery. The successful management of the crisis on that day and during succeeding months is a testament to the high-quality staff and strong leadership at P.S. 234.

## CRISIS ANALYSIS

The event triggering P.S. 234's crisis typifies External-Unpredictable in that it was utterly beyond the school's ability to forecast or control. The only comparable attack in contemporary American history was December 7, 1941, and even that attack lacked the 9/11 terrorists' focus on an entirely civilian population. There was, quite simply, no way to prepare for such a crisis. This event—which destroyed 30 percent of the office space in lower Manhattan—left private and public services in complete disarray. With no contingency plans or comparable events from which to base action, school personnel forged their own path. Thinking quickly and flexibly in evolving conditions is essential during such abnormal circumstances.

Further complicating the process of managing the crisis was the patchy and inaccurate information immediately following the collapse of the Twin Towers. Phone lines were down, panic ensued and was almost total, and rescue and response crews were stretched to the limit. Taken aback by the suddenness and enormity of the crisis, the school district response relied on established procedures and policies, ignoring the fact that these had been rendered moot (at best) or actively dangerous by the type and level of crisis they were trying to manage.

Noting the district's emergency plan was appropriate for more typical crises, Switzer states, "In case of an emergency [requiring an evacuation], we were to go to Stuyvesant High School—the school across the street. That's the level of thinking of what the emergency would be." The district's emergency response plan simply did not envisage an event making the area around the school—including Stuyvesant High School—unsafe or uninhabitable. There were no support mechanisms in place to help students move two miles north to the relative safety of P.S. 41.

While there was no specific plan in place for this crisis, the school did have several strengths that minimized the physical and emotional damage to students. They had practiced other types of crisis plans and they had a leader that the teachers, students, and parents respected. More importantly, the culture of the school was one of empowerment and investment, and even during a catastrophic crisis, faculty and staff focused on safely evacuating students. While not a plan, this strong culture and general preparation is the most effective way to survive an Unpredictable crisis. Switzer explains:

> On the lowest level of that, is that kids and teachers know how to go orderly through the halls. That they don't hesitate and talk back. That they don't buck your orders, so to speak. That kids hold each other's hand, and when one kid sees another who is crying they comfort him and help him. That when parents come in, they know not just to look for their kid, but look to see if they can help somebody else's kid. That's the most fundamental way that you help yourself during a crisis—that you have certain things in place, because you run a lot of fire drills, and because you run an orderly school . . . those kinds of things were in place, and they mattered quite a lot.

Generally, a school that has a strong, positive culture is more resistant to all types of crises and is better able to handle them if they occur. Switzer's ability to balance direct and collaborative leadership resulted in a strong internal culture at P.S. 234. One of the teachers stated that, after the first plane hit, she stayed in her classroom but was able to remain calm because she "completely trust[ed] Anna."[5] These relationships and shared beliefs helped the school to survive and recover from the impact of the 9/11 terror attacks. Switzer speaks to this directly:

> You can only be the school on the day of crisis that you were the day before a crisis. I'm in schools all the time and you wonder whether . . . they have one orderly, functional system in place. You are always preparing for a crisis . . . the previous years we spent with Bruce Arnold were about helping teachers learn how to support the psychodynamic issues of families and childhood. This was one of the critical things that helped us through this crisis. Over time, over the years, teachers learned how to support a child who is frightened, who feels lost, who gets displaced, who has a good friend move away, etc. Teachers learned

from Bruce how to work with individual children and how to run a supportive class meeting. And those lessons became extraordinarily important later on. Because teaching teachers how to handle a friend who has moved away really paid off when teachers knew how to deal with losing a friend, because everyone was moving around the city. The collaborative nature of our work, the ability to communicate, the ability to make decisions consensually, everybody respecting each other during meetings—those things were in place.

Switzer faced unprecedented obstacles on and after September 11. She lacked early warning mechanisms, the nature of the crisis prevented her from gathering further information, and there was no plan in place for handling such an event. What she did have was a strong culture of community and confidence in the abilities of everyone to play an important role in the school.

**CRISIS TREATMENT**

The crisis of 9/11 provides many lessons for handling an External-Unpredictable crisis. One of these fundamental aspects is that, when faced with patchy and contradictory information, it is imperative to provide constant and clear communication within a school community. Principal Switzer maximized communication with multiple stakeholders both during the immediate crisis and throughout the recovery process.

On September 11, communication occurred with basic tools: the PA system to communicate with those in the building when the first crash happened; the phone to the district office and other local schools to update them on what they were planning to do; dutifully maintained lists of students who had left the building and those who remained in the school; and even Bernie's whistle, which allowed limited contact between teachers evacuating through a dusty cloud.

Throughout the rest of the year following September 11, the transient nature of the school community required a heightened emphasis on communication. Principal Switzer states,

> I must have sent home one hundred different letters—I sent letters home just about every single day. "Hey, we have telephones. Hey, we have a new school bus route. Hey, we have no news today." It was critical. Remember that there's no more school building, there's no more PTA office, and people are not living in their own homes. There's no physical community, people are not working downtown.

Ongoing communication also occurred internally. Principal Switzer says, "We met every single day as a staff, whether we needed to or not, whether we wanted to or not." All of these communication methods were necessary because managing the crisis required such a departure from the familiar and comfortable; constant communication was crucial to keeping all parties focused on the same goal as the school moved toward normalcy.

Principal Switzer is quick to credit others during the entire crisis from the morning of the attacks through the following months and years as they tried to recover, saying, "Looking back . . . I realize that you find partners and you find lieutenants. They're not the same. But they're very, very, very important. And I had a few partners, and I had a few lieutenants. And that allowed us to get through." Partners were equal collaborators on whom Principal Switzer became dependent, people who had a similar broad viewpoint of the school's position, strengths, and weaknesses. Lieutenants, equally as important in managing the crisis, were individuals to whom she could delegate tasks and responsibilities.

For P.S. 234, both of these groups came from within the school community and were essential during the crisis stages of damage control, secondary prevention, and community recovery and learning. A few partners and lieutenants arose from expected positions like the assistant principals and the part-time school psychologist; some, however, were more unexpected, like the new PTA president and many parents. Principal Switzer says that people came forward where they saw they could help and "there were a few folks who came into the school and just didn't leave for five months." In the months following the attacks, the school leaned heavily on its internal community resources, resisting outside "expertise" because they believed that they knew each other and the students far better than any outside agency.

Given the changing dynamics of that fateful day and the lack of any sort of previous experience to draw from, making creative decisions on September 11 was crucial. Principal Switzer states, "We broke all of the rules. You have to think out of the box—there is no box." However, with the advantage of hindsight she admits that she wishes she had left the building earlier. She states, "I'm sort of a rule-breaker, and all the while I'm thinking, 'should I leave or should I stay?' and I'm a little disappointed in me that I didn't just say, 'screw it, let's get out of here.'"

Making decisions that break the rules is risky, but it can make the difference between a bad situation and a catastrophic one. The art of knowing when
to be daring is essential to the role of being a school leader both in times of
crisis and in times of relative calm. She states that, as part of being a school
leader,

> you have to be bold, you have to have courage. If you don't have courage you
> cannot be a good principal. You have to have the courage to tell the parents
> when they want something that you can't give it to them, or that you don't
> agree with them, or that they're wrong. You have to have the courage to say to
> a staff member—"you know, you should think about a new career." You have
> to have the courage to say "NO" to the district office when they're wrong. And
> that's really hard.

This courage is necessary for making decisions as well as defending the
choices and other members of the school community. For Principal Switzer,
the weeks and months that followed 9/11 reinforced this lesson as she found
herself dictating terms to the chancellor of New York City Schools—whom
Principal Switzer insisted meet with her entire staff, not just a small subset
as requested—the teachers' union, and even First Lady Laura Bush and her
advance team.

In guiding the school community through the crisis, Principal Switzer understood that the staff's needs first needed to be met, as they were the key to
providing support to students, communicating with parents, and developing
stability during the many changes. This was the same pattern utilized by Principal Bryan Krause after the shooting at Platte Canyon High School described
in chapter 4. Principal Switzer describes her mantra as "Staff comes first, then
the kids . . . that means every single staff member, paraprofessionals, custo-
dial, everybody." They were given presents every single week—massages from
the community and goodie bags from TimeWarner, holiday parties and gifts;
"there weren't enough ways to say thank you."

One of Principal Switzer's biggest surprises was the extent that parents and
community members displaced their anger over the attacks onto her and her
leadership team. When faced with disproportionate malice or frustration from a
student or community member, she privately thought to herself, "Hey, I didn't
bomb the World Trade Center." People deal with trauma very differently, and

Principal Switzer began to quickly recognize when frustration expressed at her was displaced pain. She also understood that her own home had been unaffected, her own family had not suffered, and hers was a slightly different experience from that of some of the people with whom she was talking.

Principal Switzer is also proud that the school resisted efforts to depend on external supports for the students. Her school psychologist, who worked extensively with the students and staff, "kept on reminding the teachers that no one knew their kids better than they did, and that they had the skills necessary to help their children, and that together, we would find solutions and strategies to things that were new to them." Finally, her role as the principal of the school was "to always remember that we were an educational institution" and to ensure that her decisions, and the actions of others, were all directly aimed at returning P.S. 234 to that mission.

## CONCLUSION

The terrorist attacks of September 11, 2001, killed almost three thousand people and had global implications that are still being felt today. The enormity of the attack, however, can obscure the incredible stories of the people most directly affected, like the students and staff at P.S. 234. Principal Anna Switzer was a ten-year veteran at the school who had built a strong, collaborative staff. The school's strengths of strong relationships among all members of the school, solid leadership, and quick decision-making all enabled the school to handle the initial onset of the crisis.

The crisis experienced by P.S. 234 did not end with the safe evacuation of the school building on September 11. In the months that followed, the school continued to deal with the long-term effects of the crisis; however, the support of the community and professionalism of the teachers continued to pay dividends. The story of Principal Switzer shows a clear example of a school that was prepared in many ways to handle this External-Unpredictable crisis even though there was no way to predict its occurrence. By developing a strong culture of mutual respect, shared input from multiple sources, and a shared vision of what the school should do for students, P.S. 234 had a foundation strong enough to help it absorb the enormous blow of the September 11 attacks, manage the immediate impact, and work toward restoring a sense of normalcy for the entire school's community.

## REFLECTIVE QUESTIONS

### Reflection on the Reading

1. Principal Switzer reflected that, in retrospect, she wishes she would have acted sooner in response to the crisis. What steps might she have taken earlier?
2. Given the school's proximity to the World Trade Center towers and its history of terrorist attacks, would it be feasible for the district or school to have a more developed evacuation plan in place?
3. Principal Switzer rejected much of the help offered to staff and students from outside organizations for a variety of reasons. What kinds of support would you have accepted and rejected if you were in her situation? Why?

### Application to Theory

4. What types of "general school preparation" did Principal Switzer and the school's stakeholders engage in that helped them deal with the crisis and its aftermath?
5. What kinds of opportunities should be provided to a school's staff to help improve team effectiveness? To ensure organizational learning?
6. Principal Switzer fully incorporated her students' experiences into the year's curriculum as an important part of "community recovery and learning." What elements would need to be present to ensure the success of this strategy?

### Application on the Job

7. How often are safety drills practiced at your school? Are there established locations to which you can evacuate your entire school? Is there at least one backup in case the primary evacuation point is inaccessible or inappropriate?
8. If you had to leave the school, how would you access critical student, parent/guardian, staff, district, and emergency services information, including contact names, numbers, and/or medical concerns? Are there multiple people that have this access?
9. What external resources or nonstaff members can you call on to help in an emergency? On which mental health resources would you rely in the event of a crisis? Do you currently have a relationship with these resources?

10. How is communication carried out within your school? Are there backup methods in case the primary system does not work?

11. Is your school located near a landmark that is of political, financial, cultural, or social significance, or place at which a large number of people gather? What natural disasters is your geographic region most at risk of experiencing?

# "It Was an Area That Was Highly Devastated—It . . . Received Eight or Nine Feet of Water."

## How New Orleans's George Washington Carver High School Rebuilt After Hurricane Katrina

**OVERVIEW**

Up from the ruins, state and district leaders are fighting to rebuild and repair New Orleans' schools.

*—Education Week, October 3, 2007*[1]

Perhaps no school system in the United States has faced such a daunting and unprecedented challenge as that heaped upon public schools in the city of New Orleans. In August 2005, Hurricane Katrina stormed into New Orleans, completely flooding portions of the city and leaving it in a state of disrepair. Like so many other facets of New Orleans, the public school system was utterly washed away. Over one hundred school buildings were flooded and dozens more suffered significant damage. Employees were laid off and families were uprooted from the city. Since that fateful day, New Orleans has made innumerable strides to repair and reshape its city and public school system.

The story of George Washington Carver High School, located in the city's upper 9th Ward, exemplifies the hardships, accomplishments, and burdensome uncertainty that still looms over the city's public schools. Like so many other public schools in New Orleans, Carver High School has encountered and largely overcome unimaginable odds in the aftermath of Hurricane Katrina. Its crisis is not simply the onslaught of the storm but also the nearly insurmountable task of rebuilding in the midst of a worn-down and worn-out city. New Orleans was exhausted by the task of recreating itself from the ruins of Hurricane Katrina yet encouraged by the promises of new opportunity. This chapter tells the story of Carver High School and the road it has traveled under the leadership of Principal Vanessa Eugene since Hurricane Katrina uprooted its existence.

## CASE NARRATIVE

Carver High School has a long-standing history and proud alumni support. Built in 1958, Carver High School was originally conceived as a large, comprehensive high school graduating thousands of students annually. It drew its students from the Desire Housing Complex, as well as from single-family neighborhoods in the upper 9th Ward. Most students attending Carver High School lived in that development or in the immediate local area, resulting in a very close-knit community. As Principal Eugene described it,

> People knew each other and had known each other for years. The parents in the community knew the teachers, in fact, many of the teachers had taught them. So it was a very close-knit community, with a big alumni group.

Carver High School's strong community support, however, is inevitably entangled in the struggles endemic to the New Orleans—and Louisiana's—public school system, including its chronic under-performance, racial achievement gaps, and troubled governance. Prior to Hurricane Katrina, the New Orleans Parish board ran a district of more than 120 public schools serving approximately sixty-five thousand students. For numerous years before the storm, the system was repeatedly marked by discouraging performance indicators. In 2005, Louisiana's public schools ranked anywhere from forty-third to forty-sixth in state-by-state rankings of student academic performance issued by the U.S. Department of Education. Additionally, the Orleans Parish ranked sixty-seventh of sixty-eighth on measures of achievement among parishes in the state.[2] Unsurprisingly, over 60 percent of the city's public schools were flagged as "Academically Unacceptable" on the state's accountability system.[3]

Preceding Hurricane Katrina, the Orleans Parish school system was also "monochromatically black," more so than the Orleans parish overall, with blacks constituting 68 percent of the entire parish population. In fact, 94 percent of students in the Orleans Parish public school system were black in the 2004–2005 school year. White children composed only 3 percent of the system's student population and almost exclusively attended the more selective (i.e., non-open enrollment) magnet schools in the Orleans Parish.[4]

Additionally, during the 2004–2005 school year, over three-quarters (77 percent) of the school system's student population came from families making incomes low enough to qualify them for a free or reduced-price meal subsidized by the federal government. Forty percent of students lived below the poverty line and resided in a city hampered by higher rates of poverty and illiteracy than evident throughout the rest of Louisiana or the nation overall.[5] A school district reform plan finds that,

> New Orleans citizens earned 35 percent less annually than the average individual in the nation; one-quarter of citizens had not completed high school; and 40 percent of adults could not read beyond a fifth-grade level.[6]

Continuity of leadership in the Orleans Parish was fleeting before Hurricane Katrina. Principal Eugene so adeptly described the consequences of such a revolving door of system leadership.

> We had several superintendents come within a few years, and that made it quite difficult because they come in with new initiatives and then they are there for two years, then a new superintendent comes on, and you have to put their vision in place. So that continuity piece was not there.

The results of such turnover were inconsistent reform initiatives and frequent leadership voids. Further complicating the situation were very high concentrations of poverty and a history of dysfunction throughout the district. Clearly, the district's state of existence pre-Katrina was tumultuous.

In the midst of this harsh reality, public schools in New Orleans were no stranger to progressive, reform-minded superintendents. For example, immediately before Hurricane Katrina, Superintendent Anthony Amato led the system with a portfolio of reforms on his agenda. According to Principal

Eugene, his focus was on creating theme-based small learning communities within high schools. He also focused on reforming the ways in which teachers worked with one another through the establishment of professional learning communities and helping to address highly concentrated poverty through the creation of family advocacy programs.

To little surprise, all of these forces—records of low performance, high concentrations of poverty, unstable yet reform-minded leadership—created great momentum for change in the aftermath of Hurricane Katrina. While devastating, the storm also provided an unprecedented opportunity to reform a chronically dysfunctional school system, which had to essentially be recreated from the rubble of Hurricane Katrina. Now, the majority of New Orleans public schools operate under the umbrella of the state-run Recovery School District (RSD) headed up by a quintessential reformer, Paul Vallas.

The RSD was first created by the state legislature in 2003, inspired by the accountability measures of the No Child Left Behind Act. It gave authority to the state to take over any school that had failed (i.e., received a rating of "Academically Unacceptable" for at least four consecutive years) under the state's school and district accountability program. The November 2005 Special Session of the Louisiana Legislature broadened the definition of the RSD, allowing the state to take over any school that scores below the state average and operates within a system declared to be in "Academic Crisis" (i.e., a district with at least one school labeled as failing for four or more years).

This latter revision to the law intentionally enabled the state to take over the majority of Orleans Parish schools. In fact, 107 of the 127 Orleans Parish schools were transferred into the RSD, administered by the Louisiana Department of Education and subject to the authority of the state's board of education.[7]

New Orleans's RSD is without comparison. It operates an intricate web of diverse school choice under the leadership of a highly reform-oriented leader with little of the local political complexity so common to the operation of a public school system. Currently, there are eighty-six public schools in the city of New Orleans, sixty-seven of which operate under the RSD. These RSD schools are split between the thirty-four traditional public schools and thirty-three RSD charter schools, and more public school students attend charter schools in New Orleans than in any other district throughout the U.S. public education system.[8]

Both traditional public and charter schools operate under the two-pronged leadership of Superintendent Paul Vallas, who runs the RSD, and Paul Pastorek, the state education superintendent. This leadership structure supersedes much of the local political constraints that define the governance of public school districts nationwide. There are no local school board and teachers' union. Principal Eugene explained the implications of such an unprecedented governance structure.

> Basically, if the state says that we need to do something, or if Paul Vallas says we want to do something, he just has to go to Paul Pastorek and they can get things passed. So you don't have as much red tape. If you have teachers that aren't performing, the teacher will be evaluated and if that teacher does not pass his or her evaluation that teacher will be removed. In the past we could not do that—we basically had to accept bad teachers. And that wasn't good for our schools, it wasn't good for our students.

However, New Orleans RSD must still contend with the most challenging students in the city. Most students are those that lived through the horrendous and catastrophic events of Hurricane Katrina and those that cannot attend any other schools in New Orleans. The Orleans Parish School Board still oversees seventeen schools: five traditional public schools and twelve independently run charters. Most of these schools have select admissions requirements, giving preference to students with higher records of academic performance. And while RSD charters are technically "open-enrollment," weaker students often drop out due to the academic press enforced at those schools. Hence, open-access traditional public schools, like Carver High School, enroll a broader spectrum of students, including mid-year transfers and those who cannot pass the academic requirements of selective schools.

It is within this complex web of a troubled past and hopeful promise that Carver High School finds itself in the aftermath of Hurricane Katrina. Two years after the storm swept through New Orleans, Carver High School reopened to fewer than two hundred students. The school's leader, Principal Vanessa Eugene, faced an unparalleled challenge at the helm of a school in a community that had just faced one of the most devastating storms in recent U.S. history and was marked by such a vulnerable past. But with such unmatched obstacles has come unprecedented opportunity.

## CRISIS DESCRIPTION

Monday, August 29, 2005, is a day etched in history for New Orleans, the day that Hurricane Katrina made landfall on the Gulf Coast as a Category 3 hurricane. By mid-day, citizens of New Orleans felt as if they had escaped the worst the storm had to offer, as the eye of the hurricane actually passed to the east of the city and spared them from the most damaging winds and rain. However, it was soon apparent that the federally built levee system, protecting the metro New Orleans area, could not withstand the hurricane's surge. Hurricane Katrina breached the levees in fifty-three places, subjecting the city of New Orleans and surrounding communities to catastrophic flooding. Major breaches left 80 percent of New Orleans completely under water for days, and in many neighborhoods, the flood waters lingered for weeks.

People around the world watched in bewilderment and horror as the city of New Orleans fell prey to the mass destruction and flooding inflicted by Hurricane Katrina. Residents who had not evacuated were stranded on rooftops or trapped inside attics of their own homes. Others waded through the daunting flood waters toward the city's Superdome, hoping for refuge. The city's communication infrastructure was dismantled, as most telephone lines and Internet access were rendered useless. Local television stations were also cut off. Most major roadways going into and out of the city were in disrepair and there was no clean water or electricity. Adding to the chaos, looting, violence, and other criminal activity became rampant. To no surprise, loss of life from Hurricane Katrina was heavy, with over seven hundred people declared dead a month after the storm.[9]

New Orleans's public school system found itself in a state of disarray. In the immediate hours following Hurricane Katrina's landfall, nearly one hundred public school buildings were flooded, some severely. Students and the system's employees had either evacuated the city or found themselves amidst the city's turmoil of that day and those that followed. According to Principal Eugene, the Orleans Parish was completely surprised by the extreme devastation resulting from the storm.

> I don't think that we had a clue. I don't think any one of us had a clue. For years and years, we were told that New Orleans was below sea level, and if there was ever a problem and the levees failed, we could possibly be flooded out because the city was like a bowl. And if water from the Mississippi River, or from the lake, actually got into the city it could flood. But I don't think that we ever

realized to the extent—actually, I was thinking two, three feet of water. I don't think anyone ever realized it could be twelve feet of water and that 80 percent of the city could receive that devastation.

Principal Eugene, like so many others in the city, believed the effects of Hurricane Katrina would resemble those of so many other threatening storms. In the past, local officials would warn of a potential hurricane and a need for evacuation, but oftentimes these orders were perceived as excessive. More often than not, the storm would not head toward New Orleans so no evacuation was needed. On the few occasions that an evacuation was necessary, citizens would pack up a few days' worth of clothes and head to a nearby alternative city. As Principal Eugene recalled, previous preparation consisted of "putting tape on windows" and making sure to "remove important papers off the floor."

I took a couple of days' worth of clothes thinking that I would be gone for a few days, and everyone that I would speak to would say the same thing, that's exactly what they did. No one had any idea that we would not be coming back home.

Instead, the sixty-five-acre campus that included Carver and a feeder middle and elementary school was submerged by over ten feet of water. With school buildings largely devastated, and employees and students no longer in the city, the system was totally inoperable. The first indication of the long-term consequences for the Orleans Parish School District was the termination of all employees. Informal word-of-mouth and news from national media outlets led many school personnel to seek alternative employment as early as the first week after Hurricane Katrina hit New Orleans. And, a month later, all employees of the Orleans Parish were terminated. With no schools in operation and no students attending, the school system could not feasibly keep personnel on payroll. Even employee benefits were cancelled several months later. Lost employment and benefits, compounded by the reality of losing one's home and possessions, left many public school employees extremely disgruntled with the Orleans Parish and in a financially vulnerable state.

In the face of this destruction, the city's public school system was rebuilt with the simultaneous reestablishment of the New Orleans public school system and creation of schools under the umbrella of the RSD. Leaders over both systems were well aware of numerous challenges they would have to tackle, but they were entering unfamiliar territory. Temporary school facilities had to be constructed until long-term rebuilding of the city's school buildings would be complete. They estimated $1.7 billion in repairs and reconstruction, and only $700 million was pledged from the Federal Emergency Management Agency (FEMA), less than half of the necessary expense.[10] Sufficient numbers of administrators and school teachers had to be hired, which remains a daunting task. These challenges were escalated by the uncertainty of the number of school-aged children that would return to the city for the 2006–2007 school year.

New Orleans's public schools started the 2006–2007 school year with approximately twenty-two thousand students, which was more than the city was expecting, but only one-third of the pre-Katrina population. Consequently, "there were not enough buses, not enough textbooks, no hot lunches, no doors on the bathroom stalls," according to Principal Eugene.

As the school year continued, additional evidence of troubling facility conditions emerged. An October 2007 *Education Week* article reported findings from an end-of-year survey conducted by the United Teachers of New Orleans, which reported, "Ninety-nine percent of roughly 200 respondents said indoor-air quality in their schools was poor. Fifty-two percent said they'd seen evidence of rodents, and 43 percent reported inoperable water fountains in their schools."

There also were not enough teachers—"106 positions were still unfilled."[11] Additionally, an exceptionally large percentage of rookie teachers worked in RSD-run schools and charters. Teachers with fewer than three years of experience constituted approximately half the teaching workforce during the 2006–2007 school year. A report by the New Orleans teachers union explained that "the firing of virtually all experienced teachers and other school district staff in December 2005 prompted a mass exodus of experienced teachers." And Superintendent Vallas—who took leadership of the RSD in summer 2007—described the goal as "get[ting] a warm body in front of the kids."[12]

Carver High School did not reopen during the 2006–2007 school year, because there were not enough students back in the community to justify its opening. As Principal Eugene explained, "It [upper 9th Ward] was an area that was highly devastated. It received eight or nine feet of water. Plus it was one of the last areas to get utilities up and running." In fact, the community is still rebuilding. It has been a slow process exacerbated by the troubling financial situation in which so many upper 9th Ward citizens still find themselves. In the storm's aftermath, many did not have insurance to salvage possessions lost in the flood or to rebuild. But, as families did begin to move back home, the RSD saw fit to open Carver High School for the 2007–2008 school year with Vanessa Eugene—a veteran educator and school leader—as its principal.

In fall 2007, Principal Eugene stood at the crossroads of a critical moment in the school's history. With the crisis of Hurricane Katrina and its aftermath still so potent, she was given the opportunity—and challenge—of reopening a high school in a community still reeling from the storm's impact and in a school system with a long history of struggles.

## CRISIS ANALYSIS

The crisis for Carver High School uniquely embodies the three core features of a crisis. The school building was certainly in disrepair, as it had literally been dismantled by Hurricane Katrina, and the school's existence remained uncertain in fall 2007. This state of crisis resulted not only from the surge of the storm, but from the pressing questions that lingered in its aftermath, primarily: How would the city completely rebuild a public school system with such a long and troubled history during such unstable times?

The hurricane completely devastated the city's and public school system's infrastructure, leaving it with an unsure number of students, inadequate facilities, and a highly inexperienced teacher corps. Without doubt, when handed the school's principalship a month before the school's reopening for the 2007–2008 school year, Principal Eugene had to work with a great sense of urgency to reestablish the school's vitality, core values, and foundational practices in order to educate students in a very vulnerable community with very uncertain circumstances.

The two-dimensional typology introduced in chapter 1 illuminates key dimensions of a crisis (see figure 1.1, page 11). The first dimension classifies the "center of gravity" of the crisis; the other specifies the predictability of a crisis. The former identifies whether the crisis originates from within the organization or from external forces. The latter dimension clarifies how well a crisis can be anticipated and prepared for. Clearly, the primary source of the crisis for Carver High School was Hurricane Katrina and its impact on the city and public school system in New Orleans. And the unprecedented nature of the

storm and its extensive consequences made the situation highly unpredictable
for the school and its leaders.

Several factors endemic to Carver High School and its community—and
oftentimes, endemic to the entire school system—influenced the nature of
the school's crisis. The history of poor performance both at the school and
particularly in the Orleans Parish created a paradoxical sense of urgency and
opportunity for reform of public schools in the aftermath of Hurricane Katrina. In fact, this unparalleled opportunity likely attracted added energy and
resources from such reform-minded leaders as Paul Vallas and large quantities
of philanthropic support. Concurrently, the close-knit nature of the upper 9th
Ward community provided momentum for Carver High School's reopening.
Yet the community's struggle to reestablish itself and its uncertain student enrollment put the school's demand in question, at least for a period of time.

### CRISIS TREATMENT

Principal Eugene was largely aware of the challenging circumstances, yet gladly
embraced the urgency of the situation as the 2007–2008 school year neared.
Her initial step in leading Carver High School through the crisis was agreeing
to take on the responsibility in the first place. It was not a position she was
required or expected to assume. She was not principal of the school prior to
the storm. And when hired, she quickly—within a month's time—had to address fundamental priorities, not glamorous ones, but priorities paramount
to the school's ability to exist.

With sixteen years of experience working in New Orleans public schools,
Principal Eugene is very committed to the well-being of the school system and
the students it serves. Prior to Hurricane Katrina, she developed a great affin-
ity for the tight-knit culture of the upper 9th Ward while working on district-
initiated reforms at Carver High School. Consequently, it was no surprise to
her that she felt a strong pull back to New Orleans in the months following the
storm. Only days after Hurricane Katrina, Principal Eugene took a job in Fulton County (Georgia) public schools. By November—only a couple months
after the storm so devastated New Orleans—she knew her calling was back to
the service of the city and students she so deeply embraced. She states,

> Sitting in Georgia, looking at CNN and seeing the devastation in my city, and
> going to work every day in Fulton County, I felt that I would be more useful at

home—that I needed to be at home. I felt that I could make a bigger difference at home than in Georgia. I just wanted to come home and reach out to rebuild. I had to rebuild. New Orleans is an awesome city, we have awesome people here, and we have good kids, despite what others say. Most of the time when you talk about inner-city kids, quite often it is negative, but we have good kids here, we have hard-working kids who want something, and I wanted to come back home and impact them; that is the bottom line.

When Principal Eugene returned to New Orleans, she aggressively sought opportunities to learn about plans for rebuilding and to serve in professional positions as an active contributor. She was not immediately hired when she applied to be a principal in the first round of schools opening after Hurricane Katrina. Regardless, she continued attending planning meetings and listening to stakeholders discuss plans for rebuilding the schools. She was eventually hired as an assistant principal in an elementary school in June 2006, and served in that role until plans for the reopening of Carver High School came to fruition.

Not long before the start of the 2007–2008 school year, Principal Eugene learned of plans to reestablish Carver High School, as its catchment area finally had enough students to justify the school's reopening. She applied and went through a series of interviews with local community members and a team working with Superintendent Vallas. She was hired around July 2007—just about one month before the start of the school year—and immediately set fundamental priorities to ensure the school's livelihood. These priorities were not flashy, but simply addressed the basic ingredients for the operation of any school: Carver High School needed students, Carver High School needed teachers, and Carver High School needed a roof over its head.

When asked about her top priorities when opening the school for the 2007–2008 school year, Principal Eugene states unequivocally, "The priority was getting students." This task was made quite difficult given several circumstances of the RSD. Most charter schools in the area served elementary-aged students, so competition with charter schools was not a concern. However, competition for students among public high schools was considerable. All RSD schools are open-enrollment, meaning students can choose to attend any school. Carver High School was at a disadvantage because many students and families were not even aware of its reopening for the 2007–2008 school year.

Given her hiring in late summer 2007, Principal Eugene did not really have time to actively recruit students. The school was given a roster of students but many never showed up. When the doors opened in August 2007, 170 students were in attendance. This number grew to 250 by the close of the school year, but it was not due to any systematic recruitment effort. There was not time nor were there many formal resources for recruiting students. Rather, Principal Eugene successfully relied on informal word-of-mouth among families in the upper 9th Ward.

For example, in February 2008, the Carver High School band participated in the Mardi Gras parade, which served as an excellent public relations opportunity to promote the school throughout the city. Principal Eugene said, "As we were marching, people were saying, 'Carver's open, Carver's open.' And after that, we started hearing more people were interested in sending children to Carver."

Additionally, in late spring 2008, the district put on a recruitment fair for eighth graders to allow those families and students to learn more about their high school choices. Principal Eugene used current students as a recruitment tool, showcasing some of the students' talents including dance, poetry recitation, and musical instruments. A full year after the school reopened, the school's enrollment more than doubled. Approximately five hundred students were enrolled to begin the 2008–2009 school year at Carver High School.

But getting students through the doors of Carver High School was only the beginning of the process. In fact, when asked to describe the moment of utmost urgency during the reopening process, Principal Eugene described the chaos and uncertainty in trying to figure out the educational needs of the school's students. Some students had been in other schools across the country in the immediate aftermath of Hurricane Katrina, while others were not in school at all during that chaotic time. And many were already significantly behind grade level, not an uncommon reality for many students who had been in the Orleans Parish school system prior to the storm. She states,

> The most important thing was making sure that we had transcripts so we could get students the courses that they need. We had students who came to us and said, "I'm eighteen years old and I'm in twelfth grade." Then we got the transcripts and we saw that, no actually you're in ninth grade and you only have three units.

Principal Eugene decided to assign students to the grade level that they claimed, simply out of necessity to get students placed in classes on very short notice. To make matters more difficult, the school did not have a computerized scheduling system. So, Principal Eugene meticulously and monotonously created each student's individual class schedule by hand.

As time lapsed and she gained more information on students' past records, she was able to redirect their class schedules to ensure they made up courses necessary for progression through the curriculum. This challenge, while still a reality during the 2008–2009 school year, is now made easier with a new district-level recovery credit program.

Although students were enrolled and placed on a schedule, getting them to attend on a regular basis was another monumental struggle. Many students at Carver High School were living in New Orleans without their parents; most were with other relatives or acquaintances able to relocate in New Orleans after Hurricane Katrina. Consequently, "If you don't have a parent with you every day making sure you get to school, you can choose to stay at home, and you will," explained Principal Eugene when describing the high absenteeism rate at Carver High School.

During the 2007–2008 school year, she estimated the daily attendance rate as being anywhere between 70 and 75 percent. Principal Eugene advocated for district-level guidelines that, as of the 2008–2009 school year, now provide a clear consequence for missing school. If a student misses more than seven days in a semester, he/she fails the course. But during Carver High School's first year of operation following Katrina, such parameters were ambiguous.

Another significant challenge for Principal Eugene was hiring an entirely new faculty. Teachers were in short supply in New Orleans following the storm, and access to experienced teachers was even more limited. Carver High School essentially started from scratch, with only Principal Eugene and one other faculty member ever having worked at Carver High School in any capacity. Only 30 percent of her teaching staff was from the New Orleans area and most came with alternative teaching certifications. Principal Eugene was not too surprised, given many of the raw memories that so many experienced New Orleans teachers harbored; teachers who had worked tirelessly found their jobs and benefits terminated at a time of great distress. Whether or not they blamed the district for that circumstance, the strong emotions still made recruitment of that pool of experienced teachers quite challenging.

There was very little time for Principal Eugene to recruit teachers systematically before the school opened in fall 2007. Fortunately, in addition to its own aggressive national teacher recruitment efforts, the RSD was working closely with Teach For America and the New Teacher Project, which ran the TeachNOLA campaign. The state of Louisiana had also been providing relocation and retention stipends for certified teachers who committed to work in the RSD schools and remain there for three school years.[13]

Given the inexperience of Carver High School's teachers during the 2007–2008 school year, and their unfamiliarity with New Orleans, Principal Eugene strongly believed she had to show an abundance of support for her teaching staff. She relied on the lessons learned from past principals she had served with at other schools before the storm. Specifically, she recalled the leadership style of the past principal of Carver High School.

> The one thing he did is that he got the teachers on his side because he supported them. If they asked for something, he tried his best to make that happen for them. I wanted teachers to feel that they were supported. Because we know that it does matter what principals do—I mean, it impacts education, it impacts student achievement, but the most impact is what goes on in that classroom. And we wanted the teachers to feel comfortable. We wanted them to feel good about what was taking place at Carver.

With essentially an entirely new and highly inexperienced faculty, Principal Eugene's first priority was taking care of her staff's most basic needs. She found herself providing significant assistance with classroom management during the first year. For many of the teachers who were in their early twenties—only a few years older than some of their students—discipline was a significant challenge.

Accordingly, Principal Eugene and her assistant principal handled a lot of the disciplinary problems, even minor issues that, in a "normal" environment, would be addressed by teachers in the classroom. Principal Eugene's rationale: "We handled them so they [teachers] could do the things they do best, and that is to teach." Overall, she felt the year went really well considering so many rookie teachers were in classrooms, and "it was almost too good to be true." The success of her support is evidenced by the fact that, between the 2007–2008 and 2008–2009 school years, only three teachers out of a faculty of thirty decided not to return.

While Principal Eugene had a degree of control—albeit, sometimes limited—over her student body and teaching staff, some elements of the 2007–2008 school year were out of her hands entirely, and at the discretion of RSD leaders. First, Carver High School's location was marked by a degree of instability. The high school began the 2007–2008 school year in modular buildings on the same site as a reestablished middle school. These modulars were a challenge for the students and staff, as the lack of covered walkways exposed students to the elements when they walked from class to class.

In November 2007, the school was relocated to its original site, again in a set of modular buildings, but these were arranged in a much preferred manner. RSD officials provided a nearly seamless transition between locations that resulted in clearly improved conditions for the school. Each grade-level modular building came equipped with eight classrooms, each with advanced technology capabilities, restrooms, a science lab, and a computer lab. The school site also offered separate administrative offices, cafeteria, media center, library, and physical education center.

Carver High School continues to implement required district-level initiatives, including a Read 180 program, the extensive use of technology, and the creation of ninth-grade academies. Principal Eugene applauded the efforts of RSD leaders, explaining that "we have gone from having a school district with no policies and procedures in place to now getting manuals that describe what you do in certain situations."

The RSD's extensive provision of technology for instruction in schools and the implementation of data management systems also eased the process of teaching and learning in schools still trying to reestablish themselves.[14] However, Principal Eugene strongly resisted the district's original efforts to transform Carver into an ROTC-themed school. The staff at Carver High School successfully lobbied the district to create ninth-grade academies on creative arts instead, and now Carver has a full-time band and dance teacher.

Principal Eugene and her staff have made momentous progress in their first year back, but significant challenges remain. The school continues to struggle in meeting the educational needs of its special education students. Additionally, funding for student activities is difficult to procure, so community events are primarily self-funded. Principal Eugene is also attempting to start a parent-teacher organization, but it is currently only in its early stages of existence. Finally, a major challenge for the school is the rate at which its community is resettled; by the summer of 2008, its catchment area had recuperated only 54 percent of its original number of households.[15]

Carver High School celebrated its fiftieth anniversary in 2008, a time in which the school was still in its first year of operation after Hurricane Katrina. Upon that anniversary, Principal Eugene reflected on the school's experience, which has been marked by both success and obstacles.

As the school approached the 2008–2009 school year (its second year of operation after Katrina), its future existence was in question and significantly out of the community's control. The RSD debated whether there was significant student demand for Carver High School, that is, enough to warrant its permanent reestablishment post-Katrina. Principal Eugene and the school community immediately took action. She circulated a petition in the Carver High School community opposed to the district's master plan, and specifically, its recommendation not to rebuild the high school.

While Principal Eugene understood that the RSD often has to make "strictly business decisions" based on the demands of student populations throughout New Orleans, she and the greater school community hoped that Carver High School would justify its existence and value to families of the upper 9th Ward. Their efforts paid off, as the original recommendation in the master plan did not pass, and a permanent school is scheduled to be completed by mid-2011. Principal Eugene again stands ready to enthusiastically uphold Carver High School's well-being against future challenges.

**CONCLUSION**

Principal Eugene's eagerness to take on the unparalleled challenge of reopening Carver High School is a reminder that leading a school through crisis requires a bit of fearlessness, a lot of heart, and an enormous amount of patience. Reopening Carver High School in the aftermath of Hurricane Katrina was not a task that Principal Eugene had to assume. Rather, it is one she pursued because of the passion she had for educating students in New Orleans, especially during such a critical and challenging time in its history.

While knowledgeable of the uncertainty awaiting such a task, Principal Eugene was also keenly aware that much of the logistics for opening and running the school would have to fall into place in a very last-minute, reactive manner. In order to face such an uncertain task, she relied on multiple resources and learned that not every obstacle could be addressed immediately. She focused on the basics, making sure students were at the school—at least as much as possible—and that teachers were present and able to instruct them. Principal Eugene also accepted the unglamorous responsibilities, such as creating handmade class schedules for all students, and looked for creative opportunities to promote the school's existence in the community.

Through it all, she tried to maintain steady leadership for a school in unsteady times, to control what could be controlled, to trust others for resources that she was not able to offer herself, and to work with great enthusiasm for a school and city she loves.

## REFLECTIVE QUESTIONS

### Reflection on the Reading

1. How did Carver High School's existence in the RSD create both challenges and unique opportunities for Principal Eugene in rebuilding the high school after Hurricane Katrina?
2. In rebuilding Carver High School, Principal Eugene's biggest challenges were getting students and teachers to the school. How did she juggle such pressing demands simultaneously?
3. Only some of Carver's students enrolled with detailed academic histories. How might this have allowed a more individualized education for its students? What processes would be necessary to place students in classes appropriately?

### Application to Theory

4. Given the external nature of the crisis for Carver High School, there were many factors out of Principal Eugene's control. How did she gather some semblance of control over the very chaotic and unpredictable situation?
5. While Principal Eugene was on staff at Carver High School when the hurricane hit, she was not the principal. How might this dynamic possibly hinder or help her cause during the recovery effort?

**Application on the Job**

6. How would you reenergize a community to rebuild a school in a highly devastated community? What resources would you rely upon? What priorities would you set?
7. In what ways would you modify your current processes and oversight if you took over a school with such a high degree of teaching inexperience and youth as Carver?
8. How would you maintain the commitment of families, students, and teachers at a school possibly facing district closure (not out of a lack of performance, but strictly for "business" reasons)?

# 4

# "A Student [Came] Down and Said 'There's a . . . Guy in the . . . English Classroom with a Gun.'"

## *How Platte Canyon High School Survived a School Shooting*

**OVERVIEW**

One of the things that we did each year was, we would poll the parents and the kids and the staff, do you feel safe, and a lot of that came from—from Columbine, and everybody felt safe in the community here.

—*Principal Bryan Krause, Platte Canyon High School*

On September 27, 2006, Principal Bryan Krause received the news that every principal fears—someone with a gun was in a classroom. Initially, Principal Krause suspected a student; however, the assailant was Duane Morrison, a drifter in his early fifties who had been surveying the school for some time. According to subsequent police reports Krause received, Morrison had "no connection to our school, and that's what was scary. He just meant to do harm and meant to do evil."

Upon invading the classroom, Morrison sent everyone out except six female students. Following post-Columbine training he received, Mr. Krause focused on getting his students to safety. Students and staff annually completed lockdown drills in cooperation with the local sheriff's office and had completed such a drill a month earlier. Other than the six hostages, the other seven hundred students were safely evacuated. After hours of negotiations, and because of evidence of ongoing sexual assault within the classroom, a SWAT team stormed the room. Tragically, the gunman shot one of the two remaining hostages and then turned the gun on himself.

A school invasion and shooting epitomize the External-Unpredictable crisis. The hostage-taking and associated violence is so terrifying because of the randomness of the crime and the invariably catastrophic consequences. In Bailey, Colorado, the shooter had absolutely no link to Platte Canyon High School, leaving the school community forever questioning the motive behind his actions. While schools have increased their preparedness for school violence, the rarity of such shootings and the perceived safety of small-town Bailey, Colorado, clearly positions Principal Krause's crisis as Unpredictable.

The hostage situation resulted in a tragic student death and one school forever transformed. Although Platte Canyon's disaster preparation had helped minimize the immediate violence perpetrated on that day, the true challenge for Mr. Krause was leading the 476-student school through the succeeding months. The sixth-year principal worked to meet the emotional and mental health needs of his students, staff, and broader community, while also struggling to restore the school to its key mission of teaching and learning.

The threat of school shootings is an unfortunate reality in today's educational environment. While most administrators will not have to cope with a violent situation, preparing one's students and staff can make a tremendous difference in minimizing damage to the physical and emotional health of your school. The story of Principal Bryan Krause and Platte Canyon High School provides insight into the unique challenges of surviving an encounter with a crisis of school violence.

## CASE NARRATIVE

I believe people moved to a community like Bailey so that events like this do not occur.

—*Principal Bryan Krause*

The town of Bailey, Colorado, and its nine thousand residents are located fifty miles southwest of Denver. The town—originally a railroad stop at which ice mined from the ponds of the area would be loaded onto Denver-bound rail cars—now serves as a regional hub for mountain bikers, hunters, and fishermen. Bryan Krause, former principal of Platte Canyon High School, describes Bailey as a "typical, rural mountain town," but one lacking the isolated nature typical of most rural environments. Less than an hour's drive from Denver, many of Bailey's residents commute to the capital city to work.

The 1,300 public school students in Bailey, Colorado, are served by the Platte Canyon School District, which contains one elementary school, and a middle and high school (the latter two sharing a campus). The relatively affluent community is not particularly ethnically diverse, with an 89 percent Caucasian student body during the 2006–2007 school year.[1] Neither is it terribly economically challenged—only 16 percent of Platte Canyon High School's students qualified for free and reduced-price meals during 2006–2007.[2]

Bryan Krause came to Bailey in 2000, from a Colorado Springs high school, accepting the assistant principal position at Platte Canyon. In August of 2001, he was promoted to principal with the support of all the high school's department chairs, obtaining the job without even the formality of an interview.

Prior to 2006, increasing real estate prices—and their attendant effects— had been an ongoing challenge to Platte Canyon. With costs rising, Bailey was losing its appeal as a "bedroom community," resulting in falling enrollment within the district. During Principal Krause's five-year tenure as principal prior to the 2006–2007 school year, his biggest challenge was to reduce the size of his staff in response to the district's declining fiscal resources and enrollment. This is particularly challenging in small, close-knit communities like Bailey, in which seemingly everyone is related or has a personal relationship. "The ties are almost everywhere . . . a perfect example [is] . . . one of my secretaries is the mother-in-law of the sheriff, who has a son in the school who announces our football games . . . and also has a daughter who graduated from Platte Canyon."

The citizens of Bailey, Colorado, are appropriately proud of their public school system. Platte Canyon's achievement scores are high, performing better than the statewide average in reading and mathematics. The high school boasts several state champion debate teams. Graduating 95 percent of its students, Platte Canyon had no episodes of dangerous weapons or violence on campus prior to the school shootings in 2006.[3] Krause is particularly proud that Platte Canyon's graduates require one of the lowest rates of college remediation in the entire state.

The faculty at Platte Canyon High School is relatively evenly distributed between teachers nearing the end of their careers and those teachers beginning their careers. This contributes what Krause considers to be a good balance within the school. Krause recalls, "There was never an issue of finding a mentor for a new teacher. While many teachers were new to the classroom, there was an established, experienced core of teachers that provided consistency to the school's culture."

Prior to the school shooting, the most significant crisis event in Bailey was a substantial forest fire in 2002 that swept through the mountains surrounding the town. Many residents were evacuated, and Platte Canyon High School had actually served as a short-term shelter for displaced residents. The populace rallied, serving dinners and—according to Principal Krause—"the community really came together and helped each other."

However, this challenge was an anomaly—for the most part, in the years preceding the shooting, Platte Canyon experienced very few episodes of disorder. The anonymous "hotline" to the sheriff's department received two phone calls during the five years preceding the 2006–2007 school year. As an example of the lack of "serious" crime in Bailey, Krause observes that the local newspaper still prints the news from the police blotter—a smattering of misdemeanors and the rare felony. At the beginning of the 2006–2007 school year, Krause was the popular principal of a safe, academically rigorous high school in a quiet small town.

## CRISIS DESCRIPTION

And so I think—I think schools and communities can get lulled into complacency when it comes to safety, and I would say that we were. And we prided ourselves on that we felt safe, and that was kind of shattered all at once.

—*Principal Bryan Krause*

September 27, 2006, began as a regular school day at Platte Canyon High School. The school year had begun with a typical, high energy August, lacking any major issues. This innocence was shattered immediately before noon when

> a student had come down and said there's a—there is a man, or there's a guy in the office—or in English classroom [room 206] with a gun. And so I headed towards the classroom, and as I was going up the stairs, I remember thinking, okay, he said guy. He didn't say student or kid or Johnny . . . so that kind of gave me pause, and I—as I was reaching for the handle of the door that goes into the hallway of the classroom, that's when [the teacher] came out. She was the English teacher, and she said, "Don't go in there. There's somebody that has a gun that is holding us hostage. There's a man with a backpack."

The "man with a backpack" was fifty-three-year-old Duane Morrison from Denver. Subsequent reports by the Colorado Bureau of Investigation reported Morrison had been camping in the area for at least a few days. Post-incident review of school security cameras showed that he had been sitting in his Jeep in the school parking lot for an hour prior to the incident, and even mingled with several students when classes had changed.

Besides an arrest for obstructing police in July 2006 and marijuana possession in 1973, Morrison had no criminal or psychological history.[4] On the morning of the attack, Duane had mailed a fourteen-page letter to a relative that "apologized for events to come," but offered no additional information.[5] At present, Morrison's motivations to carry out the attack remain a mystery, as does his selection of Platte Canyon High School.

Without more information than "a guy with a gun in the classroom," Krause immediately began lockdown procedures within the school. The uncertainty at the time was particularly troubling to the school's leader:

> It was a concern, because we—we weren't sure of what the real threat was. We knew it was a gun and a hostage situation, but then there was a report from the teacher that he said that he had a bomb also in his—in his bag, which didn't prove to be true. . . . So that was the number one concern . . . getting the kids out.

Fortunately, the staff followed the lockdown procedures they practiced annually (and had practiced the previous month). Teachers locked their classroom doors and moved students into a predesignated "safe" corner of the classroom. At the same time, the local sheriff and SWAT team arrived at the school, setting up an incident command post in a field a few hundred yards from the school. After setting up a perimeter to contain Morrison in room 206, law enforcement began to methodically evacuate students from the building.

Reflecting on the experience, Krause remembers that he almost canceled the lockdown practice at the beginning of the year because of the busy school preparation. Krause credits the drill—which had been conducted in cooperation with the sheriff's office—as tremendously important in the moment of crisis:

> The staff knew what they were doing and when the SWAT team showed up to the high school—I said room 206 and they knew where to go and [the staff] knew exactly what was going to happen. [The SWAT team] responded within six minutes and we did everything we could.

The students also knew that something was seriously wrong. In chapter 2, Principal Anna Switzer discusses how her high-quality staff knew how to manage their students when it mattered. Krause reports that the same rapport existed at Platte Canyon High School:

> That's a testament to our staff, that [students] respected the teachers enough, that they knew something was seriously wrong. They had gathered in the gym and they said it was—it was quiet. And kids knew it was serious. . . . I know the media flew over and got pictures of our kids lining up, getting on the buses, and it was orderly, single file . . . the kids responded appropriately.

After sending the teacher out of the classroom, Duane Morrison had then ordered all but six females to leave. He originally spoke with negotiators, and then had hostages yell messages down the hallway. Morrison eventually stopped communicating, only saying that "something would happen at 4 P.M."[6]

During this time, Principal Krause was at the command post answering questions about the construction of the walls and number of windows, as the SWAT team investigated every method of breaching the classroom. Duane Morrison also had intermittently released four of his six hostages, who had also provided information about the layout of the room. With the vague 4

P.M. deadline and released hostages reporting ongoing sexual assault within the classroom, Park County Sheriff Fred Wegener made the decision to enter the room. Principal Krause states,

> I was so upset that I wanted to get [other high and middle school students] out of there, get them to the elementary school, where I knew they were safe, where their parents could pick them up, and that was the thing that I was just fixated on, was get them out of here, get the buses here and get the kids safe. And then [after they were safe] I knew—I knew exactly what was going to happen in the classroom. I knew [the SWAT team was] going to breach the door and they were going to go in with guns blazing and then—and I knew how that looked, because we had practiced that.

At 3:45 P.M., the SWAT team set off explosives, blowing a hole in the wall of the adjacent classroom and at the classroom door. Duane Morrison had been using sixteen-year-old Emily Keyes as a shield, and he shot her as she attempted to run away upon the breach of the classroom. He then turned the gun on himself, firing one fatal shot. The other remaining hostage in the room was unharmed. Emily Keyes was rushed to a hospital, but tragically, she was pronounced deceased upon arrival.

## CRISIS ANALYSIS

So [the staff] knew both the lockdown procedure and the active shooter routine would work. To be real honest, I was about this close to canceling it, because it was—it was, like, well we did a lockdown last year. We know—everybody knows how to do that, and it's just one more thing that we've got to do. We've got so many things going on when school starts and I almost said, "No, we're not going to do it." —*Principal Bryan Krause*

And, why he chose us was—gave me a lot of sleepless nights, but it was, like, there's no—there's no rhyme or reason. He was camping and scoping us out and why he did what he did, I don't know, but that's what was the scary part. He didn't come from within. And so I think that's maybe why it gathered so much interest. —*Principal Bryan Krause*

Perhaps the most disturbing element of Duane Morrison's attack on Platte Canyon High School is the arbitrary nature of the violence. The attacker had absolutely no history with either the school or the town, besides camping in the area. This was not a Columbine-style attack in which the shooter was a student at the school or a disturbed parent with a grudge. This attack was plainly one that originated from an external threat, external even to the broadest definition of school community.

More disturbing than the external nature of the attack is the fact that it was so arbitrary. The definition of crisis put forth in this book includes "born from complex and often unclear circumstances," and the motives of Duane Morrison are still unclear to this day. In this aspect, the crisis at Platte Canyon is fundamentally different from the crisis of 9/11—born out of a complex foreign policy history—and the crisis experienced by G.W. Carver High School, at which Hurricane Katrina wreaked havoc. The attack at Platte Canyon was neither an act of terrorism nor of God—its arbitrary nature was a unique aspect of the violence that required special attention during the school's recovery.

The distinction between a crisis that is Predictable and one that is Unpredictable is the presence—whether recognized or not at the time—of early warning signs. During the investigation of the shooting, the police discovered and characterized Duane Morrison's behavior as "predator-like" a few days before the shooting. Police suspect he may have attended a school volleyball game prior to the shooting, and know he observed the school from the parking lot the morning of September 27. He also is suspected to have dined at a local restaurant. However, these acts only seem suspicious in retrospect. According to Krause, Morrison's behaviors were nothing unusual in Bailey, which is a community that routinely has outdoorsmen come through. Krause recalls,

> People thought Morrison was a hunter, and people wouldn't take a second look when they see a gun rack or somebody dressed in camouflage—some of the kids dress in camouflage every day. It's not unheard of.

Regardless of the unpredictable nature of the actual assault, Krause and his faculty did prepare to the extent they could for this type of high-impact, highly abnormal incident. Afterward, Krause and his faculty conducted a comprehensive review of the school's security policy, struggling to identify any flaw that prevented their recognizing the danger posed by Morrison.

While in retrospect Morrison's behavior prior to the shooting may have been "predator-like," it was not abnormal for other individuals posing no threat to the school community—a school simply cannot categorize any unidentified adult attending a sports event or owning a firearm as a potential school shooter.

The insignificant interactions between Duane Morrison and the school community prior to the shooting are insufficient to constitute the "early warning signs" proposed in this book. Owing to the highly irrational and aberrant nature of the attack, it is beyond a reasonable expectation that a member of the school community would have or should have recognized Duane Morrison for the threat that he actually posed.

Finally, the crisis is different from the other two External-Unpredictable crises profiled in this book, not only because it was sudden and of short duration, but also because the school faculty had previously received training on how to react to the situation. Although there was great uncertainty throughout the entire crisis (particularly because Morrison claimed to have a bomb in his backpack), this was not as chaotic an environment as 9/11 or unpredictable a crisis as Hurricane Katrina. Instead, faculty members were able to fall back on training that they had recently completed and implement it as quickly and efficiently as they could.

## CRISIS TREATMENT

There was a time when, I was standing out there with—surrounded by deputies and SWAT team members, and, there's yelling and radios and commotion, and then it got kind of quiet for awhile, and I thought this is—this will change who we are forever as a school, and, you know, it did.

—*Principal Bryan Krause*

Colorado witnessed the most infamous and deadly school shooting in the nation's history at Columbine High School, and the event resulted in a particular focus on violence preparation within the state. Less than two months before Duane Morrison entered Platte Canyon High School, the faculty gathered to witness an "active shooter scenario." Krause states that he almost canceled the event because they had completed a similar training in 2005, and the beginning of the school year was busy. However, he chose to have it, and credits this training with setting faculty expectations for that fateful day:

> All of them got to see the SWAT team with the guns and armor, body armor, and we talked about the importance of it and how—how it would look and how it would be loud and what would happen. . . . They actually saw a demonstration of it. And it was—it was sobering again, and you think that's not going to happen here. . . . I'd rather be prepared.

The additional benefit was that this training provided preparation for the SWAT team, who gained familiarity with the layout of the school. One could imagine the haunting psychological toll on Principal Krause if he had not chosen to pursue this training.

As the crisis developed, Krause and the staff relied upon this training. Focusing on protecting the greatest number of students and faculty, the staff and SWAT team sealed off the room and evacuated the other middle and high school students from the campus. The effectiveness of this "triage" approach is one that should be implemented in a violence situation—isolate and, if possible, neutralize the problem, while simultaneously getting everyone else to a safe place.

While the shooter response protocol greatly assisted in facilitating crisis response inside the school, neither the school nor law enforcement predicted the visceral response of concerned parents learning of the school shooting. The 2008 Annual Survey of the American Public found that most schools' crisis plans suffered from the same flaw, stating that "in the event of an order to evacuate parents say that they are overwhelmingly likely to disregard existing community emergency plans . . . 63 percent [of surveyed parents] would disregard an evacuation order and go directly to their children's school in an attempt to collect their children."[7]

This was certainly consistent with the experience at Platte Canyon. Under the response plan, students from the middle and high school were evacuated to the district's elementary school, which is located at the end of a windy, two-lane road. This was a safe location with a strong staff; however, the small road was quickly choked with media trucks and panicked parents. Krause describes the situation as "chaos." Although not present at the time, he reports that parents were "[leaving] their cars in the middle of the road, running and chasing the bus on foot." It escalated to the point that the Colorado State Patrol intervened to physically hold parents back at the roadblocks.

With the tragic end to the hostage situation, Krause turned toward the long, difficult process of recovery. Similar to the crisis that hit P.S. 234 on 9/11, his first step was getting the faculty together the very next day. The staff broke into debriefing groups split by their proximity to the event, with another group for those absent from school that day who, Krause states, "had their own separate set of needs and issues." The staff was assisted by a team from neighboring Jefferson County school district, where Columbine High School is located. Therapists and counselors were available, and staff members were given "time to just spend together, eat meals together."

Another important resource during this early stage of recovery was daily briefings from members of the sheriff's office, who were slowly piecing together the history of Morrison. The randomness of the attack made information sharing very important to the faculty as they struggled to understand a potential motive and the fact that no amount of training or security procedures could have prevented this event. While the question of "why" has never been answered—and probably never will be—effective communication minimized speculation and sped recovery by understanding "what," "how," and "who."

Staff responded to the trauma in very different ways, and Krause found himself supporting their very diverse emotional and psychological needs:

> We had one teacher that says, "I'm never going to—I don't think I can come back. I can't walk inside the building," and that was okay. And we had another teacher that called me the next day and said, "You know what? I didn't pick up my midterms. I need to grade them." But that's the way that they coped with it. It's "I need my routine, I need to get back to, looking at—grading my papers." That meant a lot. And so there was a whole gamut of reaction to it.

Of particular interest is the English teacher whose class was taken over. Because of the direct threat to her life, she temporarily stopped teaching, and Principal Krause was not sure if she would be able to return. He offers, "The thing that she kept telling me was if the kids can come back, then I need to come back." This attitude was prevalent throughout the staff, as the school only had typical, expected faculty turnover at the end of the school year.

Principal Krause speaks honestly about one of his regrets during this time, as
he feels that he missed an opportunity to model the openness vital to recovery:

> I probably wasn't as open with the staff about how I was feeling . . . and looking
> back, I wish I would have been more open and shared some of my—some of
> the things I was struggling with, too, because I felt like I needed to take care of
> everybody, and, you know, you can't.

While overwhelmed with the task of recovery, Platte Canyon's leader focused
on the extremely vital tasks of managing the recovery. However, this burden
was so overwhelming that he never stopped to allow himself to be nurtured by
the community, turning instead to the private circle of his family and church.
Krause also remembers his changed leadership role during the recovery:

> My role had shifted significantly. I was pushing for providing some different
> academic programs the day before, and then you're thrust into a situation
> where you have to make sure that grief counseling is provided for the next year
> for your staff. And how do you reintroduce kids into a traumatic situation?
> What do we do with the room? . . . How do you talk to the parents? What about
> all those things? So it was—it was sobering.

Facing a multitude of important decisions about restarting school, balancing security, and supporting students, Principal Krause states that "we got
input from different people, and basically what it came down to is we decided
we needed to get back to the business of being a school."

This did not mean, however, that student needs were not met over the
crucial next semester. Times were set aside for prayer and for meeting with
teachers. Support groups were formed, and the state's victim's assistance
counseling services were available to students. Principal Krause states,

> The teachers all had a counselor available for every class. I mean, there was that
> much help. Every class had a personal counselor, and if kids wanted to leave they
> could do that, and if they needed to talk to somebody. . . . They were interested in
> talking to our counselors or their own teachers and not so much outsiders.

This theme of familiarity, of talking only with their own teachers, aligns
with the teacher who wanted to return to the routine of grading papers. There
is a lot of comfort in the familiar, and reestablishing the "calm routine" is a

key mental health objective throughout a proper crisis response.[8] The school appears to have achieved the proper balance of restoring a regular pattern to the school day with the necessary support and decoupling from this routine for those who needed it. Principal Krause credits the advice and counseling of the Columbine team with being particularly important in shaping the ways in which he and his staff processed student needs:

> When we returned, yes, we were back in school, but, we would preface every-thing by saying, "If you're not ready for this, that's okay." We'd have some kids that would show up for an hour and then they would have to go home, and that was okay. I mean, we didn't take attendance, it wasn't what we're going to do.

Support arrived from both a counseling and policy side, as the Colorado Department of Education informally informed Principal Krause that Platte Canyon should concentrate on recovery and not worry about the results of the annual accountability assessments. Not all offers of support were appreci-ated, however—Krause states that the school received a "dizzying" number of offers of help, and even though they meant well, some "don't know how to help." Krause found himself serving as an "information gatekeeper," de-termining the sincerity and quality of offers of assistance, and directing the resources to the group he felt would most benefit. He states that, ultimately, you "have to go back to who do you trust and who has gone through some-thing like this."

Perhaps the most unexpected secondary result of the crisis was struggling to recover from the crisis amid national media attention. In Krause's opinion, the national media was very aggressive, going as far as stationing a news truck outside his home. Krause found himself managing the "city of trucks and satellite dishes next to our football field." Throughout the period of intensive media focus, he "felt my responsibility was to no one except for our students and our community." The community did give interviews at first, but soon grew wary of the attention and resisted interview requests.

In Krause's estimation, a more worrisome aspect of the media was the risk of unrealistic criticism of the school and its response to the crisis, hampering ef-forts in the community to "rebuild" after the crisis. Krause voices his concern:

> They were going to say that we did something wrong, that we should have ac-costed him when he was at the Cutthroat [a local restaurant] or at the volleyball

game. Or you should have—should have, should have, should have. And there was that fear that, that they would continue digging and, try to find where we had failed.

It was quickly apparent, however, that the school had performed well during the crisis. The community had rallied quickly, and with—very unusually—almost no dissenting voices regarding the school's handling of the crisis. This extended to Emily Keyes's parents, who—even while attempting to cope with their daughter's death—were privately and publicly supportive of both the school administration and the SWAT team.

Another challenge for the school administration was in choosing how to handle the impacted classroom upon the reopening of the school. After much discussion, the staff decided that they would "allow memorials and then clear [them] out." Cards and flowers were left at the door, and at the end of the week they would be cleared away. Krause describes the process as "very loose." As time passed, items were no longer left at the door and the classroom was eventually sealed with materials donated by the local Home Depot.

As healing progressed, the community began to discuss what steps should be taken in order to increase the safety and security of students. The superintendent led several community forums, receiving input from parents and students. Krause describes the challenge of finding the optimal balance between security and maintaining the character of the school:

> That was the balance we had to try to find after it was over. Do we want this to be a prison? Do we put up razor wire and check everybody's ID as they come in the door? . . . Like any school, we had people come in and out daily. We had parents, we have friends, deliverymen. It was just any typical public school.

These discussions resulted in no significant physical changes to the school environment; instead, parents volunteered en masse for the Pass Program, which stationed parents at the doors to welcome students and provide "an extra set of eyes." This program provided a conduit for community participation in the healing process and, in Krause's estimation, provided students with the additional emotional security coming from the proximity of their parents.

When pressed to identify a point of closure at Platte Canyon High School, Principal Krause remembers the "very important" one-year anniversary of the event, stating, "We knew it [the anniversary] was going to be very important from Columbine['s experience] . . . and it was a good healing time, and we moved on." The day was spent at a local camp with volleyball and grilled hot dogs during the day and a candlelight service in the evening. With this day complete, and the 2007–2008 school year well underway, Platte Canyon High School's recovery process came to a point of closure.

## CONCLUSION

I was very guilty of thinking it can't happen here, it wouldn't happen here. . . . Like I said,—we're this close to Columbine and I remember that day, and I thought, wow, that's going to change a lot of things in school safety. I never thought it would happen [to us], and I was certainly in that camp, but you had to be prepared. You can't ever be fully prepared, but you can at least have a plan in place. And I think that's what got us through in the media's eyes, and maybe the community's eyes, was we did what we thought we should do and we were prepared for it—as well as we could be.

—*Principal Bryan Krause*

The indiscriminate nature of the attack at Platte Canyon High School shocked both the community and the nation. Overnight, Bailey, Colorado, transitioned from a peaceful, small town to a grieving community under intense scrutiny. Bryan Krause struggled to meet the urgent priorities of grieving and reopening the school, and the longer-term needs of balancing security and openness and returning the school to its previous level of intellectual rigor. Throughout the recovery process, he and his staff remained focused on returning to the core mission of the school—teaching and learning.

Advisors from Columbine predicted to Krause that the school would lose both students and staff throughout the school year, as many would decide that they could not return. Surprisingly, the school saw increased enrollment. Several parents enrolling their children for the first time at Platte County volunteered to Krause, "This is probably one of the safest schools in the nation right now."

One of the most significant challenges for the community within the first year was balancing the desire for stronger security against creating "prison-like" security conditions at the high school. Imperative to resolving this issue were community-wide conversations—led by the superintendent—resulting in greater parental involvement at the school. With the implementation of the parent-driven Pass Program, Krause states that, after the crisis, the involvement of the community and the parents "tripled" and greatly improved both the community's interest in and support of the school.

Ultimately, the major lesson of Platte Canyon High School is that school preparedness can sometimes prevent a crisis situation from becoming catastrophic. Postincident reports credit Krause's decision to hold a "lockdown" practice at the beginning of the year with greatly facilitating law enforcement response and limiting Morrison's options. Upon being alerted to an intruder with a weapon in the building, Krause initiated a predeveloped series of responses, permitting the safe evacuation of more than seven hundred students. Additionally, because of law enforcement's prior knowledge of and experience in the school in responding to a "drill" situation, Morrison was quickly and effectively contained to a single classroom. Krause credits the virtually automatic response to the news of the shooter's arrival as being essential to limiting the tragedy to one student. Noting that during the ten minutes prior to the hostage-taking more than two hundred students were "milling around" the school's lobby, Krause notes, simply, "it could have been much worse."

## REFLECTIVE QUESTIONS

### Reflection on the Reading

1. What aspects of the hostage and evacuation situation were impacted by the event occurring in a small, rural district? What elements of the crisis might have been heightened or lessened if the crisis occurred in a larger and/or urban school district?

2. Krause states that he served as the school's "gateway" for external offers of assistance, separating offers that would benefit his students and community from those that would have been distractions—or were a proxy to exploit the school's crisis for the benefit of those who made offers. In a crisis like Platte Canyon, what resources would a principal most need to address and remediate the crisis? How would you identify these resources and ensure effective deployment of them, particularly in light of logistical challenges posed by a crisis?

3. Immediately following the crisis, Platte Canyon implemented a practice of stationing parents at external doors to the school, believing that this would help prevent a repeat of the crisis. Would it have? Is such a practice likely to be sustainable in the long term—for example, the seven-year period separating the shootings at Bailey and Columbine? Does such a practice serve as a placebo, preventing the school from considering other alternatives that are more likely to prevent a school invasion or shooting? What other realistic, attainable, and sustainable steps could Platte Canyon have taken to prepare for this crisis?

## Application to Theory

4. Principal Krause—and the entire town of Bailey—resisted the spotlight of the national media. In what school violence circumstances might the media be utilized as a tool by a school's leadership team during "damage control and secondary prevention" or during "community recovery and learning"?

5. External-Unpredictable crises, by their nature, are difficult to predict and seldom occur from circumstances within the school's direct or indirect control. How might the broader school community assist in identifying the early warning signs of school violence?

6. What structures of K–12 schooling might aid in the recovery of a violence event? What structures might hinder in the recovery?

7. In what ways could a return to a focus on teaching and learning assist in a school's recovery process?

## Application on the Job

8. One of the most important elements identified in containing the crisis at Platte Canyon was school and law enforcement familiarity with a lockdown policy and annually practicing it. Does your school practice a lockdown procedure annually? Does all of your staff know how to act in a school violence situation? Do they appreciate the noise and chaos accompanying school violence crises?

9. Do you have a close relationship with local law enforcement? How knowledgeable are they about your leadership team and the layout of your school? Do they know what social and organizational behaviors your school is likely to exhibit during a crisis in which their intervention is required?

10. Krause identified the visceral response of many parents—ignoring the directions from law enforcement and the school to stay away from the site—as an unanticipated and confounding consequence of news spreading of the school invasion. Does your school's current crisis management plan envisage the probable behavior of individuals beyond the school's control—such as parents? Is, for example, the scene of evacuation sufficiently wide to allow for the orderly pickup of students? For managed chaos? What similar "bottlenecks" can you anticipate that might hinder or prevent you from managing the chaos of an External-Unpredictable crisis?

11. Reflect on the crisis at Platte Canyon and consider how your school would likely respond—today—to a similar crisis. Specifically consider the security of your school campus and whether you have processes in place to prevent intruders from entering your building.

# INTERNAL-
# UNPREDICTABLE

# 5

# "I Thought, 'Oh, God. This is Bad.' Then I Found Out It Was Much, Much Worse."

## *How Greenacre High School Addressed the Discovery of Systemic Grade Fraud*

**OVERVIEW**

I thought, "Oh, God. This is bad." Then I found out it was much, much worse.

—*Gwen Richardson, superintendent, Greenacre School District*

Most case studies in this book address principals' experiences encountering and surmounting crisis in their schools. This chapter differs. The crisis in the Greenacre School District arose from a principal's *failure* to recognize or lead during a time of turmoil, ultimately requiring his superintendent to intervene. Systemic academic dishonesty within the district's schools—specifically the unethical changing of students' grades by teachers—eventually became the superintendent's crisis to overcome, given the principal's willful ambivalence to the mounting consequences of such practices for the system's core values, ability to educate students, and confidence of the community.

Deepening the distinction between this chapter and the balance of the book is the authors' decision to preserve the anonymity of the principal, the other administrators involved, and the district, employing pseudonyms where necessary. To increase anonymity, the case includes elements from similar crises, and changes not affecting the nature of the crisis have been made. The reasons for doing so will become apparent in the chapter. As a result, any similarities between individuals in the chapter and actual persons or events are purely coincidental.

## CASE NARRATIVE

For years, people had been saying [Greenacre] is the "worst" school system in the state, and you just ignore it. What do they know—they don't have our students, et cetera. But when it's the state department of education saying it, and you're on the school board, you know you have to do something.

—*a member of the Greenacre Board of Education*

Greenacre is a small school district located in the rural mid-south. Greenacre County is relatively economically depressed, with approximately 30 percent of the county's households below the poverty line. The average household income—less than $26,000—is approximately 60 percent of its state average. The school district is the county's largest employer, with a small manufacturing plant following. With most of the county's residents working in construction or seasonal employment, "[public school] teachers have a relatively high status locally," explains one school board member. Thirty-five percent of the school district's students live in single-parent homes, and almost 90 percent qualify for federal free or reduced-price meal status.

While Greenacre County is relatively racially balanced (approximately 55 percent black and 39 percent white), its public schools are not—approximately 99 percent of the district's one thousand students are black, as are 75 percent of the teaching faculty, 80 percent of its classified staff, and—prior to 2002—all seven of its school board members. The county's white students are primarily educated in the two small, church-affiliated private schools.

In July 2001, Gwen Richardson became superintendent of schools, following the board of education's decision not to renew the contract of Dr. John Johnson, a Greenacre native. A former teacher and principal in Greenacre's system, Dr. Johnson served as superintendent for six years preceding Richardson's appointment. When questioned about Dr. Johnson's superintendency, a board member opines, "He enjoyed the power and status that came with being superintendent, but it was clear that he knew next to nothing about budgets, personnel, or instruction."

Board members characterize the district's hiring practices during Johnson's tenure as appearing to be largely based on patronage. "The first place [district] job vacancies were announced was the pulpit of his church. Literally." Johnson's lack of focus on education was evident in the superintendent's office as well. Richardson recalls,

> When I entered the superintendent's office, it was apparent [that] mandatory [state and federal] reports had never been filed. My inquiries for personnel records . . . ran from, "It doesn't look like we have a file" . . . to—my personal favorite—"I found this in the bathroom." It was amazing. The only reason I can imagine [Greenacre] avoided state takeover is that the state department of education didn't want it.

Efforts to change the complacency and ineffectiveness of Johnson's superintendency began in fall 2000, when five community members—three black and two white—challenged five sitting school board members for their seats. The candidates campaigned on the district's ten-year history of student standardized test scores falling within the bottom 2 percent of those in its state, despite having relatively high property taxes and one of the lowest student-teacher ratios in the state. In an election with relatively low voter turnout, the five new board members were narrowly elected and seated in January 2001.

Predictably, the board began to experience tension with Johnson. The most troubling development to the new board members was discussions of the recent reauthorization of the Elementary and Secondary Act of 1965. After attending a state conference, one board member recalls,

> It seemed like every other speaker was talking about No Child Left Behind and how every child had to pass the state test or the school system failed. Later we learned this was not true, but it scared us to death. We knew our students—who scored at the bottom in the state—were not going to pass a state test.

The new board members returned with a directive for Johnson—hire an assistant superintendent with the ability to improve teaching and learning in the district or be replaced. This directive resulted in Johnson's recommending Richardson as assistant superintendent in February 2002. Richardson was a former director of instruction and assessment in a much larger, academically successful county. Richardson applied for the job knowing both the "challenges" apparent in the position and the opportunity for promotion. "Of course, there is some ego in wanting to be an assistant superintendent—even in a district like [Greenacre]."

Richardson immediately encountered a major "culture" problem in the school district. She discovered what she characterizes as a culture of complacency operating for "the benefit of the teachers and not the students." Almost immediately, Richardson began regular observations in schools, revealing systemic ambivalence and incompetence: "We had teachers who did not know subject matter, as in teaching—literally—'opposite' means 'the same as.'" Students were unsupervised and wandered the hallways. "It was impossible to tell a difference between class time and changing class time. The hallways were always packed with kids." Seemingly oblivious to their instructional responsibilities, teachers would leave the schools during the day for personal errands, with some "sit[ting] at their desks and openly play[ing] solitaire on the computer. I was so angry, I thought I would explode."

Further cracks became evident as teachers' personnel files were rebuilt from records requested from the state. Teachers were teaching outside their areas of certification, and some lacked any teaching certification whatsoever. While hiring had mushroomed during Johnson's tenure, it was not accompanied by an increase in performance: "We simultaneously had the lowest class sizes and lowest test scores in the state. It was appalling." Richardson identified the teachers as the point of immediate intervention.

Teachers whose skills were inadequate were placed on aggressive professional development plans. "Anyone who was capable of remediation, I was willing to remediate; however, we made it very clear that the current situation was not going to continue." By May, approximately one-quarter of the district's teaching faculty members (fifteen of the fifty-five teachers) resigned, retired, or were removed. "We didn't know what to think," a board member states, "until she showed us her observations. Then we couldn't believe we didn't fire Johnson sooner." On July 1, 2002, Richardson replaced Johnson as superintendent.

One of Richardson's supporters for the superintendency was Darren Roberts, principal of the high school. Roberts was an important resource for Richardson—one of the district's two white board members characterized Roberts as "a visible black supporter of hers when she needed a visible black supporter." Richardson confirms a friendship that predated Greenacre. "I had nothing but respect for him. He's incisive, articulate, funny—I love him. When he left [county] to assume the principalship at [Greenacre], I was happy for him." When asked if she was surprised to find the high school in the condition it was in after a year of Roberts's tenure as principal, she notes,

> Well, yes. But he told me that he had no support for changes in the central office and, "You should have seen this place before last year." He was my friend, I respected him, so I gave him the benefit of the doubt. And assurances that he would now have the support he needed.

Board members were less certain. Typifying their responses was one's observation that "Roberts talked a good game, but I didn't see *any* difference in the way the high school was before he got there. He wasn't as involved in classrooms in the high school as principal as Gwen was as assistant superintendent" (original emphasis).

Substantial changes followed Richardson's assumption of the superintendency. She replaced two of the district's three principals, retaining only Roberts. An instructional coach was hired for each of the district's schools, discipline was enforced, and students refusing to obey the directives of teachers were given in-school suspension and placed on computerized instruction. As expectations increased for both students and faculty, teachers continued to leave—over the next two years, approximately another one-third of the district's veteran teachers retired or resigned. They were replaced by individuals with stronger pedagogical training, who were "hand-selected" by Richardson and the principals. Recalls Richardson,

> In three years, we basically replaced or remediated almost the entire teaching faculty. This had a huge impact on instructional quality. We integrated after-school programs and test-taking strategies. With our socioeconomic demographics, we also knew we had to take the battle "home," convincing parents who had not personally seen the benefits of education that their children could benefit from good schools, and teaching them how to help, support, and occasionally cajole their students at home.

The results were significant. By spring 2005, the district's performance on state standardized tests soared from the bottom tenth of the schools in the state to performing nearly at the state average. More impressively, Greenacre ranked in the top 10 percent of performance among schools with comparable student demographics. The district's performance brought state and national recognition. The district's schools received Title I "Blue Ribbon" honors and "distinguished schools" status, with the elementary and middle school earning the state's highest recognition for improved school performance. "It was amazing," summarized one board member, "simply amazing."

## CRISIS DESCRIPTION

I'll never forget it. It was late May and the school year was ending uneventfully. That should have been my first clue.

—*Superintendent Gwen Richardson*

As the 2006–2007 school year drew to a close, Richardson was in her office when a high school teacher asked for a moment of her time. "He informed me that he had been approached by another teacher requesting that a senior's grade be changed." While he refused to do it, he believed other teachers had already done so. Taking the student's file, Richardson immediately saw that the student's semester average in two of his classes was a full grade higher than the arithmetic mean of his quarter grades. This was particularly astonishing to Richardson given the school board's policy explicitly prohibiting the changing of quarter or semester grades by teachers.

Curious, Richardson began to pull grades for other graduating seniors. She noticed similar discrepancies. "I started to feel sick, because of our school board policy and apparent flagrancy with which this policy was violated." She noted that two of the senior-most teachers in the system—teachers with almost thirty years of experience in the school district—had the most significant number of discrepancies:

> If you had asked me earlier in the day who were the two biggest problems in the high school, I would have identified these two teachers. They were both decent at instruction [but] they were vocal critics of changes made in the system, they were constantly accused of playing favorites with the students by students and parents, and they constantly openly longed for the "old days." I was repeatedly told they referred to me as "that white bitch."

As Richardson continued her investigation throughout the summer, evidence mounted that this was not an omission, misunderstanding, or oversight. "A clear pattern emerged regarding the seniors whose grades were altered. In most cases, they were either the children of district employees or went to a particular church to which both teachers belonged." Richardson continued pulling student grades, going back several semesters, and expanding her review to the rest of the students in the high school, and subsequently to the middle and elementary schools. She recalls,

> I must have reviewed grades for two weeks, but I needed to know how wide-spread the problem was. Listen, we had done remarkable things, things no school system that looks like us is supposed to do, and I immediately knew that if we did not get this problem contained it would destroy all of our gains. A school system that makes tremendous progress on test scores cannot have the integrity of those scores—or any other academic indicator—validly questioned.

By the end of June, Richardson knew that she had to reprioritize her investigation. "I had to know whether the academic dishonesty extended to the standardized test scores, on which all of our national and state awards—and pride—were based." She contacted the state department of education and informed them of the grading irregularities and requested state assistance with an immediate investigation of the validity of district test scores. The state verified testing protocols, making certain no teachers oversaw the testing of their own students. Several "miserable" weeks later, the state department of education determined there was no evidence of academic impropriety on state tests. "In fact, they actually commended us on steps taken to ensure testing accuracy." Richardson returned to the "local" investigation.

As the 2007–2008 school year commenced, Richardson closed her records investigation, concluding that eight of the county's fifty teachers had grades that were inconsistent with the board's policy on grading.* Of the eight, six were in the high school and two in the middle school. Looking at patterns in the altered grades, Richardson was troubled. "Any academic dishonesty is

---

*Richardson lowered the number of teaching faculty from fifty-five to fifty to produce additional revenue for staff development and other initiatives. She observes, "We were still well below average class sizes in our region."

problematic . . . but some of these grades were actually *lowered* by the teacher.
. . . I thought, 'Lord, here comes the lawsuit.'"

## CRISIS ANALYSIS

It was immediately clear that this was going to be a world-class mess. I
thought that when the press gets this, it will undo everything we've worked
so hard to do.

—*Superintendent Gwen Richardson*

Initially, it may be unclear whether the academic dishonesty detailed in the
case above rises to the definition of a crisis—after all, "cheating" has been a
perennial and chronic problem in education, both in the United States and
internationally[1]—and schools have persevered. However, the events giving rise to crises occur within specific cultural and organizational contexts
that—in isolation—might not rise to the level of crisis. As Denis Smith notes,
it is precisely these cultural and organizational dynamics that make "service
sector" industries—such as schools—*particularly* vulnerable to crises.[2]

Greenacre makes an important contribution to the analysis of school
crises by demonstrating the role of context in crisis evolution. It was not
the academic dishonesty by 20 percent of the teachers at Greenacre High
School—which Richardson would unquestionably categorize as a "serious
problem"—but the potential effects of its discovery that actually brought the
events to the level of a crisis. Greenacre was in the middle of transformational
organizational change when the grade-changing discovery unfolded. Had
the facts of this case emerged in 2001, they would have posed a logistical and
financial problem to Greenacre, but its core values—which were, in 2001,
very much built around a "culture of complacency"—would not have been
threatened.

However, between 2002 and 2005, Greenacre made a remarkable—and
difficult—transition from a low-performing school district to a relatively
high-performing one. Richardson believes these successes "robbed" the administration's critics of the "tremendously powerful" phrase "that will never
work here." Securing "wins" heartens supporters and minimizes critics when
attempting transformational organization change,[3] while "victories" encour-

age followers and build commitment, communicating that leaders will do what they say they will do.[4]

By contrast, nothing strengthens opposition as showing that a leader promotes insincere values, providing opponents with an opportunity to question credibility.[5] The effects of "wins" are particularly important in organizations—such as those typified by public education—that culturally and structurally resist change.[6] Reflecting, Richardson seemingly concurs:

> I was . . . most worried about the potential erosion of community support for the way the schools were changing. [The grading inaccuracies] gave the district's critics the ability to say, "See. We told you that they must have been cheating." That would destroy support for the changes we were trying to make.

As noted in other chapters, correctly identifying the true source and predictability of a crisis significantly facilitates response (see chapter 1). This crisis falls within the Internal-Unpredictable typology. The source of the crisis is the academic dishonesty practiced by those teachers within the school system. The crisis is classified as Unpredictable because Richardson—and the rest of the administrators in the system—were completely taken aback by the news of grade changing. It was not a crisis for which she had adequate early warning. Rather, it was a crisis that fell in her lap and required immediate action without advance planning.

## CRISIS TREATMENT

We had to publicly demonstrate that these teachers were not part of our school's community and their actions did not represent the school district.

—*Superintendent Gwen Richardson*

The crisis response model suggests that successful crisis response requires quick and decisive leadership—leadership anticipating and planning for crisis situations prior to onset to the extent possible. It also requires the development of leadership dispositions upon which a leader can almost instinctually rely at the onset of crisis.[7]

This is precisely what Gwen Richardson did when faced with the crisis in Greenacre. A teacher reported falsification of student grades and Richardson moved immediately to personally investigate the situation. This uncovered further evidence of widespread and systemic grade changing. Most concerning, these practices threatened to dismantle the integrity of all the district's recent efforts to climb out of a chronic past of dismal performance and into a season of transformational change.

Richardson immediately called a meeting of her three building principals to discuss her findings. "Since it was an issue occurring in two of their schools, I did not want to overstep my bounds as superintendent and intervene directly—well, any more than I had, already." All three principals agreed that an investigation was needed to discover both the extent of the grade changes, any reasons why the grades might have been changed, whether there was insufficient awareness of the board's policy, and any other contributing factors.

They all attested that they covered the board's grading policy during in-service with the faculty, and it was doubtful that teachers—particularly veteran teachers—were unaware of the policy. The elementary and middle school principals recognized that the next logical step would be to conduct interviews with the grade-changing teachers and ultimately notify parents. However, Roberts—the high school principal—balked at this. "He asked if we just could 'fix' the grades and tell the parents that it was some sort of internal error. I told him that we had enough 'grade fixing,' and we had to notify the parents," recounts Richardson.

Roberts's reticence to talk to parents paled beside his resistance to confront the teachers involved:

> He just shook his head and said, "That will be suicide," or something like that. He then became an apologist. He said, "I'm sure it's extra credit, teachers have the 'right' to consider student effort," that sort of thing. I told him that the teachers would have an opportunity to [explain] that during interviews.

The other two principals and Richardson began to discuss an interview protocol and questionnaire, discussing how to question teachers without disrupting instruction and, since the investigation would include questioning six of the high school's twenty teachers, how to "contain" the effects of the interviews. Richardson had two primary concerns. First was controlling the dissemination of information about this investigation, knowing it could easily spiral into the chain of gossip in the small Greenacre community. "After the [principal] meeting, I added [Roberts] to my list of concerns. I didn't think he was 'hiding' anything, but he was so resistant to doing this, I didn't know."

After the other principals left, Roberts remained to talk to Richardson. He explained that his hesitancy had nothing to do with a lack of courage, but stemmed from "political reality":

> He told me "as a friend" that this was my first superintendency, I had a long career ahead of me, I was committing "career suicide," they would come after me in the churches because I was white and four of the six teachers were black, this would affect my whole career, that sort of thing. I think he was genuinely concerned.

Richardson responded by asking him if it was fair to the students involved to "ignore it":

> He asked me if it would be more beneficial to the 95 percent of students who weren't affected if I were removed as superintendent, the board lost the next election, and all the changes we made were undone. And you have to remember that this is coming from the person I use as my sounding board for decisions. Before talking to him, I thought I clearly knew what I needed to do, but his comments were unnerving.

Instead, Roberts suggested a "quiet" internal investigation, "correcting" any "misunderstanding" by teachers regarding grading practices, and "quietly fixing" the fraudulent grades. Richardson told him she would think about it, but she wanted the principals to meet the next morning and start putting together a process for interviewing the teachers. "His final words were 'make sure you talk to me before that meeting.' I told him I would."

Roberts's observations gave Richardson pause. "The more I thought about it, the more terrified I became." Particularly concerning Richardson, however, was Roberts's forecast of the racial tenor of the ensuing controversy:

> I hate to say it . . . his remarks on the black/white thing scared me. I was accustomed to being . . . called a racist by just about every black teacher I corrected, removed, said anything he or she disagreed with, [and] I lived through several [Equal Employment Opportunity complaints] accusing us of racial animus in employment decisions—all of which found no evidence of racial motivation

. . . [but] Darren said this would be different. He said we'd have marches, it would be in the news.

That night, Richardson reports, she was so concerned she did not sleep:

> I asked my husband to seriously consider how we would make it if I got fired, and we talked about the financial impact on our family. I mean, we got out our financial records—that's how scared I was. There was no scenario in which it was not bad. I sat in my living room that night after everyone went to bed and got to the point of wishing that teacher had just changed the grade.

Early the next morning, Richardson believed that she needed the perspective of a more experienced superintendent, and one further removed from the crisis. She called a friend she characterizes as a veteran and well-respected superintendent. Her advice to Richardson was that this is a *principal*, not a *superintendent*, problem, and it only becomes a superintendent problem if the principal doesn't do his job or doesn't do it appropriately. Richardson took this advice to heart.

Richardson then called Roberts as promised and told him that she decided to go forward with the investigation. Roberts reiterated his concerns, saying this was "a huge and career-ending mistake." He also told her that he was now uncertain if he had adequately explained the board's grading policy to his teachers, which Richardson found doubtful. Richardson said she wouldn't do anything until she talked to him, and asked Roberts to come to her office before going to school, which he agreed to do.

In preparation for her meeting with Roberts, Richardson called five of the high school teachers, asking them if Roberts covered the grading policy during the high school in-service. Each of them confirmed that he did so adequately, accurately describing the policy prohibiting quarterly and semester grade changes.

Once Roberts arrived, "the discussion became awkward in a hurry. I remember he came in looking very tired, and I guess a little relieved." Any relief Roberts felt disappeared quickly when she told him that they had an "ethical obligation" to continue with an investigation. Switching tactics, Roberts agreed to investigate, but again raised concern that perhaps he had not been as clear about the board's grading policy as he could have been with his teachers. Holding up her hand, Richardson interrupted him, informing him of her conversation with the five high school teachers that morning. Richardson began to question Roberts's ability to investigate this matter, noting "he was subconsciously—if not consciously—already looking for a way to exonerate the teachers involved."

Upon the other principals' arriving, Richardson asked each of them—starting with Roberts—how they would proceed with an investigation. "I anticipated that his suggestions would not be workable, [but] I needed to preserve our relationship, and I had enough confidence in [the other two principals] to critique Darren's suggestion—which is what happened." As Roberts began to outline a plan—one informing individual teachers of their discrepancies and allowing them to go home and "think about it" before being questioned—the other two principals "tore it apart," noting it was likely to produce dishonesty and collusion.

Eventually, the principals agreed that the investigation would require the participation of all principals and a common interview protocol. Then Roberts raised the issue of whether the district had "the legal right" to ask the teachers these questions. Anticipating this question, Richardson previously discussed the matter with the school board's attorney, clarifying what could or could not be asked during the investigation. Richardson also arranged for eight substitutes—one for each of the teachers to be questioned—and the union representative, "in case any teachers wanted him present during questioning."

Richardson and the principals then built the questionnaire, working to establish teacher familiarity with the policy and forecasting probable explanations for the grade changes, as well as appropriate follow-up questions—such as, if a student was given extra credit, was this opportunity offered to all students? After each teacher's questioning, he or she would be given a chance to fully inspect all questionable grades and document an explanation for each. The teachers would be asked not to discuss the interview with any other teacher and would be given a packet with questions requiring written responses and a copy of all their grade books and quarterly and semester grade submissions. Each would be given two days to provide a more detailed written explanation for any inconsistencies.

An hour after the principals departed from Richardson's office, she received a phone call from the elementary school principal. The principal reported Roberts's issuing similar "career-suicide" warnings to each of them as they drove to the middle school, saying, "I [Richardson] would be fired and the principals would be looking for jobs." She also said that Roberts refused to record interviews or personally ask questions of any high school teachers. He also volunteered several times that a teacher's answer was "good enough" and that no follow-up questions were warranted.

"He was positioning," observes Richardson. "When this all came out, he wanted the teachers to remember that he was against it." Richardson directed them to continue recording the interviews and that she would be there momentarily to observe—as part of their annual evaluation. When asked why she did not remove Roberts from the interviews, she responds,

> I couldn't, for several reasons. First, it was his job, and I thought—with enough pressure—he would eventually do it. Second, he had already told me that this would be a racial issue, and I couldn't remove the black high school principal from this investigation—which primarily involved his teachers—without inviting speculation as to why. I would be put in a position of not responding, or explaining why I removed Darren from the process . . . [resulting in] the board wanting me to fire him.

Upon Richardson's arrival, she sat in the corner with a legal pad and a teacher observation instrument. "It was all I could find, but the principals recognized it as an evaluation instrument, but were not close enough to see that it wasn't for principals." Roberts's posture immediately changed. He began to lead the questioning of the high school teachers, taking an active role in the process, adding a personal admonition that teachers were not to discuss the investigation with anyone at the school.

Two weeks later, the evidence showed that six of the eight teachers—two white, four black; two middle, four high school—each had in excess of fifty grade changes that they could neither explain nor justify. The other two teachers produced sufficient evidence of "extra credit" projects students did to earn additional points to justify the grade changes.

Richardson and the principals concluded that the six remaining teachers were blatantly violating Greenacre board policy, and that the children of certain school faculty were particularly favored. One of the teachers—whose spouse was the football coach—tended to increase the grades of athletes, while another improved the averages of students enrolled in her Sunday school class. "All these patterns came out while we were investigating . . . they were very select and deliberate."

The district—and the high school particularly—now faced a new crisis. Richardson could not fire four of the high school teachers at the start of the school year—"that was 20 percent of all the teachers in the high school." However, something had to be done to convey that violations of board policy would not go unpunished.

Richardson invited suggestions from the middle school principal and Roberts. The middle school principal suggested allowing the teachers to resign immediately in lieu of a termination hearing. Roberts suggested "a reprimand." Richardson explains, "I did not think a reprimand was appropriate, given the gravity of the offense, particularly as none of the teachers involved acknowledged wrongdoing in any way or showed any remorse." Plus, she knew that the news of the academic dishonesty would spread like wildfire considering the district's obligation to report grade corrections to parents.

Richardson also knew that termination hearings were not a "realistic" option, given that each one of those hearings would cost at least $10,000—potentially a $60,000 unplanned expenditure—and money the district did not have. The teachers, who had legal representation provided by their union, would face no comparable personal cost. Richardson knew she could potentially replace two teachers and afford two termination hearings—but no more. She also knew Roberts would be a key witness in the hearings of the high school teachers, and likely to testify that he did not believe termination was merited.

Despite this, Richardson knew she could not permit the academically dishonest teachers to remain in the schools without significantly eroding the community's faith in the district and support for continued reform efforts. She also had to move quickly, as grade corrections were going to necessitate parental notice—with resulting media attention—and federal and state law limited what she could communicate to the press.

After weighing options, in November 2006, Richardson offered all six teachers the opportunity to resign immediately, with an effective date at the end of the school year. While the middle school principal agreed to make the offer to her teachers, Richardson had to direct Roberts to make the offer to his. Again making the union representative available to the teachers, Richardson and

Roberts called the teachers in individually, outlined the evidence against them, offering the options of resigning with an effective date at the end of the year or facing a termination hearing.

In Richardson's opinion, the meeting "forced" a decision by the teachers, prevented equivocation, collusion, or procrastination in their decision-making, and allowed the administration to simultaneously present parents, students, and community members with the problem and the solution:

> We told them that we had a meeting with the affected parents and students at the end of the day, and they would want to know what was happening with the teachers—particularly the parents of students whose grades were lowered. We also told them that we were going to have to issue a press statement to prevent misinformation from being spread in the community regarding the crisis and report it to the [state educator ethics board]. I told them that it was my strong feeling—and this is true—that unless they resigned before this news got out, (1) the [ethics board] would suspend their teaching certification—which would require us to fire them because they couldn't teach; and (2) the parents and community would not tolerate end-of-the-year resignations. [Resigning before the news got out] was the least disruptive way this could be handled.

By the end of the day, all six of the teachers had turned in resignations effective at the end of the year. The district issued a press release, candidly discussing what occurred and the scope of the investigation. The release also addressed both the state's validation of standardized test score results and the district's "confidence" in the accuracy of all other grades.

Two months later, the crisis appeared to have passed. "We were repeatedly told by other teachers, parents, and community members that they appreciated the 'quiet' way we took care of this." However, the resigning teachers did not share this sense of appreciation, and Richardson was also told by several high school teachers that a story was circulating among faculty that "all this was my 'fault,' and [Roberts] wanted nothing to do with it." Richardson observes, "If he didn't start it, he also didn't deny it. I told him I thought he was making a mistake and—at a minimum—the rumor made the administration look divided." A board member was less equivocal. "He was responsible. We had teachers telling us that he personally told them that he did not want the matter pursued, and it was all [Richardson]."

Parents and community members were livid with Roberts's tolerance and implicit endorsement of the teachers' behavior, expressing their anger to the board of education. The mounting pressure made it impossible for Richardson to retain Roberts as high school principal, and he resigned at the end of the school year.

Richardson's handling of the crisis in Greenacre exemplifies many of the actions and dispositions that a school leader must utilize when facing an Unpredictable crisis threatening the core being of his or her school (or in this case, schools). While Richardson moved decisively, she also did not merely react—her steps were very thoughtful and deliberate, ensuring that her response focused directly upon the *actual* crisis she saw looming—the potential loss of momentum in systemic school reforms. Upon recognizing that the most potentially devastating effect of the crisis would be allowing opponents of system reform to question the validity of standardized testing results, Richardson "self-reported" possible testing inconsistencies to the state and cooperated completely with a thorough investigation of the testing process.

This investigation ultimately validated the district's testing protocol and indicated no threats to the district's test scores. Richardson seized the opportunity to control the flow of positive information given this promising find. Richardson notes, "We publicized the results extensively and prior to the 'grade changing' becoming public knowledge. In my opinion, this prevented any questions of testing validity from gaining traction." Additionally, sharing this information with stakeholders—as well as sharing information on the investigation with parents and community members at the conclusion of the investigation—indicated that the administration was operating transparently. "To the extent we could, we threw open our books on the investigation."

Richardson was similarly deliberative in considering what the probable consequences of—and responses to—the crisis would be in her stakeholder community and moved to contain responses that would be adverse to the process. While it may be difficult to foresee Unpredictable crises, leaders can occasionally forecast the primary and secondary results of crises and move to contain them. Richardson's appropriate anticipation of allegations of testing irregularities resulted in her moving to contain those allegations before even her principals knew of the looming crisis.

Likewise, Richardson anticipated Roberts's attempts to frustrate the investigation of grading irregularities. Such forecasting led her to telephone teachers, verifying that he addressed the district's policy prior to his having an opportunity to either directly or indirectly suggest that he might not have covered it.

One of the significant lessons of this case was the effect of a school leader—Roberts—refusing to recognize and contain a crisis, and the necessity of marginalizing that individual as an element of crisis response. While Richardson and other interviewees are unanimous in their belief that he was acting from "good" motives and genuinely believed he was acting in the district's—and Richardson's—best interest, Richardson could not convince Roberts that his response to the crisis would only intensify it, deepening it in length and effect, and spawn additional crises. While "containing" Roberts forced Richardson to play a greater role in responding to the crisis (and one that she believed was not ideal, given that she was a district-level administrator), by so doing, Richardson prevented Roberts from fracturing the crisis further. Although containing him was time consuming, Richardson believes the crisis required it—he could not be allowed to unilaterally participate or be removed without exacerbating the situation. "Removing Darren would have been a disaster, and would have presented me with an even bigger problem to solve, and probably would have turned this completely into a black-white issue."

Overall, Richardson used her ability to anticipate consequences of the crisis to minimize the extent to which it would undermine the district's well-being. Despite limited financial resources—leading her to a compromise between terminating teachers and simply reprimanding them—she was able to devise a solution that preserved the integrity of the district and allowed reform efforts to continue. Consequently, the momentum for transformational change was not stymied and—despite the crisis—Greenacre continued its progress toward becoming the school district that it always had the potential to be.

## REFLECTIVE QUESTIONS

### Reflection on the Reading

1. A major challenge to Richardson's decision-making capabilities in Greenacre was the realistic threat of a school crisis becoming a personal crisis, threatening her professional livelihood and reputation. How should a school

leader forecast personal variables impacting his or her ability to make leadership decisions for a school? Can—or should—these be contained? Why?

2. A significant issue in Greenacre was Dr. Richardson's inability to discharge 25 percent of the school's faculty despite their systemically engaging in unethical and illegal behavior. How would you handle such a situation in your school? Could you sustain the loss of 25 percent of your teaching faculty from a single event? How would you explain retaining "unethical" teachers to the parents of students who were actively hurt by those teachers' behavior?

**Application to Theory**

3. The crisis at Greenacre took Dr. Richardson by surprise, as she did not anticipate systemic grade fraud at Greenacre High School. One of the most significant debates occurring between the authors on this book was whether she should have assumed that academic dishonesty occurred in a system like Greenacre. What do you think and why?

4. In Greenacre, Richardson believed the discovery of systemic academic dishonesty only rose to the level of a "crisis" because of the transformational efforts occurring in the district and the dependency of those efforts on the integrity of student performance on standardized tests. Would another systemic problem not relating to students' academic performance—such as the discovery of a group of teachers' embezzling funds from activities accounts or using school computers to distribute pornography—have created a "crisis" in Greenacre, or would it have remained a "problem"? What are other examples of situational contexts or variables in schools capable of transforming a problem into a crisis?

**Application on the Job**

5. A chief issue in the Greenacre crisis was one of trust and public perception. What communication resources would you employ in a crisis to ensure that the public did not lose confidence in your leadership? How could you retain—or even build—parental and community "trust" in a crisis?

6. At Greenacre, Dr. Richardson had to work to contain one of her chief and most trusted lieutenants who was actively working against her resolution of the crisis—but with the best of intentions. Assume you are in a similar position, with one of your primary and most trusted subordinates actively working against you. How would you handle such a situation, and why?

## 6

# "He Kept Returning to 'She Cost Me a Cow!'"

*How H.W. Smith K–8 School Struggles to Integrate Somali Bantu Students*

**OVERVIEW**

The reality is, as a principal or vice-principal, you have to stand up for what you believe in is right, and you have to do what's right for kids, because that's why we're here. It's the kids. Not their parents, not the politics, not the community—although they're all part of it. . . .The moment they walk into this building until the moment they leave, they're our kids.

—*Sharon Birnkrant, principal of H.W. Smith K–8 School\**

Accommodating a refugee group newly arrived to the country involves a myriad of challenges for a school. Language support must be provided to both students and family members, staff and students may require resorting, and appropriate instruction must be arranged. More challenging is that many students bring with them incredible physical and emotional baggage associated with a refugee's past. Clearly, refugee students can be among the most high-need and disadvantaged within a school. Principal Sharon Birnkrant of H.W. Smith K–8 School in Syracuse, New York, is familiar with the challenges of educating refugee students, as her students represent *forty* different languages and *thirty* separate countries. Most districts' entire student bodies do

---

\*At the beginning of the 2007–2008 school year, H.W. Smith converted from a K–6 Elementary School to a K–8 school. Many of the stories told within this chapter occurred in a K–6 environment.

93

not represent thirty different countries, but Principal Birnkrant is responsible for them all in one school.

Under Principal Birnkrant's leadership, H.W. Smith K–8 School was transformed from its conventional background to a multiethnic, educational, and informational node of the immigrant community. Beginning in 1993, H.W. Smith began receiving groups of immigrants, and each of these cultural waves brought its particular challenges and opportunities. In the midst of these challenges, H.W. Smith has maintained an inclusive environment for English Language Learners (ELL) and their families, minimizing xenophobic reactions from the broader community.

The biggest challenge so far, and the true crisis that has yet to be fully overcome by H.W. Smith, is the latest group of refugees from the failed, war-torn nation of Somalia. This Somali Bantu ethnic group has arrived with less educational preparation than all previous groups; this, coupled with distinctive social norms and an insistence on special treatment, has stymied efforts to increase student achievement levels. The demand for special treatment and unwillingness to fully connect with the global community at H.W. Smith is an Internal-Unpredictable crisis that threatens to derail the inclusive culture of the school. Within this case study, the authors will first discuss the ways in which the staff at H.W. Smith built their multiethnic, inclusive community, then present the efforts to address the refugee crisis—not yet resolved—that threatens to swamp this uniquely American environment.

## CASE NARRATIVE

H.W. Smith K–8 School is a very different school today than what it was two decades ago. The school, located in Syracuse, New York, had a total enrollment of between seven hundred and eight hundred since the mid-1980s. The proportion of Caucasian students, however, fell from 53 percent in 1988–1989 to 27 percent by the 2006–2007 school year. During this same period, the percentage of African American students grew from 45 percent to 64 percent, and the number of Asian and Hispanic students grew from 1 percent to 9 percent.[1] In 2006–2007, 71 percent of the school's students were eligible for free or reduced-price meals, and one of every three students was labeled as ELL.[2]

The unique circumstances at H.W. Smith reveal the shortcomings of the basic racial categories promoted by No Child Left Behind (NCLB). The growth in the number of "African American" students was not an influx of

American students, but rather the arrival of the Bantu, Somali, Congolese, and Maay ethnic groups. The percent of Caucasian students fell significantly, but would have fallen even further had it not been for the influx of Bosnian students, who are categorized as "Caucasian."

H.W. Smith is located within the Syracuse City School District. Like most city districts, Syracuse City School District has struggled with maintaining consistent district leadership, going through four superintendents in the past twelve years.[3] The twenty-one-thousand-student Syracuse City School District contains thirty-four schools, with 11 percent Hispanic students, 31 percent white, and 54 percent black. Three out of four of its students receive free or reduced-price meals. Only 7 percent of the district's students are ELL, clearly revealing the extent of the clustering of immigrants at H.W. Smith— which has 33 percent ELL. [4]

Principal Birnkrant reports that the city of Syracuse is a favorite resettlement city for the State Department because of the numerous interreligious organizations that offer sponsorships to facilitate the transition, and New York State provides one year of public assistance to new immigrants. Additionally, the manufacturing and corresponding population decline within the city ensures a surplus of affordable housing.[5] The history of immigration to Syracuse is one of waves of specific ethnic groups hitting U.S. shores.

At first, H.W. Smith's ELL population was primarily Vietnamese. Over time, Syracuse—and, by extension, the school—welcomed Bosnian, Congolese, Somali, Sudanese, Somali Bantu, Liberian, Maay, Burmese, Iraqi, Bantu, and Bhutanese. As Craig Martin, assistant principal of H.W. Smith states, the students came from "wherever in the world there was a war at that moment." Families arrived and enrolled their students within Syracuse City Schools. As the primary ELL elementary site, and located within the area of town in which many of the immigrants resided, H.W. Smith enrolled the elementary students from most of these transplanted families.

Principal Sharon Birnkrant assumed the leadership of H.W. Smith after teaching within the Syracuse City School District for eighteen years and serving as an assistant principal for three years. She has the unique claim of attending H.W. Smith while it was a junior high and still lives within the neighborhood. Her master's in urban education was conferred by Syracuse University, although she admits that meeting her ELL challenges required "learning very quickly" on the job. Because of her success with and passion for working with immigrant groups, she reports that the district leadership has accused her of being the "Statue of Liberty." There are currently two assistant principals—Craig Martin and Laureen Lane—who have been at H.W. Smith for four years and one year, respectively.

The staff at H.W. Smith deserves deeper investigations, as they embody the welcoming spirit of the school. When Principal Birnkrant took over the school in 1992, it was clear to her that, because of declining enrollment, the school needed to take in additional students in some way. It was the staff that pushed to become an ELL center. Assistant Principal Laureen Lane says that the staff is "very flexible in implementing instructional strategies appropriate to what students need." The dedication and buy-in of the staff is revealed in the 2006–2007 School Profile compiled by the New York State School Report Card, which shows in the last two years an astonishing 0 percent staff turn-over rate for staff members with fewer than five years of experience.[6] This record of teacher retention within an urban ELL center is a testament to a strong community at H.W. Smith.

H.W. Smith staff have identified commonalities among the waves of immigrants they have received, particularly when new refugees arrived from a war zone. Principal Birnkrant reports that the first students to arrive at the school are usually children of the intelligentsia, whose families have the connections and resources to escape the country. Most of these students have at least some academic preparation and assimilate into the school fairly quickly.

Based on rules from the U.S. Citizenship and Immigration Services, the other immigrants who generally arrive first are individuals with physical disabilities, as these rules assign greater priority to this group. Some disabilities would be familiar to American administrators, and others are associated with war and violence, such as shrapnel injuries. Lastly, a larger group of nondisabled students arrive. Many of these immigrant groups bring with them violent backgrounds; Assistant Principal Laureen Lane states that "[new students talk] about learning how to identify a landmine the way most of our kids would talk about the way to use a yo-yo."

The staff at H.W. Smith is proud of the skills that they have developed through welcoming multiple waves of immigrants. They have developed a few guiding principles by which the school has so successfully handled de-mographic changes. Principal Birnkrant openly admits that she started her job at the school "without knowing anything about [ELL]," saying that she "learned from each crisis and brought that to the next one." Outlined below are broad lessons discovered by H.W. Smith staff that held for each group of immigrants.

### Do Your Homework

In 1992, H.W. Smith learned that they would soon be receiving a number of Vietnamese Hmong students and planned an elaborate multicultural café in order to welcome the families to the school. Right before the event, the refugee center that was facilitating the resettlement called the school to say that the Vietnamese families refused to show up. The reason? The glass bridge at the entrance to the school, at which flags of the nations represented within the school are displayed, was flying the official Vietnamese flag. As supporters of the U.S. government during the Vietnam War, the Hmong families were offended by the "North Vietnamese" flag. It was only after the official flag of Vietnam was replaced with the flag of former South Vietnam that the Hmong felt welcomed by the school.

This anecdote reveals that borders of a country—sometimes arbitrarily drawn—can include a wide variation of ethnic groups; many of the immigrants arriving to U.S. shores are from an oppressed group or from the losing side of a war. These are incredibly important nuances to understand as one attempts to meet the educational needs of students within an existing ethnic social structure. Principal Birnkrant describes a parent meeting during which a Somali father describes the differences within Somali ethnicities. Referring to another ethnic group from Somalia, he described for her, "They're Maay. They're bad. Me good. Me Mushunguli." Just as the United States contains a multitude of ethnic groups with different histories, other countries may not be homogenous, and understanding the uniqueness and historical animosities of the previous culture will help meet the educational needs of incoming students.

One of the most valuable resources for Principal Birnkrant and her staff to come to greater understandings of their new students is through an important relationship with both the refugee center and with Catholic Charities of Onondaga County, which helps new immigrants find housing and jobs within the United States. Their cultural capacity and resources are shared freely with the school, which leans closely on the organizations for both background information and to serve as a liaisons or mediators in challenging individual circumstances. This capacity-building research—through the refugee center, Catholic Charities, State Department, educational networks, and Internet research—allows the staff at H.W. Smith to see the world through the eyes of their new students.

One such example of the benefits of research is the tragic background of Somali Bantu students arriving from refugee camps in Africa. These camps held tens of thousands of displaced peoples dependent on international charity groups for their survival. Tragically, atrocities were still occurring at the camp, as marauding bands of thugs preyed on refugees in and around the temporary quarters.

One of the primary modes of transportation for these bandits was by secondhand yellow buses. Children within these camps knew to run and hide whenever a bus drove through, as these vehicles brought perpetrators of violence. Imagine, then, the fear newly immigrated students must have felt when they were introduced to their new school—a place that should be a safe and secure place for them—and it is surrounded by yellow school buses. Knowing the history of their students and the environment at the refugee camp allowed the staff at H.W. Smith to appropriately and gently handle their students' fears, introducing and processing the presence of yellow buses in a safe environment.

**Lean on Your Students**

It quickly became clear to Principal Birnkrant and her staff that, no matter how much preparation they completed before the arrival of students, the individual who knew most about the cultural experiences of a particular student was usually another student within the class. The creation of a welcoming school culture begins with the staff, but what continues to amaze H.W. Smith staff is the extent that students can take up that mantle themselves. On a daily basis, students can serve as important resources to overcome language and cultural barriers, both for other students and for their parents. Staff members routinely receive assistance with interpretation and issues of cultural competency from other students.

The school supports this behavior and serves as a conduit for student social action. One such example is the H.W. Smith student who approached Principal Birnkrant insisting that the school cafeteria begin serving yogurt every day because her new classmate was a vegetarian. This led to a schoolwide letter-writing campaign to the district protesting the lack of a daily vegetarian option, and the eventual change of cafeteria policy. In another example, students planning to fundraise for their class trip to a Rochester amusement park switched their efforts mid-year, raising $1,600 for victims of the Southeast Asian tsunami.

### Expect to Bend the Rules

Principal Birnkrant expresses a lot of frustration toward educational policies that may not be appropriate for the unique situations of international students. She states that special education rules are "made for American kids, not international kids with shaky birthdates, unique learning needs, and rare medical conditions." But, she adds that "the teaching goes on regardless of who joins the class." The birthday issue is particularly challenging, as many students have different birthdays on their passport than they have on their native birth documents. Principal Birnkrant reports that she was advised by the Department of Homeland Security that even if the parent admits that the passport birthdate is fabricated, the school must accept it as accurate. Some of her families arrive with multitudes of children, all supposedly from the same set of parents even though their birthdays are too close together to be feasible.

Principal Birnkrant continues that there "are no rules that we can find, and there are no guidelines about where you place immigrant students in grade levels." New students at H.W. Smith are placed in their age-appropriate grade, which can be a challenge if a student that has never been to school for a day in his life is placed in a sixth-grade classroom, and is then expected to read and write at that grade level. This gets more difficult in upper-grade classrooms, especially in the current NCLB environment, in which below-proficient test scores have led to a "failing school" label for H.W. Smith. Sometimes, there are no perfect answers, and an administrator will have to balance the educational needs of the students with state and district requirements. As stated by Principal Birnkrant, "We often find that we can't do what's best for kids because it doesn't fit the neat little chart."

Her staff, however, does find itself accommodating needs that are unique among elementary schools and goes to great lengths to meet the educational and cultural needs of its students. Principal Birnkrant reports that the month of Ramadan is particularly challenging, because some of her students will not eat anything during the day. Other experiences are just irreplaceable. In one particularly funny anecdote, Principal Birnkrant discusses the challenges of meeting religious requirements for Muslim students, some of whom pray five times per day. She has Craig Martin, her assistant principal, chaperone the prayers, which are held in her office, and states, "This may be the only place where a Christian man chaperones Muslim prayers in a Jewish lady's office."

### Address Racism from Current Students

Those who study the economic impact of immigration have observed that racism most strongly comes from groups that feel most economically and socially threatened by new immigrants.[7] In Syracuse, immigrants compete for jobs and subsidized housing with multigeneration, urban American families. Principal Birnkrant states, "Students who are new to our school from other [Syracuse] city schools are very different than our homegrown kids. They sometimes demonstrate racism towards new arrivals, make fun of them, and don't appreciate diversity. This is also true of their parents, in many cases." This last point is something that staff must deal with "discreetly," saying that "[neighborhood Americans] view refugees as people who have taken away their jobs and [refugees] have supports they don't have."

H.W. Smith has attempted sessions in association with the refugee center for inner-city parents but has not had too much success. The school continues to struggle with this issue. It is worthwhile to quote Principal Birnkrant at length:

> First, you have hard-core American families that have never gotten out of poverty, and they see "new" people coming in who are upwardly mobile and very motivated and it causes problems. Second, they have people coming in who are nomadic and they don't place the same value on keeping a house or area neat and clean. Third, the Muslim families have a great deal of problem with the American families where the [American] women would go out and drink and smoke—these things are anti-Islam. And the African American women were very much enthralled with the African males who gave them respect, and the African men were polygamous so having an affair with a[n American] woman was no big deal.

These issues are a struggle to overcome because they are deeply ingrained and are caused primarily by situations external to the school's control. What a school can control is stringently curbing racist expressions within school, creating a safe environment, and modeling respectful actions for students.

### Communicate and Educate

As "outsiders," the staff at H.W. Smith often struggle to communicate basic standards and expectations to newly arrived immigrants. For example, when speaking with Bosnian parents about their child's achievement, Principal Birnkrant was told that "it's not that important to be smart or graduate high school; you just have to be a nice person." Overcoming this Bosnian cultural norm requires constant and consistent efforts.

Another challenge facing schools with immigrants is students who travel back to their homeland for weeks at a time. A parent may return to Bosnia, promising to return for school "sometime in September." Assistant Principal Laureen Lane states that they do not understand "that the focus needs to be having your student here at the beginning of the year." Communicating expectations of attendance, homework completion, and the parental support role has been a constant struggle for H.W. Smith, and direct, continuous communication is attempted to set the proper expectations for parents.

As part of the school's communication strategy, Principal Birnkrant maintains diligent relationships with the local press in order to minimize potentially negative reactions to immigrants. A simple web search reveals quite a number of TV and print media reporting on summer school, the latest field trip, or the challenge of learning in a school that does not have air conditioning.[8]

One particularly revealing episode occurred late during the 2007–2008 school year, when a newly arrived student was diagnosed with pulmonary tuberculosis.[9] H.W. Smith worked closely with the health department to assuage community fears and communicate with the families of the students in the same classroom. Fortunately, the disease was not in its contagious stage, and no other student or teacher was infected. However, during an informal briefing with a member of the media, a reporter told Principal Birnkrant, "Look, you're one of my heroes. I'm not going to screw you." Such a statement, and the reporter's refusal to promote a fearful reaction from the community, reveal the relationship and trust between the local media and the H.W. Smith staff.

The United States has a long history of welcoming the oppressed and the downtrodden from around the world, and our nation has been richly rewarded by their contributions. The process of assimilation has always been a struggle, and has sometimes taken generations to fully accomplish. Through the efforts of the staff at H.W. Smith, newly arrived immigrants—many of them who come from horrific pasts, from war and tragedy—are provided the tools necessary to fully seize the American Dream. Numerous ethnic groups have arrived at the doors of the school to be welcomed into the community, treated with dignity, and provided solid academic preparation for middle school and beyond. The successes of H.W. Smith contrast greatly with their inability to effectively integrate one ethnic group into the culture of the school. A variety of interventions have been implemented to exhaustion, but academic and cultural barriers continue to prevent success with the recent immigrant Somali Bantu group.

## CRISIS DESCRIPTION

As a persecuted minority group in Somalia, the Bantu refugees had endured continual marginalization in Somalia since their arrival as slaves in the 19th century. Although they have lived in Somalia for approximately two centuries, the Bantu are, in many ways, viewed and treated as foreigners. This history, coupled with their cultural, linguistic, and physical differences, distinguishes them from other Somali refugees who have been resettled in the United States. The culture of subjugation under which most of them have lived may present special challenges to their American resettlement case workers.

—*The Somali Bantu: Their History and Culture*[10]

As formal education has only begun to be available in the refugee camps, educators in the United States may find Bantu parents reluctant or unable to participate in their children's education.

—*The Somali Bantu: Their History and Culture*[11]

Although the lack of value-added scores makes it challenging to measure the true impact of H.W. Smith's contribution to student achievement, in 2007–2008, H.W. Smith met New York's accountability targets in mathematics and science, but—predictably—failed to meet standards in English/language arts.[12] The school is celebrated as a model of successful student integration, with profiles appearing in *Education Week* and on NPR.[13] These successes, however, contrast a crisis with a group of Somali Bantu students who have presented more challenges than all other immigrant groups. This Internal-Unpredictable crisis is one that threatens the inclusive nature of the school, therefore jeopardizing a core value of H.W. Smith.

The crisis at H.W. Smith begins with the history of the Somali Bantu peoples, as the tragic circumstances that brought them to the United States illuminates the school's current inability to fully assimilate them into American culture. Somalia may be best known in the United States for the failed American military action in 1992 and 1993. This military action took place within a completely failed state, torn apart by civil war between and within competing clans. The United Nations was also involved with peacekeeping operations and had short-term success in alleviating a devastating famine. However, after suffering multiple casualties, the United Nations pulled out its troops in March of 1995, leaving increasingly violent and competing clans brutalizing the nation.[14]

The Bantu people are actually spread throughout all of sub-Saharan Africa, belonging to over three hundred groups, each with a distinct dialect. They were considered the lowest of the low within their own country, taking undesirable jobs and excluded from economic, educational, and political opportunities.[15]

Many Somali Bantu fled southern Somalia after the civil war broke out in 1991, ending up in dangerous refugee camps within neighboring Kenya that grew throughout the decade to hold 160,000 people. With inadequate security, refugees who stayed in the camps were under constant threat of bandit attacks, looting, and even rape.[16] Principal Birnkrant adds that, ironically, the Somali Bantu's history of persecution raised their priority for resettlement. In 2002, the U.S. Immigration and Naturalization Service began interviewing Somali Bantu for resettlement; groups have settled in New York City, Atlanta, and Detroit.[17]

H.W. Smith first received Somali Bantu children four years ago, in 2004, and the students were generally placed a year behind their age-appropriate grade level. While there are only forty Somali Bantu students enrolled within the school, Principal Birnkrant reports that they account for disproportionate levels of discipline and achievement problems. The staff at H.W. Smith has encountered several characteristics of the Somali Bantu that—together—have interacted to create an unprecedented crisis within the school.

The phenomenal academic and cultural results achieved by H.W. Smith ethnic groups have come because of the mutual respect and sense of equality within the school. Students are treated with dignity and are expected to treat their fellow students and teachers with dignity.

This culture, however, has been threatened by some members of the Bantu community demanding special, separate treatment for their students. During the previous summer, they attempted to utilize district funding to run a summertime Bantu-only program staffed by noncertified teachers for Bantu children. Additionally, Principal Birnkrant reports that—following a legal settlement in Pittsburgh—the Bantu have threatened to sue Syracuse City School District for failing to provide a separate educational path for Bantu only, and she is very worried about the precedent this would set. If special treatment is granted to the Bantu, the Hutu could then demand separation from the Tutsi, the Sunni from the Shiites, and the Karen from the Chin (Burmese). These other groups may have arrived in America with generations-old issues, but as stated by a Tutsi man, "We've learned very quickly that if we can't learn to live together [in America], then we're in big trouble." Integration is a core value at H.W. Smith, and the creation of a separate but equal educational path for the Bantu would create a dangerous precedent for the district.

This separate attitude manifests itself in the Bantu style of dress and pace of assimilation. Principal Birnkrant reports that the Bantu are very pious with their Muslim religion and that her Bantu girls have not adopted Western dress. Parents also show very little interest in learning English. Although they consider themselves experts at welcoming and absorbing new immigrants, the staff at H.W. Smith has struggled with a Bantu population that has made little effort to adapt to their new surroundings. The staff members encourage maintaining one's cultural identity, but not at the expense of academic achievement.

The staff at H.W. Smith is also challenged by a culture that has very little background in formal education. Principal Birnkrant states that no one was surprised when Bantu students scored a 1 out of 5 on New York's achievement test their first year, but her students continue to score at the lowest rung after five years of extra tutoring and summer school.

Much of these educational challenges are due to the history of persecution of the Bantu. Principal Birnkrant reports that the Bantu came from an environment with no economic system beyond bartering. The concept of numbers is foreign to them, so even simple math problems are challenging. Principal Birnkrant describes students who verbally express complex, creative thoughts, with extremely limited capacity at writing these thoughts on paper. One online history of the Bantu reports that other Somali call the them *ooji*, which is Italian for "today," conveying the Bantu cultural practice of focusing on the short term only.[18]

Cultural gender norms are also a struggle, with persistent rumors of girls being married at fourteen years old. Men in the Bantu culture have not necessarily given up their polygamous ways within America, causing social strife both within their community and between Bantu and their inner-city neighbors. Additionally, some Bantu women were offered monetary payments by non-Bantu men if they reported to the refugee camp staff that they were married and were then able to escape. Some children, then, arrived with men that had no connection to the family other than one of convenience to escape the violence of the refugee camp.

It would be easy to blame one of the factors above for the academic challenges of the Bantu, but the staff at H.W. Smith has overcome individual challenges with other ethnic groups. The Hmong arrived with no written language, but both students and parents actively learned written English. Other ethnic groups did not have number systems but more quickly picked up an understanding of number sense. During the fall of 2008–2009, the staff was shocked to discover that the newly arrived Burundi immigrants had walked five miles in order to attend their parent/teacher conference. The challenge is both the lack of an educational background and an extremely limited community academic push from students' families. The staff is discouraged, "banging our head against the wall . . . this is the first ethnic group that is not Americanizing well." The academic challenges—and legal threats to force separate educational resources—threaten the unique, integrated culture of H.W. Smith.

### CRISIS ANALYSIS

Immigrant men are sometimes mad that the women don't have to obey them in America. One father told me that the kids are *his* because he paid a cow for his wife. . . . This is the first ethnic group that is not Americanizing well.

—*Principal Sharon Birnkrant* (original emphasis)

The crisis of the Bantu is a threat to the integrated, multiethnic community at H.W. Smith. The school prepared for the arrival of the Bantu similarly to other ethnic groups, through working with the refugee center to study their background and history. What has become apparent—nationally, as well as in Syracuse—is that the Bantu arrived with more cultural barriers to the American formal education system than previous groups. These integration problems are internal to the school community and were unexpected by the school's staff. This Internal-Unpredictable crisis continues to resist efforts at a long-term solution.

The crisis is unique compared to the other case studies profiled within this book. It is atypical in that the crisis has originated from a subset of the school's community that has, so far, failed to accept the integrated educational model of H.W. Smith. The other case studies of Woodland Elementary School in chapter 12 and John Dewey High School in chapter 13 describe the challenges of a changing school community, but the demographic transitions profiled in these two chapters were externally imposed by district policy. Principal Birnkrant reports that the H.W. Smith staff members are "really excited when a new country comes," and they did not initially view the Bantu as a threat to the school's culture. The challenges of and resistance toward full integration continue to surprise the school's staff and place this crisis in the category of Unpredictable.

This crisis challenges the school because it has always found the resources and capacity to adjust to the trials of integrating new immigrants to America. Other ethnic groups have arrived with little educational preparation, and many arrive without an ability to speak English. These challenges, however, have been overcome through the cooperation and hard work of the school's staff and community resources. Additionally, parents immediately enrolled in English classes and supported the academic press of the school. The Bantu, however, are the first group that has lacked the community values that accept a common responsibility for working toward the American dream.

It is currently unclear as to the extent to which the crisis threatens the existence of H.W. Smith K–8. The Bantu may set a trend of demanding separate educational accommodations for their students, and the multicultural environment of H.W. Smith will end. It is difficult to imagine the school itself ceasing to exist; instead, what is at stake is the integrative and achievement successes experienced by successive waves of Syracuse immigrants.

## CRISIS TREATMENT

The staff of H.W. Smith had welcomed a variety of ethnic groups to their school, and their preparation for the Somali Bantu followed the same pattern as with other groups. They met with staff from the refugee center, were briefed on the background of the Somali Bantu, and researched the refugee camps; however, there were no early warning signs that the new immigrants would not be as amenable to integrating to American society.

It may be clear, in retrospect, that the low social status at which the Bantu have lived for generations may have inhibited their integration into the United States; however, in 2004, H.W. Smith did not have the benefit of knowing the common challenges currently being faced by refugee advocates across the nation. As more and more Somali Bantu began arriving, problems have appeared across the nation as the growing community began making their voice heard.

As an Unpredictable crisis, H.W. Smith did not experience a state of school preparation and primary prevention, but the school did apply the interventions that had served them successfully with other ethnic groups. Students attended summer school, received additional tutoring in the morning and during teacher planning periods, and both college groups and senior citizens volunteered their time to mentor students. However, achievement levels for the Bantu refused to budge.

Principal Birnkrant and her staff are now in the crisis state of damage control and secondary prevention. The highest priority is convincing the Somali Bantu and H.W. Smith stakeholders that the best, long-term solution to the crisis maintains the inclusive, interactive nature of the school and its students. The refugee center has served as a powerful voice in this debate, but the district has not yet made a strong statement, perhaps because of fear over a lawsuit. Principal Birnkrant has stated that she knows of some fissures within the Bantu community that have appeared, as some parents are advocating for maintaining enrollment at H.W. Smith. Whether she will have success in utilizing these individuals to co-opt the Bantu dissenters remains to be seen.

The staff has also expanded their search for solutions to worldwide resources but has not found anyone who has found academic success in working with the Bantu. Communities from Nashville to Pittsburg to England have struggled to address the academic needs of the Bantu. Additional pressure comes from NCLB, which requires testing with the first year of enrollment. H.W. Smith is a "failing school" in the black subgroup in which the Bantu fall (although Principal Birnkrant claims that she is "proud to be the principal of a failing school").

The crisis stage of community recovery and learning remains to be written, as does the concluding chapter of the crisis currently threatening H.W. Smith K–8 School. The school staff continues to hope that the academic answer lies in the intensity of services, and that, in time, the academic performance of Somali Bantu students will rise. More importantly, they continue their attempts to be inclusive of the Bantu community, communicating high expectations and a respect for other cultures. It is their hope that efforts are successful to maintain H.W. Smith's role as a community that continues to welcome and educate "your tired, your poor, your huddled masses yearning to breathe free."

## REFLECTIVE QUESTIONS

### Reflection on the Reading

1. Other district officials interviewed attributed the success of H.W. Smith to the presence of an extremely dedicated principal who shaped the school culture for over a decade. What potential challenges might you forecast arising from a school culture that is so leader-driven or leader-dependent? Is it sustainable?

2. Since the United States Supreme Court's decision in *Wisconsin v. Yoder* (1972), schools have struggled with the tension between a parent's right to limit their child's education for religious reasons and the probable long-term effects of that decision, including, as Justice Douglas forecast in his dissent, "forever barr[ing] [the child's] entry into the new and amazing world of diversity that we have today." At H.W. Smith, Birnkrant faced balancing the Bantu parents' right to practice their religious beliefs against the right of their children to an educational experience enabling them to be productive members of a pluralistic and diverse society. Where does one right end and the other begin?

3. What are the key elements of H.W. Smith's successful integration of students from historically adversarial cultures? What are some likely organizational threats to this culture?

4. What specific issues would arise if the Bantu were given the opportunity to start their own educational track?

**Application to Theory**

5. The facts of this case led to significant discussion among the authors as to whether the crisis was Predictable or Unpredictable (ultimately deciding that the crisis was Unpredictable). Given the fact that H.W. Smith had an established history of successfully integrating students from diverse cultures, do you think Birnkrant and her staff could or should have predicted the resistance of the Bantu parents to their children's assimilation into H.W. Smith's pluralistic culture? Did their previous successes limit their ability to forecast this problem?
6. Describe H.W. Smith's core values and its foundational practices. How do the Bantu parents' demands threaten these?

**Application on the Job**

7. All schools have a culture. What steps does your school take to assimilate new students, faculty, and parents into your school's culture, connecting them with the broader school community? What resources does your school or external organization(s) offer to assist with this transition?
8. Birnkrant greatly attributes the success of her school to the assistance of the immigration center in proactively training teachers and staff on the challenges they are likely to face from forthcoming immigrant students. While few schools will have the assimilative challenges of H.W. Smith, American schools increasingly face challenges stemming from the educational needs of English Language Learners (ELL) and migrating students. What resources do you currently utilize to address the academic and social needs of your ELL students and their families? What training do you provide your faculty and staff?
9. In *Bethel School District No. 43 v. Fraser* (1986), the United States Supreme Court recognized that "the role and purpose of the American public school system . . . is to prepare students for citizenship in the republic," including teaching "tolerance of divergent political and religious views." How does your school accomplish this (if it does)? Is this an appropriate role for your school to play?

10. How much do you know about the histories of your immigrant students and their families? From what types of environments did they come? Is your entire faculty and staff—not just your ELL faculty and staff—familiar with this information?

11. Does your school consider the education and integration of ELL a school-wide responsibility or that of an isolated subset of your faculty? If the latter, in what ways can you broaden the responsibility for ELL education?

# INTERNAL-PREDICTABLE

**7**

# "I Think That We Finally Have the People That We Need to Get the Job Done."

## *How Johnson Elementary School Addressed Annual Teacher Turnover*

### OVERVIEW

You never know when people are going to leave. . . . We cannot stop them; it is going to happen one way or another. In my experience, we have to have systems in place to maintain the level of consistency and rigor necessary to keep students learning.

—*Dr. Sallie Pinkston, principal of Johnson Elementary School*

Two years after assuming the principalship, Sallie Pinkston was confronted with a crisis that is frighteningly common at schools around the nation. For two years in a row, she retained only 50 percent of her staff. Despite this high turnover rate, she built a culture of high-quality teaching and learning at Johnson Elementary School. Located in Chicago, Illinois, Johnson Elementary is confronted with many challenges typical of urban areas: widespread poverty, highly diverse students, and low performance on standardized assessments. High teacher turnover can be endemic in schools that struggle with these challenges.[1]

A summary report released in 2005 by a national community group studied sixty-four schools in low-income Chicago communities. The average annual teacher turnover rate among these schools was 22 percent, but in the 2001–2002 school year, four schools had turnover rates that exceeded 40 percent.[2] One of these schools was Johnson Elementary. Principal Pinkston faced the significant challenge of maintaining rigorous teaching and learning while acculturating a new staff to the high expectations of the school.

The issue of high faculty turnover is a too-frequent occurrence, but it falls to the school's leaders to strike the delicate balance between maintaining staff continuity while at the same time demanding excellence from the entire teaching staff. This means, as Dr. Pinkston notes, that the ideal level of teacher turnover is *not* zero: some teachers are not suited to a particular school or to teaching generally, and they should be removed either from the school or the profession. The challenge lies in keeping the "right" teachers, getting rid of the ones who are not a good fit, and ensuring that teaching and learning in the school is not negatively affected by these changes. This point is further driven home by a report from the Consortium on Chicago School Research, which states that loss of teachers can be good if it is "the loss of weaker teachers."[3]

All schools face teacher turnover issues, but only in a small subset do the frequency and intensity rise to the level of a crisis. Teacher turnover can ruin a school's ability to effectively carry out the fundamental task of helping students learn, and therefore, constant, multiyear turnover can rise to the level of a crisis if it prevents the solidification of the school's core values. This was the crisis at Johnson Elementary School, which struggled to implement a rigorous academic program and professional learning community while losing a significant percentage of their teaching workforce.

## CASE NARRATIVE

There was some teaching going on [at Johnson Elementary], but the level of learning wasn't enough to raise student scores.

—*Principal Sallie Pinkston*

Johnson Elementary School is located in North Lawndale, on the west side of Chicago. A K–8 school with approximately 450 students, Johnson served a population that was almost entirely African American. Approximately 90 percent of students were on free or reduced-price meals, and around 13 percent were receiving special education services.[4] Serving these students was a teaching staff of fewer than thirty. The school is part of Area 8 of Chicago Public Schools, the third largest district in the country. With a student population of four hundred thousand in over 650 schools, CPS is actually more diverse than Johnson, with a student population of roughly 46 percent African American, 39 percent Latino, 8 percent white, and a small percentage of other racial groups. The Limited English Proficient numbers are also dramatically different, with a negligible number of such students at Johnson while 14 percent of the district's population is LEP.[5]

Dr. Pinkston was elevated to the position of principal at Johnson in 2004. At the beginning of her time as principal, student scores on the ISAT assessments were around the 20th percentile. She states that "there was a lot of unemployment [in the neighborhood]. Over 50 percent of incarcerated folks came back to North Lawndale, and there was not a high level of respect for education overall." This lack of respect expressed itself through a multitude of student behavioral problems, some of which stemmed from school issues, and some of which came from the "poverty-stricken environment" of the local neighborhood.

This description portrays an environment familiar to other school leaders in Chicago and around the country. Like other schools, Dr. Pinkston struggled with raising the rigor of teaching within the school. Dr. Pinkston's predecessor had led Johnson Elementary for sixteen years, so the staff and students had a comfort level with the status quo that would prove difficult to overcome. The new principal needed to engage the impoverished community and address the lack of academic rigor in the classrooms, while simultaneously addressing her dramatic teacher turnover rates.

Addressing the challenges faced by Johnson Elementary required a proactive and longer-term turnaround plan for the school. High teacher turnover had historically been a problem for Johnson Elementary; the innovation of Dr. Pinkston was utilizing strategic turnover to remove teachers who were not contributing to student achievement within the school. She accomplished this through interventions that were slow-acting and relatively simple, focusing on increasing accountability and cohesion among the staff.

With increased staff cohesion and an improved school environment, teacher turnover at Johnson Elementary fell to a more manageable level. Changing the foundational principles of the school required more work on the front end but ultimately established a positive culture as teacher turnover decreased and the remaining staff committed themselves to student achievement.

## CRISIS DESCRIPTION

Our scores were going down, and my AIO (Area Instructional Officer) had a conversation with me, and she asked me what types of things I was going to do to turn around the direction my school was going. So that next year, I moved some people around—by that time, I knew who the stronger teachers were—and I changed some grade levels, and some teachers left when I did that.

—*Principal Sallie Pinkston*

Dr. Pinkston began at Johnson Elementary School as a curriculum coordinator, so she was familiar with the mediocrity of the school before she took over as the lead administrator. At the time of her promotion, the school was struggling with low levels of student achievement and high rates of behavior problems; there was also a fair amount of tension between the teaching staff and the administration. Each of these factors was uniquely related to the crisis of teacher turnover within Johnson Elementary School.

When she took over the role of principal, Dr. Pinkston chose not to make wholesale changes. She states, "I didn't come in changing everything at once, because research says that that's not a good way to go right away." As part of her initial review, Dr. Pinkston completed a comprehensive assessment of the school. She found a school that had very low performance on standardized assessments, "there were a lot of suspensions, students . . . being disrespectful to teachers," and, within the teaching ranks, "some of the teachers were not as friendly as others. And new teachers needed to feel accepted, and coached . . . some of the veteran teachers weren't as committed to that feeling as others." Combined with low community support and high poverty, it is easy to see why many teachers were not staying at Johnson Elementary School for the long term.

Dr. Pinkston also witnessed a concerning lack of teacher professionalism in areas other than just teaching. She cites cases of "insubordination . . . when I asked them to turn in lesson plans and they did not. Not being professional to parents—talking to them as if they were children, just things that they were not supposed to do as professionals." With such a pervasive culture, it was clear that a few surface changes would be insufficient to turn the school around.

The reality was that over the sixteen years under the previous principal, many teachers had become complacent with the "status quo" and student learning inevitably suffered. Scores on the ISAT from 2005—taken by third, fifth, and eighth graders—showed that the highest rate of meeting or exceeding standards in reading was 34.6 percent by the eighth-grade cohort; only 25 percent of fifth graders and 13.2 percent of third graders met this standard. In math, 32.4 percent of the fifth-grade cohort met or exceeded standards while 23.7 percent of third graders and a paltry 7.7 percent of eighth graders could say the same.[6]

Speaking about those who left the school in her first few years as principal, she states, "It was teachers fighting change. . . . So some of them left because they didn't want to do the things that were being asked by not only me, but the district as well." From the very beginning, Dr. Pinkston was thinking in a longer time frame than most who feel they need to bring about instant and dramatic change: she says she "didn't want to come in and take these drastic changes right away." Because she started slowly in her first year, none of her teachers left after her initial year as principal, a marked difference from the turnover rates of closer to 40–50 percent the school experienced in most years prior to that.

Instead of taking drastic action, Dr. Pinkston used both informal and formal pressure to influence teachers. For formal measures, she simply used the teacher evaluation tools already mandated by the district. She also held teachers directly responsible for their actions through letters and reminders, setting a strong tone of change.

> I basically used the tools provided by Chicago Public Schools, as far as the ability to follow the policies and procedures. I had to write a few teachers up . . . I just went by the procedures already in place, but I don't think they were being affected by them until I arrived.

This was not change for the sake of putting her stamp on the school; rather, it was empowering teachers who were effective and holding every teacher to the same standard to ensure the best for the students. In the end, Dr. Pinkston turned the crisis of teacher turnover—over 50 percent in some years—to her long-term advantage by creating a situation in which the strong teachers stayed and ineffective teachers unwilling to improve left.

Turnover spiked following her second year, which was the year she began increasing expectations and accountability among her staff. Following the 2005–2006 school year, ten of the school's twenty teachers left, and after the 2006–2007 school year, nine of seventeen teachers were lost. This turnover rate decreased in the following school year when only five out of sixteen teachers did not return. Teachers who were not willing to change with the school left, and this created opportunities to hire teachers whose values and efforts aligned with Principal Pinkston's vision for the school. Associated with a decreased turnover rate was the formation of a new culture among the teachers; Principal Pinkston states that "a professional learning community manifested itself."

It is important to again point out that teacher attrition did not drop to zero, nor was that the goal. The aim was to ensure the retention of teachers who held the same vision for the school. Principal Pinkston expected and wanted some teachers to leave so that the school could change for the better. In order to meet her long-term goal, teacher attrition rates needed to remain high. The key was seeing how this short-term setback was actually a greater benefit for the future of the school.

As turnover was managed at the school, Dr. Pinkston's new teachers would enter a school full of peers ready to mentor them to become effective teachers. This focus has resulted in all of Dr. Pinkston's hirees remaining on staff. While never shooting for a goal of zero teacher turnover, Dr. Pinkston knew that a lower level of teacher turnover would be an important component of the school's transformation into one that more effectively helped students learn.

## CRISIS ANALYSIS

Jack Welch, the former CEO of General Electric, famously stated that 10 percent of an organization's workforce should be fired every year.[7] These departures then create openings for "new blood" to come in and revitalize the organization.[8] Teacher turnover in schools should be viewed through the same lens: it is both expected and good that some people leave because it provides an opportunity for new teachers to join the faculty and bring in energy and new ideas.

Another important distinction is that *who* leaves and stays is just as important as *how many* leave and stay at the school. Losing five teachers from a small school can be a crisis, but this challenge may have a significant silver lining if those teachers are ineffective. Chapter 8 describes how an NCLB restructuring allowed Sobrante Park's principal to weed out a subset of his teachers who had not committed to the school's mission. Hence, teacher turnover is not something for principals to prevent; it is something for principals to manage.

The significant teacher turnover at Johnson Elementary was an Internal-Predictable crisis. High teacher turnover is an Internal crisis, as the decision to renew a contract or seek other options is held by individual teachers and influenced by the atmosphere and leadership of the school. High teacher turnover can be a necessary step in school reform efforts if staff members are not willing to make necessary changes in their instruction. Therefore, high teacher turnover can be a crisis either directly instigated by the actions of the school leadership or as an indirect derivative of those actions. Such actions do fit into the theoretical crisis model proposed in this book, because a crisis threatens the core values of a school.

The core values at Johnson Elementary when Dr. Pinkston was promoted to principal were the continuation of the status quo and acceptance of low student achievement as the norm. Dr. Pinkston initiated a crisis of staff turnover in order to successfully confront and oust these values, replacing them with a collaborative staff environment that promoted a higher rigor of learning.

The word *crisis* commonly has a negative connotation. The model proposed in this book recognizes that a crisis is associated with high levels of uncertainty and change. These adjustments, however, can serve the important purpose of exchanging a flawed school culture for one that is more focused on student achievement. In these circumstances, the crisis—while bringing short-term pain—is a necessary purging step in order to reach the school's higher goals.

The crisis at Johnson Elementary was also Predictable because school leaders usually are aware with some degree of warning that teachers are not returning. The window of notification may be a few months or even shorter in individual cases, but leaders typically have some warning if a large number of staff members choose to leave. Teacher turnover due to retirement, promotion, or changes in family circumstance will always be present in schools as they are in businesses and other institutions.

As Dr. Pinkston so accurately stated, "You never know when people are going to leave . . . people leave for a variety of reasons. . . . We cannot stop them; it is going to happen one way or another." What is controllable, however, is the type of environment and relationships that are mindfully developed by school leaders. As stated by Dr. Pinkston, "In my experience, we have to have systems in place to maintain the level of consistency and rigor necessary to keep students learning." Creating a school where standards are high and expectations are clear, providing opportunities for honest communication, and allowing teachers to help each other are all important factors in creating an environment that teachers are less likely to leave.

Teacher turnover in urban schools is high across the nation, with the National Center on Education Statistics (NCES) calculating annual teacher turnover at 16 percent; that number, however, increases for beginning teachers as well as for teachers who are in schools that serve 35 percent or more minority students. Of sixty-four schools in Chicago Public Schools surveyed by a national nonprofit, only three had single-digit turnover rates; across the surveyed schools, thirteen of the schools lost over 30 percent of their teachers and seven had turnover rates exceeding 40 percent.[9] Even more disheartening is a 2007 report by the National Commission on Teaching and America's Future that calculated each teacher turnover costs the Chicago Public School System almost $18,000 per leaver.[10]

The issue of teacher turnover is commonly connected to other negative educational variables. According to a national study on teacher retention from NCES, teacher turnover is also often related to schools in urban areas with large amounts of student diversity,[11] low amounts of parental or community involvement, high rates of discipline issues, and low student achievement.[12] It is difficult to know if teacher turnover or the related challenges are the "chicken" or the "egg" in these schools; what is important is that they are intricately linked and must be addressed simultaneously in order to ensure a successful school. While some turnover is good—and even necessary—good schools maintain low levels of staff turnover.

**CRISIS TREATMENT**

Teacher turnover isn't in itself a bad thing, but you want to make sure that the people that want to stay are the ones who you want to stay. And the environment that you create minimizes teacher turnover and ensures that the ones that are leaving are not the ones that you need in the environment.

—*Principal Sallie Pinkston*

In addition to high teacher turnover, Dr. Pinkston struggled with the related issues of student behavior problems and low student achievement. Many principals facing such an array of daunting challenges spread themselves too thin, trying to handle each situation as a separate and discrete issue. Principals can also make the mistake of focusing only on the outcomes instead of examining the underlying causes of these problems. This is just as shortsighted as a doctor who treats a fever without examining further to see what ailment actually caused the fever.

While looking for fundamental causes to problems can take more of an initial time investment, it is the only method of finding a true solution to a school's issues. Dr. Pinkston could have attempted to tackle each discrete problem confronting her in her first year. By putting in place long-term steps that would help to change the culture of the teachers within the school, she was able to bring about positive, potentially enduring change. When faced with a long-term crisis, it is crucial that leaders investigate and address the underlying causes of the crisis, not simply try to take each fresh wave as it comes.

Dr. Pinkston began this process by reviewing each member of her teaching staff. Specifically, she focused on the core interaction between teacher and student within the classroom, "watching the way the teacher communicated with the students, and in turn, watched how the students perceived the teachers." She describes the ideal teacher-student relationship "like a marriage . . . you just know when you walk past the classroom, and you see the kids engaged." Once she determined in which classrooms high-quality instruction was taking place, she began the process of assisting teachers not engaging their students to improve or leave.

While it sounds like a superficial change, Dr. Pinkston started by simply using the district procedures that were already in place to hold teachers accountable. In most cases, this simply meant

evaluations, and just going into their classrooms, and observing their teaching. Ensuring that they followed through on submitting their lesson plans. Just having those conversations with them: "Are your students learning? How do you know? What evidence do you have?"

Crucial to her success were other methods she employed to bring high standards for teacher performance to the forefront.

> I would let them know the importance of coming to school on time and setting a good example. Also, professionalism . . . a lot of teachers missed a lot of days. . . . I just thought that teachers should realize the impact that they have on students in more ways than just academics . . . and just being professional, and leading by example. There was one teacher—a special needs teacher—I would go into her classroom, and she would just be sitting all the time. Students would not be engaged. So I talked to her, and I asked her if she had considered retirement, because she was at a retired age. I told her that her performance was not conducive to good teaching, and that she would have to make a decision before I made one.

Each of these steps could be utilized at any school. What turned around Johnson Elementary School was the setting of high expectations and holding everyone in the building accountable to them. While this likely means, as it did for Dr. Pinkston, that teacher turnover will increase in the short term, it starts to lay the foundation for supporting effective teachers and those who want to get better.

Just as important, it makes the school an unwelcoming place for those who are not as willing to be held accountable, as Dr. Pinkston did when she informed a teacher that "she would have to make a decision before I made one." While individual teachers leave for any number of reasons, a revolving door of teachers in and out of a school on a yearly basis is indicative of larger issues than simply promotion or retirement.

Fortunately, Dr. Pinkston had been working on her dissertation, and she chose to focus on the topic of teacher retention in schools. Her research gave her practical knowledge to apply at Johnson Elementary as she recruited teachers to the school. Her second source of insight was that she "was one of the members of a committee that was trying to keep teachers in school. . . . We felt that teachers needed a mentor at their school, and an effective induction program." Her membership on this committee allowed her to complete research directly on this issue, including opportunities to gain insights through interviews into what teacher concerns were when deciding whether to leave a school.

Dr. Pinkston entered this crisis with a solid understanding of education research, which provided a basis for planning effective change. Seeing the teacher turnover crisis as being inextricably linked to the other problems of low student performance, poor discipline, and a lack of a supportive teaching environment, she implemented a plan to create professional learning communities within the school. While some teachers were not on board, those that were took advantage of the increased communication and openness in the school. She states,

> That is why it is so important to have leadership teams, and to ask people's opinion, because if they feel involved, they take more of an ownership approach, and that is what I've been able to do. It is like they take stock not only in the school, but in the school being successful and students being successful. So I think based on my ability to delegate, and not be the type of leader that needs to be out in front. I can easily be in the background and let teacher leaders make decisions based on their expertise.

As an example of teachers stepping forward, one of her teachers approached her about developing a new lab for struggling students; as Dr. Pinkston says, "When I first started in my school, no one came to me with an idea like that."

Accountability, in combination with increased autonomy and authority, started to change the culture of the school from one in which ineffective teachers could hide in their classrooms to one in which teachers were rewarded for innovation and effectiveness. When this culture began to take hold at Johnson Elementary, unwilling teachers voluntarily left while strong teachers stayed within the school. This culture had additional spillover effects, contributing to increased student achievement and decreased discipline problems.

Dr. Pinkston's methods of addressing her teacher turnover crisis hold several lessons. Dr. Pinkston addressed the root of the problem—the lack of instructional rigor and lack of peer mentorship—instead of simply struggling each year to convince each individual teacher to stay. Maintaining a long-term vision requires a commitment to a course of action, something that is hard to do in today's culture of rapid changes. In this case, it allowed Dr. Pinkston to slowly build up a staff that was committed to her vision of a collaborative work environment based on excellence and accountability.

Because teacher turnover is always going to be present, the key to successful school leadership is managing this inevitability to your advantage. The first step in this process is to minimize it by being careful in your selection of teachers to bring into the school. This means evaluating them for how well they will fit into your vision for the school's culture. For example, if cultivating an atmosphere of shared planning time that revolves around continuous evaluation of teacher and student work, the school's hiring process should have a component that evaluates candidates' experience with and commitment toward this vision. In this way, teachers are hired who are more likely to "fit" with the school and be less likely to leave.

A second fundamental aspect that was clearly evident in Dr. Pinkston's story is creating accountability structures based on transparent evaluations of effective teaching. In many schools and districts, these measures are already in place in the form of observations and other methods of assessment. What is not done as often, unfortunately, is using these tools to honestly evaluate the strengths and weaknesses of teachers. This means not just going through the exercise of evaluating teachers but establishing high expectations and then ensuring that teachers meet those expectations.

In her time at the school, Dr. Pinkston has made efforts to both retain teachers who are performing well and identify teachers who are not performing and "assist[ing] them with their departure." Making people accountable not only improves outcomes, it also provides a principal with clear indications of the specific areas a teacher needs help with in their practice. In the worst-case scenario, these evaluations also are essential if it comes time to make the decision that a teacher would be a better fit in another school.

The third important component to minimizing teacher turnover is fostering collegiality among staff. Dr. Pinkston attempted to facilitate this in her school through the development of a professional learning community. As she says, "One of the things I learned is teachers want someone that they can talk to, that they can talk to freely, and that they can tell their problems to. I [am] an active listener to them." A professional learning community creates an environment that builds instructional skills, enhances communication, and supports a more positive organizational culture.

Teachers who have the freedom to critique others and be critiqued by others help to create a powerful force for learning. The benefits are also immediate to students and families as they receive consistent messages from among the school staff. Within the school, it also helps to identify and communicate special aspects of children, whether struggles or strengths, so that each teacher has a clearer picture of each student they have in their classroom.

Finally, principals need to establish a level of trust with their teachers so that they know when someone is going to leave. Teacher turnover can be unpredictable because teachers can choose to leave for a variety of reasons. While some ambiguity must be accepted, efforts should be made to maximize the time between the notice that a teacher will be leaving and the start of the next school year. The more time that is available before the need to fill the vacancy, the greater chance that an appropriate candidate can be recruited and put in place.

Dr. Pinkston reflects on how that was developed at her school: "Now, there is a teacher who is leaving, and she told me that she is leaving, so now I am prepared to have someone take her place when she leaves. You have to win people's trust, and that is done in a variety of ways—it depends on the individual—and hope that the person respects you enough to let you know."

## CONCLUSION

The significant challenge for school turnaround specialists, as stated by Dr. Pinkston, is that "effective change takes five years." Reform efforts, such as the creation of a professional learning community within a school, can address many ills at once, but it requires several years and significant investments of time and resources to take root in the school. The necessary steps of improvement, however, will successfully distinguish teachers who are on board with the vision from those who need to be shown the door.

Dr. Pinkston points out that there was no turnover in her first year as principal. In her second year, however, when she started to make the changes of increased accountability and a more collaborative focus, turnover increased significantly. In order to establish a culture in which effective teachers were happy to stay, she first had to go through a period during which she lost even more teachers overall. While the pessimist might have seen this as a step backwards, it was clear that this needed to take place in order to differentiate those who were willing to buy into her vision and those who were not.

It is crucial for all leaders to understand that it is the teaching staff that drives a school's ability to promote effective learning. The teachers hired and lost play a crucial role in determining student outcomes from behavioral indicators to academic achievement on standardized tests. Dr. Pinkston was able to manage the inevitable teacher turnover to her advantage, ensuring that teacher evaluations centered on retaining those teachers who were adding the most to the students' success and identifying those that were not up to the task.

By managing this one aspect, a range of outcomes were addressed, putting the school in a much better position going forward than it had been previously. Teacher turnover of some degree is present in all schools; when it rises to the level of an Internal-Predictable crisis, school leaders are presented with a unique opportunity to reshape the school to their vision.

## REFLECTIVE QUESTIONS

### Reflection on the Reading

1. While teacher turnover is a common occurrence in urban public schools, it is generally not well publicized. Would it be beneficial to bring this issue to light? What would be the most effective ways of gaining public attention for teacher turnover issues?

2. Dr. Pinkston felt that addressing the school's teacher turnover would take five years. Do you think this is an appropriate time frame? Too long? Too short?

### Application to Theory

3. The authors have determined that losing approximately 50 percent of a school's teaching staff from year to year amounts to a crisis. Do you think that this is accurate? If not, what percentage of teacher loss from year to year would meet the definition of crisis (a larger percentage or a smaller percentage)? How might it depend on which teachers in addition to how many?

4. What are ways that Dr. Pinkston could have capitalized on the teacher turnover during the "Community Recovery and Learning" stage of the process?

5. What are some early warning systems a school can put in place to identify potential teacher turnover issues in time to react to them successfully?

### Application on the Job

6. Describe your school's teaching faculty. Is it disproportionately experienced or inexperienced? How many of your staff have aspirations for new positions?

7. What percentage of teachers do you retain at your school? How does your retention rate vary between beginning, mid-career, and late-career teachers?

8. Are there patterns in terms of teacher characteristics or reasons for leaving among those teachers who decide to leave?
9. What good teachers are most likely to leave your school this year? How can you best encourage them to stay?
10. What teachers are not meeting expectations? What formal or informal ways can you begin to lay the groundwork for their remediation and/or departure?
11. Describe the characteristics of your ideal faculty in five years.

# EXTERNAL-PREDICTABLE

# "Very Typical Teaching Within a Large District—Dysfunctional and Comfortable."

## *How Sobrante Park Elementary School Capitalized on NCLB*

**OVERVIEW**

People think that growth just started last year. Well, that's not the case. . . .
I've been doing this for six years and just last year felt like, "Okay, well, it's
coming together."[1]

—*Principal Marco Franco, Sobrante Park Elementary*

In the entire state of California at the beginning of the 2005–2006 school year,
401 of the state's 9,600 schools had entered the restructuring phase in the No
Child Left Behind Act.[2] This chapter tells the story of Sobrante Park Elementary School, one of the ten schools that—through hard work and instructional
innovation—successfully recovered from this accountability crisis.

Sobrante Park Elementary School serves a diverse, poor student body—91
percent minority, with over 80 percent qualifying for free and reduced-price
meals.[3] While the school showed some growth in the early 2000s, the gains
were not enough to attain adequate yearly progress. Nearing the more punitive end of the No Child Left Behind sanctions in 2004–2005, Principal Marco
Franco and his staff realized that one more year of not meeting performance
thresholds would lead to the implementation of a major restructuring plan.

The crisis at Sobrante Park was occasioned by pervasively low expectations and performance, and administrative obstacles hampering efforts to address them. Although the school historically struggled with low performance, by 2004, external accountability pressures transformed the school's low performance into a full-blown crisis. Fortunately, the efforts of Principal Marco and his staff throughout the stages of primary prevention and damage control ensured a successful resolution of the crisis.

An accountability crisis—like the one at Sobrante Park—may be the most likely crisis that current public school leaders face during their careers. While NCLB reauthorization will undoubtedly modify the law, the predictions are that the central tenet of externally applied school accountability is a force schools will face for the foreseeable future. In this context, exploring the methods utilized by Sobrante Park to successfully overcome its accountability crisis holds lessons for current and aspiring principals.

## CASE NARRATIVE

Something had to change at Sobrante Park. Year after year, the elementary school in the poor flatlands of Oakland failed to meet test-score targets that, under state and federal laws, have consequences attached.

—*Christian Science Monitor*[4]

Sobrante Park Elementary School is located in the urban district of Oakland Unified, which has experienced significant challenges in the past five years. The district is composed of approximately forty thousand students and demographically includes 37 percent African American, 34 percent Hispanic, 16 percent Asian, and 7 percent white. Strikingly, Oakland Unified was and remains a district in which two out of every three students qualify for free-or-reduced lunch, and English is not the first language of one out of every three students.

In 2003, budgetary shortfalls and academic challenges pushed the district into a unique relationship with the state of California. In exchange for an emergency loan of $100 million, the state superintendent of public instruction "assumed all of the rights, duties, and powers of the governing board of the Oakland Unified District, and appointed an Administrator to act on [his] behalf."[5]

Urban school systems are notoriously complex, with budgetary battles and racial politics imposing tremendous distractions to the business of educating students. Within this environment, the Oakland Unified School District was driven to invite a state-level educational entity to share in the daily management of the school district. It is in this politically charged, budgetary-shortage context that Sobrante Park Elementary School operates.

Described by Franco as your "typical inner-city school," Sobrante Park Elementary serves approximately three hundred students in grades K–5. In 2005, the majority of its enrollment was Hispanic students (65 percent), with African Americans constituting 26 percent and Pacific Islanders and Asians 5 percent. Over 80 percent of Sobrante Park's students receive free or reduced-price meals, and 56 percent of its students are English Language Learners.[6] The school's neighborhood is described by Franco as "depressed," without a large number of businesses with which to partner. The school is located in eastern Oakland, a poorer part of the city. Indicative of the school's environment, the school's portable classrooms were set on fire by vandals three different times during the 2007–2008 school year.[7]

Additional student support resources are a necessary component of success in inner-city schools, and Sobrante Park is no exception. The school benefits from an active homeowners' association, an after-school program, cooperation with the health department to provide checkups and immunizations to students, and support from city council members; however, unlike more established—or affluent—schools, Sobrante lacks a culture of significant parental involvement or engagement.

Principal Marco Franco, a straight-talking consensus-builder, has led Sobrante since 1999. He began his educational career teaching within the Oakland School District and describes his experience as "very typical teaching within a large district—dysfunctional and comfortable." In 1997, Franco was appointed as the assistant principal at Sobrante Park and states that the school's culture upon his arrival was "old guard, very well entrenched." He became principal two years later and set about to change the culture of the school. While a number of teachers appreciated his change efforts and sought opportunities to increase their performance, many did not. It did not appear to Franco that the school community (and particularly some of the faculty) had a significant incentive to change.

Franco describes his first attempts at utilizing student data to guide Sobrante Park's instructional decisions:

> What do you do when the data is all bad? Seriously, you're just depressed as hell.
> So [myself and teachers] said, forget the data, the answer is with us; it's not with
> the district, it's not with the Clintons, it's not with the administration—it's with
> us. It's as simple as that.

Franco states that as a result of his investigation into data, during the first year
as principal, he and his staff chose to "pick one thing and do it really well."
During his first year, the focus was on improving writing skills. The next year,
the school implemented a formative assessment system called "Open Court,"
allowing for regular internal evaluations of instruction. Sobrante Park teachers also utilized Open Court to administer self-created assessments; a shifting
focus toward student achievement within the school had begun.

Another major adjustment made by Franco was based on his first years
of teaching. He jokingly says that he should "be locked up for thievery" for
those years because—like most new teachers—"I didn't do anything because
I didn't know how, and nobody helped." He was shocked then, when he "received these glowing evaluations [from his supervisor]." Remembering the
lack of useful feedback he received, Franco supplied constructive criticism to
his faculty. He states,

> [It was] key when we started tying achievement into evaluations. It was hard
> and took awhile—but it started to change and many of the teachers started to
> improve. . . . With evaluations, you have to tie them into achievement. Other-
> wise, you are just spinning your wheels.

Franco and his staff were not yet aware of NCLB on the horizon but were successfully displaying continuous innovation in teaching.

Franco also evaluated the school's bilingual program at the beginning of
his tenure. Franco describes his viewpoint:

> The key to doing that successfully was that the audience must understand the
> reason for the change . . . if they don't see why you are doing this, it's hard to
> convince people . . . you have to be honest and transparent. That's why we use
> data. And this data was beautiful. This data showed kids who were trapped in

bilingual programs were already behind the other, lowest-performing kids. . . . [The bilingual programs in Oakland] were totally ineffective, segregated, only for one group of students.

Although Franco was accused of being antibilingual, his defense rested on the data that convincingly showed the "dismal" results of the bilingual program in grades 3–5. He became convinced that students should be mainstreamed, but faced resistance from the community, district, and faculty. Utilizing achievement results, he convinced stakeholders one-by-one that such a shift was best for students. The victory, however, came from convincing the teachers who would have to personally shift their instruction that this change would be in the best interest of students:

> There was one very good bilingual [teacher] who was more idealistic than others. . . . This was a guy who was committed. He came, knocked on my door, "Look, man, I'm not sure I agree with you about this. . . ." But he said "I'm willing to do what I think is best for the school, I like where it is going."

In promoting this major curricular shift to his staff, Franco was able to co-opt a key stakeholder of the opposition. Franco was convinced of the need for the change because of his analysis of student achievement results, and he was able to utilize these results to sell the change to an individual who would be most affected by the change. With a key bilingual educator on his side, opposition to the shift quickly melted, and the school removed the bilingual program from third through fifth grades in 2000–2001.

Franco states, "Each year we do or add something new or different to our instructional program—always our instructional program. Whether it is a writing program, new library, new schedule, new intervention program, new transition program for English Learners . . . we keep looking at ways to do teaching better." This improvement is evidenced in the achievement scores from this era, as from 1999–2000 to 2001–2002 the percent of students scoring above the 50th national percentile on the Stanford 9 increased from 17 percent to 26 percent in reading and from 19 percent to 26 percent in mathematics.[8]

Reforming the writing program and improving the teacher evaluation process did contribute to increased test scores among Sobrante Park students, but not enough for the school to make adequate yearly progress. It would take a full-blown accountability crisis in the form of impending restructuring to create the urgency required to commit all Sobrante staff members to the vision of learning at the school.

## CRISIS DESCRIPTION

Like many schools, Sobrante Park only slowly realized the paradigm shift associated with the No Child Left Behind Act. Franco says that under the Clinton administration, schools were "spoiled" because there were many resources but no accountability. Until the fifth year of failing adequate yearly progress (AYP), he says that the district and schools struggled to disentangle the complex law and determine its effects: "There was no sense of urgency . . . until the [fifth year of failing AYP], that's when everybody from [the district] came down." Even though incremental student progress was being made, the school found itself moving further down the punitive accountability steps of NCLB. He describes the district's communication more fully:

> Even though we'd been making these advances, it came to a point when the district said, "Get your staff together and let me talk to them" and this director came down and said, "Oh, my God, oh, my God!"

The reason for the district official's dismay was the possibility of extreme measures if the school continued to fail AYP. After another year of incremental progress in 2003–2004, Sobrante Park entered the 2004–2005 school year in the first phase of Restructuring I. During 2004–2005, they would have to create a turnaround plan for their school that utilized one of the following options: turn the school over to an outside organization, reopen as a charter school, replace all or most staff including the principal, or "any other major restructuring."[9]

Through negotiations with the district, and because of the progress the school had been making in previous years, Franco committed to the option of "any other major restructuring." The 2004–2005 school year would be spent putting a restructuring plan together, which would be implemented in 2005–2006 if the school failed to make AYP one more time. Unfortunately, the district insisted that in order to meet the definition of restructuring, Sobrante Park would be required to turn over half of its teachers.

The possibility of the forced removal of half the school's staff caused great consternation among the faculty. Franco states that "there was a lot of anxiety, but it was mostly reflected by those who knew they would get transferred [if the school failed again]." Union leadership became informally involved in an attempt to determine which staff members would be favored if Franco was required to remove a subset of teachers, and the faculty lounge was abuzz with speculation and fear.

Franco states that the threat of restructuring "brought NCLB alive for us." Sobrante Park Elementary had a choice about how they would respond to the increased pressure and possibility of further transformations that would have involved the loss of more staff or reconstitution of the school. Instead of reacting with dismay, a group of staff gathered at a teacher's home to immediately begin planning for the school's "any other restructuring" that would be implemented in the next school year. The staff considered further instructional innovations beyond those already attempted, and Franco proudly describes that the teachers already had a solid foundation on which to build:

> We were already committed to increasing achievement of kids. Our school was better mentally prepared, in a way, to deal with everything that comes with NCLB so even though there was a sense of urgency, it was not an immediate kind of thing to say "We have to look at everything now—oh, my!" We already looked at it every year.

As part of their academic plan, the school planned to implement a new schedule that would provide opportunities for targeted assistance aimed at failing students and increased levels of shared planning time between teachers. They were prepared to put this plan into action upon failing AYP at the end of 2004–2005.

The school's stakeholders were overjoyed, however, when the results from the 2004–2005 school year showed that the school had met AYP goals. All of Sobrante Park's preparations for restructuring proved to be superfluous, as the school would not be required by the district to implement their restructuring plan after all. It could be shelved and forgotten about. Amazingly, Principal Marco Franco and his staff chose to implement their restructuring plan regardless of Sobrante Park's 2004–2005 achievement results.

## CRISIS ANALYSIS

Entering Restructuring I at the beginning of 2004–2005 placed Sobrante Park in a crisis state. The External-Predictable accountability crisis threatened to remove at least half of the school's staff or even, at the extreme, cause the closure of the school. The low achievement at Sobrante Park resulted from a complex interplay between neighborhood impacts and failing elements within the school. Finally, the event necessitated urgent decision-making on the part of the staff of Sobrante Park to increase the slow, upward trend of student performance.

While Sobrante Park did not appreciate the magnitude of NCLB until the end of 2003–2004—when the district official gave a panicked presentation to the school's staff—the school did have significant time to prepare for its accountability crisis. Information on the consequences associated with the failure to meet No Child Left Behind standards was presented early. While the staff perhaps did not foresee the crisis from five years out, they did have over a year to modify the school's instruction while in Restructuring I—hence the "Predictable" label. Additionally, the crisis was created by the school's failure to meet NCLB achievement standards—an external accountability pressure—hence, the "External" label.

This accountability crisis of NCLB did allow Franco to replace a few staff members that he would not have been able to otherwise and did assist in focusing efforts and resources. The unique aspect of accountability crises is that, as with Sobrante Park, schools sometimes have to reach very punitive stages of NCLB before institutional and bureaucratic obstacles are overcome to induce change. Franco explains that without the impending threat of restructuring through NCLB he believes that he would have eventually made AYP,

> but it would have taken me longer. By that time, I already changed four teachers and was working on others. I think we were already going in that direction. It certainly played a part in commitment . . . it increases [teachers'] sense of ownership because we all know that it's up to us. The district didn't get us into this mess, the district isn't going to get us out of this mess. It's all up to us. Without that sense of urgency and without the sense of accountability—that in many ways comes from NCLB—that cultural complacency would still be ever-present.

Instead of responding to Restructuring I with dismay, the school saw it as an opportunity to further implement its reform plan—even though they were not required to.

The efforts of Franco and his staff did result in the school making adequate yearly progress in both 2004–2005 and 2005–2006, moving the school to "good standing." In fact, the school also met AYP in 2007 and 2008, demonstrating the long-term and continued impact of the faculty's efforts. Franco remembers receiving scores in 2005–2006 and says that he was "euphoric . . . it was like winning the Super Bowl." Instead of panicking or relinquishing control over the school, the staff implemented common planning time between teachers, strategically adjusted student scheduling, and made necessary changes to instruction. Sobrante Park had manipulated its accountability pressures to its advantage and produced the necessary test scores to overcome its crisis.

## CRISIS TREATMENT

For a teacher to be terminated, it is a lengthy process. It goes union.
So when restructuring came about, it was in a certain way a very good
opportunity to replace staff who were not onboard with the vision.

—*Principal Marco Franco*

Franco remembers the fear and uncertainty that permeated the school at the end of the 2004–2005 school year:

> There was a sense of urgency. . . . There was a sense of panic from some teachers who were in trouble with me already. Teachers want to protect themselves in those times . . . there was a lot of pressure from outside, not only our internal pressures, but all of a sudden we had all these other people in our school [and] that created a sense of confusion.

When an organization comes under stress, its leader has the power to set the tone with his or her response. Instead of panicking himself or feeding the frenzy, Franco wisely took advantage of the sense of urgency associated with possible takeover, seeing the crisis as an opportunity to make necessary curricular and staffing changes to Sobrante Park. Franco responded to the district representative's panicked speech and his faculty's frenzied acts with coolness. He states,

> I spent a lot of time reassuring teachers about what I was going to do. I couldn't say who [would be transferred], but I was very clear about the process. One way to deal with crisis is transparency, letting people know what happens every step of the way.

He began planning for restructuring by determining what teachers would not contribute to the school's turnaround, and which were integral to its success. He describes the response of his staff to the restructuring plan and outlined expectations: "You were either working [toward improvement] or you were not."

However, the district was still insisting that he would have to replace at least half of his staff in order to meet the requirements of restructuring. The great irony of this requirement was that the threat of takeover had motivated the very changes that had needed to occur at the school. The replacement of half of his staff would have actually been a step backward because, by this point, the majority of his staff bought into Franco's vision of improvement for the school. He states, "At that point, I didn't need to lose half—strategically, I could not afford to lose half. So I had to go argue my case. And somebody listened."

By fighting this bureaucratic battle, Franco was able to gain some flexibility from the heavy penalties of NCLB, and he transferred only four of his staff to other schools. However, this flexibility was only provided because Franco was able to convince district officials—using student achievement trends—that his core staff members were already moving the school in the right direction.

Franco states that one of his biggest challenges throughout his exposure to the punitive sanctions of NCLB was controlling the many external organizations attempting to "help" the school: "It's very easy to let these outside entities take over, but once you lose your influence over the school, forget it."

Two anecdotes reveal the ownership one has to feel as a leader both for the issues facing your school and the solutions to those issues. Increasing amounts of state intervention is associated with failing AYP, and assistance is offered in several forms. In the spring of the 2004–2005 school year, the district selected an external nonprofit agency to partner with Sobrante Park on its improvement plan. Franco states that the educational interventionist wanted to "bring her own vision for what [she] thought Sobrante Park needed." Describing his staff as "pretty daunting," the external individual quickly understood that she would be a facilitator, not a dictator.

A similar interchange occurred with supplemental educational service (SES) providers, who are private and nonprofit agencies paid to provide after-school tutoring to students. Franco explains:

> All these people coming out of the woodwork for this SES money. It can be very disruptive to a school. So one of the things I said is that if you are going to come in here, you are going to come in under the umbrella of our after-school coordinator. She'll tell you where to set up. . . . You have to control those outside influences.

One of the unique challenges of accountability crises is that, many times, there are a variety of external influences that are all clamoring for attention and action. Not all of these entities are motivated by idealism—such as for-profit SES providers. Other entities, such as district leadership, may have the students' best interest at heart, but not the in-the-trenches knowledge on how to best serve their educational needs. The examples above show that Franco handled the external pressures with the appropriate exertion of executive authority.

With the impetus for improvement on his shoulders, Franco continued to build a collaborative culture of learning at Sobrante Park. He reiterates that he's "not smart enough to have all the answers," and advises that school leaders should listen to their teachers and attack the root causes of instructional problems immediately and unequivocally:

> I like asking [the teachers], "What do you guys think?" I see many principals and administrators get lost in that kind of theoretical thinking. . . . [I've heard other] principals say, "We're going to change the culture of our school—we're going to be about learning, not about teaching." My point is that we need to stop looking at things like systems. When you tell me that we're going to do this within a certain system, I forget about the mission and concentrate on the system. . . . I just don't see us taking a straight line to the problem—we get lost in all this other stuff. . . . With NCLB and the threats of reconstitution—you have to think about what I need to do day-to-day to make sure Johnny and Anisha learn.

Contrary to many calls for reform around the nation, he adds, "I'm not the instructional leader . . . I am the excuse remover, that's what I do. I remove any reason teachers might say why Johnny can't learn." This statement demonstrates the degree to which Franco empowers his teachers to be successful, giving them the resources to be successful and holding them accountable to that standard.

Franco emphasizes that once he successfully removes reasons that students cannot be successful, it is important to extend the line of accountability in a fair manner to the teacher level. Sobrante Park's formative assessment system, Open Court, made achievement levels measurable and transparent, and this tool became even more crucial during the school's two-year turnaround. Open Court made it clear to teachers and administration whether a curriculum change was working and steps to ameliorate problems were successful.

> I think the best thing that the principal can do to change the academic course of any school is evaluation. You have to be comfortable using data, and using achievement directly to assess performance. . . . I tell my teachers right up front—your evaluation is all about achievement, not about how many times you were here, not about lesson plans—I don't even want to see them. I need to know where you are and where you are going. It's all about results.

This singular focus on results drove the entire school mission and every decision that was made.

Although Sobrante Park did utilize formative assessment results and had a strong teacher evaluation system in place, Franco admits that doubt was ever-present in the improvement process. Users of assessment results know that data can sometimes produce nuanced or contradictory results, and decisions are rarely black and white. When asked if he ever had any doubts about the instructional decisions that he made during restructuring, Franco states, "Always! If I could have put Ms. [X] in the second grade instead of the first, we could have gotten five more points. Always thinking about the how, especially—how do we do this, how could we do better, what did we miss."

In 2005–2006, Sobrante Park's "any other restructuring" took the form of a series of instructional reforms that increased the scale of targeted assistance for students and faculty collaboration. The school implemented a new schedule that pushed the beginning of school forward by thirty minutes to allow for tutoring to struggling students early in the day. The school also brought in substitute teachers twice per month to allow teachers collaborative time to analyze data and prepare curricula.[10] These interventions continued the school on its positive path, and—with the staff's willingness to experiment and collaborate—the school achieved AYP both in the 2004–2005 and 2005–2006 school years, thereby coming off the High Priority list.

## CONCLUSION

I believe that the "secret" to our success is not a particular curriculum or set of practices. And it is certainly not "wise" policy-making from above. Our "secret" is hard work and willingness to think outside the box. It is the opportunity to have a say in how we do our jobs. It is who we are as individuals and professionals that have helped us bring our students up.

—*a Sobrante Park teacher*[11]

What broader lessons can be drawn from successful turnaround experiences at previously low-performing schools? The Institute of Education Sciences, the U.S. DOE's research division, released a report entitled *Turning Around Chronically Low-Performing Schools*, which recommends four actions leaders should take to turn around a school. It concludes that successful efforts share four common components: signal the need for dramatic change with strong leadership, maintain a consistent focus for improving instruction, make visible improvements early in the school turnaround process (quick wins), and build a committed staff.[12]

The lessons of Sobrante Park align with these four components. Franco showed strong leadership by insisting to external policymakers that the shift in achievement would come from innovations conceived and implemented by his staff. He already had confidence in many of his staff, and he utilized the accountability of NCLB to transfer those who were not contributing to increased student achievement. His statements, and the gains made by Sobrante Park's students, reflect his singular focus on student achievement.

Perhaps the only disconnect between the restructuring provision of NCLB and the experience of Sobrante Park is the expectation of NCLB that transforming a school can be successfully completed within a year. Franco suggests that the school's transformation was an effort that began years before the school began thinking about restructuring. NCLB may have helped quicken the transformation, but coming out of restructuring would not have been possible without the strong faculty, focus on student achievement, and instructional innovations put in place by the school prior to the accountability crisis. The ultimate expression of this ideal is that Sobrante Park believed in its instructional reforms so much that they were implemented even after meeting AYP in 2004–2005.

Franco also admits that his singular focus on student achievement can serve as a frustration for district leadership, as he sometimes has trouble finishing district tasks. He states, "If you call up the Oakland School District, you'll get a sigh. I get in trouble because I miss principals' meetings and stuff like that, but oh, well." However, he quickly adds that even though he is "often late with things for the district," he spends his time on what he considers paramount to the success of Sobrante Park, stating, "I'm never late on evaluations. You have to prioritize what's important—my staff and school are what's important. . . . That's why I'm successful."

The experiences of Sobrante Park Elementary School hold valuable lessons for school leaders facing accountability crises. Innovations and an instructional focus flow from the school's leader and permeate throughout the faculty. One of the most effective ways of accomplishing this is by completing periodic, student-achievement-based evaluations of your teachers. Most importantly, an accountability crisis can be utilized as an opportunity to harness the sense of urgency and increased resources to make changes that were previously bureaucratically blocked. By maintaining a strong instructional focus and utilizing the pressures of restructuring, Sobrante Park Elementary School overcame the accountability crisis that threatened the very existence of the school.

## REFLECTIVE QUESTIONS

### Reflection on the Reading

1. In what ways did a cooperative district allow Principal Franco to implement his desired reforms? What pressures might have contributed to the central office's cooperation? Do you think the school's turnaround would have occurred if the central office was not cooperative?
2. Principal Franco appears to have partnered with faculty members in turning around Sobrante Park while being intentionally vague as to the impact of

potential transfers. What do you think of this management decision—one that kept the real threat of Internal and External crisis ever-present? Is this a necessary element of building a successful faculty? Or a drawback to building one? Is this sustainable in a longer term?

3. Why did Principal Franco and the school implement their turnaround plan even though they made AYP? Would you have done this in your school?

## Application to Theory

4. Could you argue that Franco did so well with "preparation and primary prevention" that he skipped "damage control and secondary prevention"? Why or why not?

5. In what ways can Franco use "community recovery and learning" to ensure that Sobrante will continue to make adequate yearly progress and that its performance crisis is not cyclical—particularly as accountability expectations are likely to increase?

## Application on the Job

6. Do you use teacher evaluations effectively? Are they meaningful, centered around student achievement, and ongoing? Do your teachers understand their importance to effective instruction? Are they provided with guidance and resources to make needed improvements?

7. Do you understand the way adequate yearly progress works in your state? Do your teachers? Do parents and other community members know your proficiency targets for this year, as well as the potential effect of not meeting those targets? Do your teachers?

8. If you were facing a performance crisis, what would be the major shifts you would make to your curriculum and/or instruction? To your staff? What barriers have prevented you from making these changes already, and how can you circumvent these barriers?

9. In Sobrante, Franco credits effective data use and disclosure for allowing him to communicate both the reality and nature of the crisis to teachers. Are your decisions and communications based on data? If not, on what are your decisions based? In what ways do you not have the data necessary to make good decisions?

# "There Weren't Enough Affluent White Kids to Spread Out."

*How Accountabiility Pressures Pushed Manual High School to the Brink of a State Takeover*

**OVERVIEW**

Perhaps no other issue evokes as much community passion and angst than the method of distributing students from high-, middle-, and low-income families among schools. As a result of a decision by the Denver, Colorado, school board in the mid-1990s, Manual High School—a seeming model of ethnic integration and high achievement—was transformed into a neighborhood school serving almost exclusively poor students. This chapter describes the tremendous adversity faced by the school and the remarkable efforts made by its staff to provide a quality education to Manual students.

Throughout the 1980s and the early 1990s, the district of Denver held up Manual High School as an example of successful ethnic integration. Manual's half-minority, half-Caucasian student body routinely produced high achievement scores on standardized examinations and went on to attend Ivy League schools. However, Manual's success was largely due to the aggregation of its students' test scores—an aggregation masking a very large achievement gap. Despite public accolades, most of Manual's minority students were neither performing at high levels nor graduating.

This gap became apparent in 1995 when a new student assignment plan transformed Manual's student body from one of mixed socioeconomic status (SES) to almost exclusively low-SES students. As the higher SES students left Manual, its test scores plummeted. By 1997, Manual moved from an ostensible model of ethnic diversity to a decidedly "majority minority" school, with the percent of minority students rising from 58 percent to 95 percent in those two years. The percent of students eligible for free and reduced-price meals rose from 27 percent to 75 percent within one year.

The departing students took their disproportionately high test scores with them, revealing that the school's high achievement scores were an illusion borne out of the aggregation of test scores. Despite a committed faculty and a broad array of instructional tools, Manual faced increased accountability pressures and a threatened state takeover. With the assistance of the Gates Foundation, Manual converted into three small schools, but even this move was unsuccessful and the school was eventually closed by the district.

This chapter reviews the crisis at Manual High School caused by district rezoning, when within a year, its student body was transformed from a diverse reflection of the city of Denver to one exclusively containing high-poverty students. The demographic transition that occurred at Manual High is an External-Predictable crisis. The crisis was predictable because the change in the district's student assignment policy took place after some debate, which provided the school time to prepare for the coming changes. The crisis was external because the rezoning decision was made by the school board, outside the immediate school community. The crisis eventually was overwhelming, as Manual High School was closed by the district in 2006.

## CASE NARRATIVE

"There are a lot of people with good will and intentions," said David M. Dirks, a member of the Manual decision-making council whose twin daughters graduated this spring. "But it's going to be real hard, and I'm apprehensive about what the end result will be."

—*Education Week, 1998*[1]

Denver's desegregation journey began in 1969 when a group of parents sued the district charging deliberate racial segregation. The case went all the way to the United States Supreme Court, resulting in the influential *Keyes* decision. In *Keyes v. School District No. 1*, the Court ruled that African Americans and Hispanics should be placed in the same category when considering both the impact of segregation and the availability of remedial measures "since both groups suffer the same educational inequities when compared with the treatment afforded Anglo students."[2]

As in many cities throughout the nation, the courts imposed a desegregation plan bussing Caucasian students from affluent areas in Denver into the inner city. The desegregation plan remained in place until 1995, when it was lifted by the United States District Court. Manual Lead Teacher Santo Nicotera believed that "white flight," while not an express part of the court's rationale, outpaced the remedial measures originally imposed by the court: "There weren't enough affluent white kids to spread out."

District statistics support this assertion. The school district grew from just over sixty thousand students in 1990 to just under seventy thousand by the turn of the century. This growth was primarily due to the aggregate increase of minority students enrolled in the district, growing throughout the decade from 71 percent to 77 percent of the total student population. This growth—both in real numbers and as a percentage of student population—was primarily due to the large numbers of Hispanic students enrolling in the district. Between 1994 and 2000, the number of Hispanic students increased from twenty-eight thousand to thirty-six thousand. This resulted in a continuing erosion of diversity in the district as a whole.

The resulting impact of the shift to neighborhood schools affected Manual High School dramatically. The 9–12 high school, located directly east of downtown Denver, has a long and proud history. Founded in 1896, it counts former mayors of both Denver and Seattle among its alumni. The demographic transition at Manual High School occurred after the 1996–1997 school year, when Denver's new school assignment plan was implemented. Manual's total student enrollment hovered around one thousand students throughout the 1990s both before and after the new assignment plan.

The makeup of the student body, however, drastically changed between the 1996–1997 and 1997–1998 school years, when the percentage of minority students increased from 58 percent to 87 percent. The remaining 13 percent of white students were holdover eleventh and twelfth graders that were grandfathered in under the old student assignment policy. Within two more years, the school was 95 percent minority.[3]

The school's staff struggled to adjust to this dramatic shift, and the community wrestled over how to best address the dismally low achievement scores. The demographic shift at Manual High School caused tremendous stress while also providing unprecedented instructional opportunity; unfortunately, the accountability pressures eventually pushed the school into a sweeping restructuring that ended in failure.

During this transition, Manual was led by Principal Nancy Sutton, who had been recruited from Indianapolis as the result of a national search for someone to lead Manual through its transition. One of the key members of her leadership team was Lead Teacher Mr. Nicotera, who began his career at Manual as a social studies teacher and served as the chair of the committee that brought Principal Sutton to Manual. In the 1997–1998 school year, Mr. Nicotera's role was formalized as the position of the Assistant Director of the Reform Initiative, overseeing instructional reform and faculty initiatives within the school. Along with a few other lead teachers, Principal Sutton and Mr. Nicotera helped prepare Manual High School for the end of desegregation, implementing instructional reform throughout the demographic transition.

## CRISIS DESCRIPTION

There were three [proposed rezoning] plans drawn up: One was—that I thought was very equitable—was this rectangle drawn from Northeast Denver over Manual all the way through the city south, just pulling this slice of the Denver central population. Another was this zig-zaggy thing that wrapped around this central core of blight where most people were in poverty. It was a fight. I went using U.S. census data and just compared on either side of the boundary drawn around Manual, what the difference in household income was and it was between ten thousand and twenty thousand, the difference between those outside of the boundary and those inside Manual's boundary. [The accepted boundary] was just so badly drawn.

—*Santo Nicotera*

In the early 1990s, Manual High School's student body spanned the socioeconomic spectrum. The student body, made up of 50 percent Caucasian students, 39 percent African American, and 9 percent Hispanic, were offered advanced placement, regular, and remedial coursework, and they routinely had a graduation rate that was ranked in the top three in the district.[4] An *Education Week* article provides a vivid picture:

> Superintendent Irving Moskowitz, who sent his own children to Manual in the 1980s, said the school became "a flagship for the integration program" in part because of its striking socioeconomic mix. As Manual English teacher Barbara Ingram put it, "We had kids whose families were on the society pages, down to kids living in shelters."[5]

This glowing picture of integration, however, masked significant achievement gaps within the school. Santo Nicotera recalls that, in 1994, the school had graduated *only nine* of the one hundred African American males who had entered Manual High School as freshmen. These hidden achievement gaps, masked by aggregated data, exemplifies why NCLB requires that schools dis-aggregate results by race and student status.[6]

The mid-1990s witnessed the city of Denver undertaking several efforts to improve the quality of life and stem the growth of the suburbs. The new airport was built in 1995, as was the home of the Colorado Rockies, Coors Field. The new, $215-million baseball stadium was built in a blighted area of downtown and jump-started the development of the condo-saturated, pedestrian-friendly downtown.

One year after the beginning of downtown's revitalization, in 1996, the Denver school board approved a student assignment plan that focused on creating neighborhood schools, sending students to the school closest to their home. This shift changed the zone from the combination of some neighborhood students and a larger, predominantly white satellite attendance area to one that was exclusively neighborhood students.

Neighborhood school advocates sold the plan on the promise that students would perform better closer to home; however, the Denver school board also might have hoped that the return to neighborhood schools would entice families back to the city. Whatever the motivations resulting in the neighborhood schools rezoning, the result of the rezoning (and the gerrymandered zone drawn for Manual) was drastic. Best stated by former school board member Sharon Bailey, "We're pretty much back to where we started with the resegregation of the schools."[7]

Educational researchers have bemoaned similar trends that show the increased segregation of African American and Hispanic students throughout the nation.[8] A 2002 report by Harvard's Civil Rights Project found that, among districts with greater than twenty-five thousand students, "the last 10–15 years have seen a steady unraveling of almost 25 years worth of increased integration."[9] Another study concludes, "The Clinton Administration [had] presided over a period of substantial and continuous increase[s] in segregation without any initiatives to offset these trends."[10] Throughout the 1990s, Denver was not the only city implementing pupil assignment plans that significantly increased the extent of segregation within urban schools.

Between the 1991–1992 and 1995–1996 school year, the school was between 51 percent to 56 percent minority. Over the next three years, with the school's total enrollment staying relatively constant, the percentage of minority students enrolled in the school went to 58 percent in 1996–1997 and then exploded to 93 percent in 1997–1998.[11] As expected, the percent of students receiving free or reduced-price meals ballooned from 27 percent in 1996–1997 to 75 percent in 1997–1998 and 81 percent in 1999–2000.[12] The paradigm of two separate groups within Manual High School—one affluent, and one poor—had ended, and in its place was exclusively put high-poverty students.

The school's staff had time to instructionally prepare for the shift in student population, but the immediate concern at the opening of the 1997–1998 school year was the threat of violence on the very first day of school. What appeared to be missing from the redrawing of school zones was appreciation for the potential gang implications from shifting students around. Santo Nicotera describes:

> The summer prior to the end of desegregation, the police department of Denver came to us and said, "We are really worried that the first day of school there will be a gang war between the Crips and the Bloods on the Manual campus." . . . because the way they'd drawn the boundaries, it took in an area above 40th Avenue that is traditionally a Blood neighborhood whereas the neighborhood around Manual was more of a Crip neighborhood.

Fortunately, the Manual staff concentrated on team building with the incoming ninth graders, and Santo Nicotera considers the lack of violence that first year to be one of the school's most significant successes. He states that the school did a "pretty good job of that first year of creating a new group of kids," and the retention of so many ninth graders supports this:

> The successes at first were that that first ninth grade we didn't lose anybody . . . they all came back next year . . . we used to just lose them all, they'd just drop out, we would never see them. . . . It was like 98 percent retention into the tenth grade, so that was amazing success not that they had necessarily all passed their classes, there was still a failure rate happening at high levels. . . . The personalization variables, we definitely had addressed that. We definitely had addressed that and succeeded in making it a much more "home" place for the kids of the neighborhood.

The "failure rate" described by Mr. Nicotera was the defining issue associated with Manual's demographic crisis. When analyzing the strengths and weaknesses of its incoming students, Manual's faculty found that 75 percent of the incoming freshmen were not reading at their grade level. Their even greater shock was that half of these 75 percent were actually reading at below a sixth-grade level.[13] These dramatic student achievement results—of incoming ninth graders that had not yet enrolled in Manual—reveal the scope of the crisis faced by the school's faculty.

### CRISIS ANALYSIS

This chapter describes the demographic crisis experienced at Manual High School. Integrally connected to the demographic shift is the achievement crisis, which ultimately forced the school into a major restructuring. This demographic/achievement crisis was a significant challenge, but it is a challenge for which the school had time to prepare. With the bureaucratic wrangling among the school board and necessary planning time, Manual's faculty had over a year to get ready. Principal Sutton states that "the quality of the faculty and the intensity of the community support were two key elements that would help get us through this change." While these two key elements were certainly strengths of the school, they were not enough to prevent it from being overwhelmed.

The rezoning decision was made by elected school board members over whom the Manual School community had little control. With so many constituencies clamoring for their needs, one cannot hold the Manual community primarily responsible for the shift to neighborhood schools. Indeed, Santo Nicotera and others attempted to influence the debate by advocating for a more balanced student body, but as described by Mr. Nicotera, "It's a typical urban situation where the poor don't have anyone representing them." Principal Sutton adds that "Manual wasn't as strong politically as the neighboring school."

The ability to prepare for the crisis and the origination from outside the Manual community make this demographic shift an External-Predictable crisis. As with Franklin Career Academy (chapter 11) and John Dewey High School (chapter 13), the crisis at Manual High School had a multiyear duration, fragmenting continuously and spawning new crises. However, unlike these two cases in which conditions gradually deteriorated, Manual's adjustment was of short duration—the school transformed from a relatively socioeconomically and ethnically balanced student population to an overwhelmingly poor and minority student population in a single year.

Compared to other case studies profiled within this book, lessons from Manual High School do not as readily appear. The school formed a great leadership team, implemented a variety of instructional reforms, and attempted to influence district policy in order to solidify its restructuring. Without greater control over its hiring decisions and without more support from the district for the reforms they attempted to implement, the school was eventually forced to undergo a complete restructuring into three small schools. Continued policy inflexibility, inadequate resources, and an accountability system that failed to credit the school for student growth all contributed to set the school up for failure.

## CRISIS TREATMENT

Overcoming the staggering challenges faced by Manual High School would require strong leadership, a tremendous commitment from teachers, and increased instructional rigor. These resources were delivered to varying degrees throughout the four years between the demographic shift and transition into three small schools. Santo Nicotera chaired the search committee tasked with finding the right principal, and he states that the district "gave us a lot of leverage" with the hiring decision "because they knew they screwed us [during the rezoning process]."

The past decade has witnessed a growth in research investigating the strong correlation between strong school leadership and increased student achievement. Indeed, a comprehensive literature review completed in 2004 found that, among school factors, school leadership is the second most important factor in contributing to student achievement.[14]

The research base is best applied to the school context within the Educational Leadership Policy Standards: ISLLC 2008, which provides "guidance to state policymakers as they work to improve education leadership." The standards include "facilitating the development, articulation, implementation, and stewardship of a vision of learning" and "understanding, responding to, and influencing the political, social, economic, legal, and cultural context."[15] Fortunately, Manual's new principal fiercely executed these standards, even in the midst of traumatic changes.

The newly hired principal, Nancy Sutton, immediately began promoting her "vision of learning" to her new faculty. When describing the first faculty meeting at which Principal Sutton was introduced, Mr. Nicotera states that,

> she walked in, the faculty was hoping to become a magnet school that would continue to have the same population it had always had, and the people had taught and had that kind of success . . . and she walks in and said "if you're not wanting to teach the neighborhood, the kids that come to us from this neighborhood, there's the door because that's what we're teaching."

Principal Sutton adds that she communicated that Manual was going to "address head-on the needs of the community. And I felt that we had the faculty resources, leadership resources, and community support to get the job done." Some faculty did choose to continue their careers elsewhere; Principal Sutton states that the teachers that stayed were "a superior faculty; they had a lot of talent, and a lot of leadership, they were particularly dedicated." The staff was also aging, and through retirements and voluntary transfers, twenty-six out of the fifty-eight faculty members left the school within two years of the transition.

One of Principal Sutton's first instructional moves was implementing a summer-school program for incoming ninth graders, "to get them prepared for the rituals, routines, and cultures of the high school." After receiving some pushback from the community concerning the loss of summer job income,

Principal Sutton—in a controversial move, but one she says she would definitely repeat—procured funding from the mayor's office to pay students $25/week for being active participants in summer school. This also allowed the school faculty to begin building relationships with the new student body.

Principal Sutton also began replacing the teaching staff that had left, and fortunately, she was able to formulate an agreement with the central office that the district would no longer consider Manual the "dumping ground . . . for teachers that couldn't fit anywhere else." She states that without an influx of lemons, the school's leadership was "able to build a really premier faculty." Mr. Nicotera adds that the faculty was one "that would be able to pull this off if lots of those other variables were more stable."

Many of the new faculty members were bilingual teachers, because the district had sprung a surprise on Principal Sutton after she had been hired by turning Manual into a bilingual school. She states that she and the faculty began "retooling ourselves" to learn how to best serve their bilingual population, and they had success building relationships with the Children's Hospital, which utilized Manual student volunteers as translators. Principal Sutton also describes raising $200,000 annually from philanthropic groups to pay for professional development covering how to teach reading for Manual's faculty; she adds that "Manual had never been a school that had needed to teach reading."

Fortunately, the school's rezoning had allowed for a negotiation over student scheduling, and teachers were granted a ninety-minute planning block every day. The teacher's union was also supportive of these efforts because of the strong teacher voices Principal Sutton had built into her decision-making process. She states that the school really became a "darling of the teachers union," and this strong relationship allowed the administration flexibility in implementing its reform programs.

One of the most powerful, but difficult, of these efforts was utilizing the teachers' planning block as an opportunity to have thoughtful conversations about student work. This initiative, called Critical Friends, trained teacher and administrator facilitators to critically discuss teacher lessons and student output in a group setting. Principal Sutton states that these were the "early days of Critical Friends . . . it was very hard . . . there was an enormous amount of discomfort." Mr. Nicotera adds,

The one thing we didn't anticipate about the faculty was the resistance to making their work public. . . . The issue of dealing with faculty who are just resistant . . . I don't think we were prepared for how much resistance we started to get from faculty members about just being collaborative about their work.

Teachers also formed research action teams that were designed to review on a biweekly basis data around student attendance and performance. Further efforts concentrated on increasing the rigor and longitudinal consistency of instruction. As told by Mr. Nicotera,

It was teachers looking at their own work and creating goals for themselves. So we were doing that. Where every teacher in the school was supposed to be designing units of instructions, not just lessons, but whole units using the Grant Wiggins [*Understanding by Design*] stuff.

Manual High School utilized some creative strategies to expand the level of fiscal support that they were receiving from the district. National data show higher levels of free and reduced-price meals (FRM)—which determines Title 1 allocations—at the elementary and middle school tiers. Statistics from the U.S. Department of Agriculture show that the disparity is due almost entirely to the social stigma that exists at the high school level.[16] Knowing that an accurate count of FRM would result in increased funding for the school, Manual's staff made a "massive effort" to collect the free and reduced-price meal sheets. The district was then forced to label Manual as a Title 1 school, and this designation provided funding for additional reading teachers at Manual.[17]

The curriculum for students at Manual focused on rigorous and relevant offerings, as students enrolled in one of four programs of excellence: math/science/medicine, business/entrepreneurship, cultural studies/law/government, or arts/humanities/communications. Students were offered postsecondary coursework through the Community College of Denver, and they participated in job shadowing, internships, and a self-designed service-learning project.[18] The concrete learning experiences appeared to have the desired impact on test scores, as continuously enrolled Manual students were making an average of one-and-a-half years' worth of academic gains annually. Nonacademic outcomes were also showing improvement, with the suspension rate falling from 50 percent to 36 percent from the 1998–1999 to 1999–2000 school year.[19]

Manual's relationship with the district was a challenge, according to Principal Sutton: "Frankly, the rest of the district didn't go along with what was going on at Manual." Mr. Nicotera had lobbied the district to receive the school's per capita staffing allocation in a lump sum in order to end what was—in effect—Manual's subsidization of other high schools in the district. Paying the average district salary for each staff member due to Manual would have shifted thousands of dollars to the school because their staff was less experienced and less educated than the district average. This request was denied by the district.

Another effort blocked by district personnel was the school's request to require students to maintain 85 percent regular attendance in order to stay enrolled. At the time, students and their parents were required to sign a pact with Manual at the beginning of the year to attend regularly, but the school had no way of enforcing this. The lack of student attendance was particularly punitive because the instructional reforms being implemented by teachers were longitudinally linked as part of larger lessons. Students who then missed a few days were lost and disassociated upon their return to the school. Denver's central office, however, feared granting special treatment to a school and refused Manual's attendance policy appeal.

Principal Sutton states that many central office administrators were extremely supportive, and that the central office "wasn't mean or mean-spirited." She states that the barrier was that the central office

> didn't have an infrastructure that was designed to support this type of change . . . I've learned in spades that central office administrative staff in large districts are really huge barriers to school change and school leadership. The standards also changed everything in schools, and these central office folk didn't have a clue. So they said, "We have the reading program de jour," but that really didn't address the cultural issues, the organic pieces that had to bubble up in order to be real with the kids, authentic with the teachers, it just destabilized the school immensely . . . it was the type of infrastructure that said "Top-down, my way or the highway."

Principal Sutton, Mr. Nicotera, and the rest of the school faculty attempted a broad array of instructional and policy reforms with Manual. A school with its concentration of poverty requires a multifaceted solution. Patrick

McQuillan, a University of Colorado at Boulder professor who worked with the Manual faculty during this time, succinctly sums up the approach of the staff: "There's no secret or magical solution. . . . It's people struggling day in and day out trying to figure out what the hell to do. That's what Manual is doing."[20] These efforts, however, were causing powerful incremental change throughout Manual; the school even won the Governor's Distinguished Improvement Award based on gains made in the 2001 school year.[21]

Unfortunately, the challenge the Manual staff would not be able to solve—and the component that eventually resulted in the transformation of the school—was low student achievement. Mr. Nicotera describes a dilemma faced by far too many high schools in the nation:

> One of the things we found at Manual . . . was that out of the four hundred freshman we were getting into the school, 180 had not passed a class in middle school and were just being sent up because that's the age they were. So out of four hundred, we had 180 kids who had just skipped middle school . . . they'd skipped three years. So we were just behind the eight ball and I guess it's the urban situation, across the country . . . it's just what happens when you've got ineffective teaching going on, the worst teachers in the middle schools, and the feeder population coming up is a mess.

With 75 percent of the incoming freshman class not reading on grade level— Principal Sutton describes them as "first generation everything"—Manual High School would have to produce historic growth in order to bring students up to the test's passing rate.

By 2006, Colorado would implement a statistical process that tracked student value-added scores; however, at the time of Manual's transition, the Colorado Student Assessment Program (CSAP) accountability stucture was based solely on meeting an absolute proficiency level. Even with strong leadership and a faculty endeavoring to meet students' needs, Principal Sutton and Mr. Nicotera knew what was to come. Until given credit for growth, Manual High school would continue to fail within the accountability system and was destined for state takeover. As described by Mr. Nicotera,

> [19]98, was going to be the first year of CSAP . . . and then as soon as the first [reporting of results] came out we knew we were dead. It's the issue that everyone

is dealing with still, with AYP, you start with a kid in sixth grade, you might have two years of improvement, but they're still not at grade level and it's just part of teaching urban kids who are way behind . . . until they compare the kid with himself from a year earlier, urban schools are screwed.

Principal Sutton adds, "What was happening was more incremental change rather than the dramatic change that [the district] had hoped for." Seeing the writing on the wall, the faculty began investigating more drastic measures to maintain their efforts to serve the students of Manual High School. The ticking clock of Colorado's accountability system presented what Principal Sutton calls an "opportunity" for Manual, and they met to choose between three options: "make an application to become a charter school, make an application to become a Gates small school, or remain as they were and wait for state takeover."

In August 2001, Manual High School became the first "large-to-small high school conversion in the country funded by the Bill and Melinda Gates Foundation."[22] The movement to personalize high schools has been a major reform movement throughout this decade, with results that have not fulfilled the promise of increased personalization. Two researchers, Valerie Lee and Douglas Ready, found that one of the consequences of small schools was increased SES-division.[23] This finding is ironic, considering that before the zoning change, Manual was described as "two schools."

Manual's movement toward small schools was not primarily motivated by a commitment to the principles of the movement. Mr. Nicotera explains:

> I'm going to be really honest about the going to small schools: The way that Colorado had set it up, we knew if we went to separate building locators . . . if we created three small schools, each one of them would get their own [building locator] number if we pushed for that; total autonomy which means they start from scratch . . . all CSAP scores from before, don't mean anything anymore . . . we'd start with a clean slate. . . . From my point of view, we were trying to buy time in an initiative that was running out of time. And [we] ended up running out of time.

Principal Sutton was promoted to assistant superintendent soon after the transition to small schools, and Mr. Nicotera took a position consulting with other small schools around the nation. The story of the demographic crisis ends with these departures, as this changeover was a definitive break in the leadership of Manual High School.*

## CONCLUSION

But kids reading at sixth grade level were not reading at tenth grade level by the time . . . so there were still failure rates and we were using [Iowa Tests of Basic Skills] back then and getting ready for the state test which was going to be inaugurated in, I think, [19]98, was going to be the first year of CSAP. We knew it was coming, that we were going to get nailed and then as soon as the first CSAP thing came out we knew we were dead.

—*Santo Nicotera*

Attempting to draw lessons from the story of Manual that are applicable to other educational leaders is challenging, because although the school succeeded in creating a strong community, low achievement, faculty resistance, and central office obstacles prevented the school from reaching externally validated success. Its story, however, does provide school leaders a few broad lessons that are applicable to the proposed crisis model.

First, a demographic shift can act as a tremendous opportunity for a school's leader. The increased concentration of poverty at Manual—from 27 percent to 75 percent FRM within one year—could have overwhelmed the school community. Instead, Principal Sutton utilized the dramatic shift to create a commanding vision for the school, rallying community groups, neighboring districts, and her faculty toward serving Manual's students. These community relationships and faculty efforts were resulting in incremental improvements in student achievement.

After experiencing early success with high retention and greater than average student academic growth, Principal Sutton and Mr. Nicotera pushed for more drastic innovations. Without the district's support on the proposed

---

'Manual High School spent a few years split into small schools, but the school struggled to increase personalization and instructional rigor. With falling enrollment throughout the beginning of the decade (due partially to Manual's feeder schools closing for nonperformance), a new superintendent announced in February 2006 that the school would be closed during the 2006–2007 school year and started anew in 2007–2008. The school continues to struggle with achievement, failing AYP in the 2007–2008 school year.

waivers of student-based budgeting and a required attendance rate, Manual High School was destined for incremental improvement only. Principal Sutton, who left Manual High School to serve as the director of the University of Indianapolis's Center of Excellence in Leadership of Learning, states that, with the benefit of her national exposure to the importance of a district's participation in a reform effort, "I wouldn't touch [the conflict between Manual High School and the district] with a ten foot pole today . . . they didn't have an infrastructure that was designed to support this type of change."

Manual High School was also challenged by an accountability system that did not give credit for progress. Without the statistical capability to calculate value-added scores, Colorado's accountability model held schools responsible for an absolute achievement level. Reaching this level with Manual's student population would have required the perfect alignment between all stakeholders' resources and political agendas, and historic gains in student achievement.

If there is a positive outcome to the demographic crisis at Manual High School, it is that states continue to move toward crediting schools with making progress toward proficiency. Manual High School did not have this luxury, so Denver's 1995 shift toward neighborhood schools caused a substantial increase in the concentration of poverty at the school. The resulting achievement decline ensured that Manual High School would continue to swim upstream, constantly fighting the current with no salvation in sight.

## REFLECTIVE QUESTIONS

### Reflection on the Reading

1. Denver's reassignment plan appears to have decreased ethnic integration among the city's schools. Do you think the national trend is greater or less integration in U.S. urban districts?

2. As a long-term teacher at Manual, Santo Nicotera played a very important role in the reform process. Describe how Principal Sutton's reform efforts might have been more challenging without his partnership.

3. What role did the state's accountability system play in this chapter? In what ways might a school like Manual still be challenged by an accountability system that did incorporate value-added scores?

## Application to Theory

4. In what way did both the proposed changes to Denver's zoning policy and the lack of a permanent principal hurt the school community's ability to act on "early warning signs"?

5. Did Manual High School ever make it to the stage of "community recovery"? Explain.

6. How did Manual's process of "damage control and secondary prevention" differ from other case studies in this book? Do you think these differences eventually led to its closure? If so, how?

## Application on the Job

7. To what extent do you provide a rigorous curriculum to all of your students, from the lowest to the highest performing?

8. Describe your relationship with your school board representative. Would he or she (or other district leadership) advocate for your school in any district rezoning conversations?

9. Does your state or district report or reward based upon value-added student achievement gains? If not, do you and your data team calculate student gains yourself, in order to evaluate teachers?

10. Do you think that the free and reduced-price meal rate reported for your school accurately reflects the poverty level of your students? If not, in what ways can you encourage students and parents to enroll in this program?

11. Are reform efforts at your school completed with the cooperation of the teacher union? Why or why not? In what ways can this relationship be improved?

# "If You Want to Do Good, But You Don't Want to Fight for It, Then Go Raise Puppies."

## *How LEAD Academy Overcame Bureaucratic Obstruction*

### OVERVIEW

We come in risking failure, and when you come in with that attitude, you're so much more optimistic, so much more open to change.

—*Jeremy Kane, founder, LEAD Academy*

As many charter school petitioners in the United States have discovered, creating a school from the ground up is a difficult task. Like the proverbial double-edged sword, the price of "freedom" from traditional school district-level oversight is often the lack of "traditional" school support mechanisms. Unlike other public school principals, charter school principals seldom assume their duties with staffing in place, a secure and renewable source of funding, capital and maintenance needs primarily externally funded, and a central office on which to draw for support and expertise.

Instead, charter principals often experience an ongoing battle to recruit and retain students and staff; manage fiscal and instructional uncertainty; and locate, procure, and maintain a school building. Additionally, they also might experience active and passive resistance from the public school district housing the charter school—despite the fact that "charter" schools are also public schools. This case study details the experience of Jeremy Kane, a twenty-seven-year-old graduate of Stanford and Vanderbilt universities, who carried a vision of a high-performing, innovative Nashville, Tennessee, charter school through a multitude of bureaucratic and logistical problems into reality.

While opening a charter school is difficult in the most receptive of states, Kane's challenge particularly merits classification as a "crisis." Tennessee is not considered a "charter-friendly" state. The Center for Education Reform ranks Tennessee thirty-second of the fifty states on the receptiveness of its charter school legislation.[1] As a result of the state's seeming reticence to support charter schools, by the 2007–2008 school year, Tennessee contained only twelve public charter schools—all of which were located in the state's major population centers of Nashville and Memphis. If the traditional challenges of charter schools were not sufficient, the challenge is greater in Nashville, where the local newspaper—and even some school board members—had criticized what they perceive to be the Metro Nashville Public Schools' hostility toward charter petitions.[2] It is in this less-than-accommodating environment that twenty-seven-year-old Jeremy Kane envisioned beginning a charter school to serve at-risk students in West Nashville in 2006.

Jeremy Kane's three-year process of planning LEAD Academy culminated in the school's opening in July 2007. Building on research from nationally successful charter schools, LEAD Academy exudes a college focus, with homerooms named after local universities and a requirement that a student be accepted into a four-year college or university in order to receive their high school diploma.

In its first year of existence, LEAD has received numerous accolades and much media attention, with visits by the mayor of Nashville and Jim Cooper, a U.S. congressman. First-year test scores reveal the school's meeting expected state gains in mathematics and science and achieving 18 percent and 21 percent of a standard deviation greater than expected state gains in reading/language arts and social studies, respectively.[3] Perhaps the most remarkable thing about this remarkable school, however, is that it almost didn't exist—and not because of any deficiency in its academic or business plan, or lack of commitment by its bright and energetic leader. As Kane quickly discovered, the charter school authorization process is far more political than educational, and "if you run away from a crisis . . . it just gobbles you up."

## CASE NARRATIVE

LEAD Academy was, in many ways, born while Jeremy Kane was completing his master's degree in public policy at Peabody College, Vanderbilt. Kane, a Nashville native and graduate of Stanford University, wanted to do something significant with his life. A commitment to the less privileged led him to an internship at the White House during the Clinton administration, and then a stint as a speechwriter for Senator John Kerry (D-MA). He held positions at a variety of nonprofit corporations (including one focused on teacher training in New York), which ultimately led him, at the age of twenty-four, to return to Nashville and found Raising Hope, Inc., introducing "at risk" Nashville students to community programs.

In 2005, he assumed the executive director's position of the Tennessee Charter School Resource Center, the primary charter school advocacy group within the State of Tennessee. His experiences aiding other charter schools throughout the application and opening process would subsequently be instrumental in the creation and negotiation of LEAD's opening in Nashville.

Metropolitan Nashville Public Schools (MNPS) is the second largest public school district in Tennessee, serving approximately seventy thousand from pre-kindergarten through grade 12. The district is 47 percent African American, 36 percent Caucasian (non-Hispanic), and 13 percent Hispanic, with 70 percent of its students receiving free or reduced-price meals. With a 9 percent ELL population, MNPS has the highest number of Limited English Proficient students in the state. The district spends $9,300 per student—$1,400 more than the state average—allowing for higher-than-average compensation for teachers.[4] However, the school district serves much poorer students than the city's suburbs.[5]

It was not long after beginning work with the charter school association that Kane was attracted to the idea of opening a charter school and becoming directly involved. Kane perceived that "traditional" schooling was failing students in the poorer areas of West Nashville, containing primarily African American, Vietnamese, and Hispanic families—all sharing the commonality of poverty and a cycle of underperforming schools. A "Hope VI" public housing project is located in the neighborhood area, along with various industrial developments. In researching the area, Kane discovered that many of the tenement homes were originally placed in the neighborhood for families of men incarcerated in the local prison.

The process of opening a charter school within Tennessee at the time of LEAD's application was one of the most comprehensive in the nation, requiring charter school petitioners to complete a twenty-one-section instrument that, when successfully completed, may be over two hundred pages in length. Tennessee's charter school authorization law both limits the number of charter schools (within individual districts and the state as a whole) and constrains charter schools to a relatively small pool of students. Unlike the traditional "choice" model in charter schools, LEAD Academy would only be permitted to enroll students from schools failing to meet adequate yearly progress or those who individually fail to achieve better than at the 11th percentile in mathematics and the 9th percentile in reading/language arts on state assessments.

While an arduous process may successfully cull well-intentioned but unprepared applicants, Kane notes that it also challenges all applicants. As the executive director of the Tennessee Charter School Resource Center, Kane witnessed both motivated, high-quality charter-school entrepreneurs and unprepared groups whose applications were denied by local boards of education—often on technical details that could be easily remedied. Public schools are sometimes percieved as "anti-charter" and can take actions toward charter school students that are, in the characterization of one charter school board member, "just mean-spirited."[6]

As evidence of the difficulty of the process, Kane cites an application by Knowledge is Power Program (KIPP)—one of the nation's most successful charter school models—to start a school in MNPS. The KIPP application experienced considerable "bureaucratic" resistance from MNPS, even though the application was directly solicited by the district's superintendent of schools.[7] Kane states that the district was not, in his opinion, necessarily "anticharter," but it had more of a pragmatic, cynical approach believing that eventually the school will fail and "[the district was] going to be responsible . . . so they just decided that they would kill that from the beginning." Based on his experience assisting charter petitioners in preparing and defending their applications, Kane knew that any charter approved by MNPS would have to be academically rigorous—and politically connected.

In order to maximize time and resources, in 2006, Kane arranged to make the charter school application for LEAD his culminating thesis toward his master's degree in public policy at Vanderbilt. Cognizant of needing to provide research-based evidence of demonstrated success of charter school models, Kane visited over fifty high-performing public, private, and charter schools around the country. Based on his visits, he constructed the charter application for LEAD Academy, comprising elements from YES College Prep, KIPP, Cristo Rey, Green Dot, and other successful charter models.

The LEAD model focuses on a 100 percent graduation and acceptance rate to a four-year college or university. Unlike other charter petitions, LEAD's could hardly be characterized as "well-intentioned but unprepared"—the 267-page document applies theoretical and empirical poverty and educational research to the specific challenges facing students in West Nashville, substantially integrating research-validated "best practices." If the application was rejected, it certainly would not be on the basis that LEAD's charter petitioners lacked an appreciation of the challenges of educating students from areas of highly concentrated poverty.

In the summer of 2006, Kane reached the point of no return—he left his job at the Tennessee Charter School Resource Center, committing himself full-time during the next year to completing the application. To fund the project, Kane and his wife took a second mortgage on their Nashville home. While both these steps seemed highly risky at the time, Kane attributes them to later demonstrating to West Nashville stakeholders that he had a genuine commitment to offering a better educational choice to their children, and a commitment meriting their time and attention. Offers Kane, "No one's going to trust you until you have skin in the game."

Having established a sound theoretical basis for LEAD's educational model, Kane turned to the more difficult part of most charter approvals— the political process. The experiences of previous successful and unsuccessful charter petitioners taught Kane that he would have to ensure sufficient political support for LEAD prior to the board of education's undertaking its review of the charter application. He describes his experience of building political capital as a "snowball process . . . one person led me to another, which led me to another . . . I still remember that first phone call; I was shaking."

Kane initially sought the advice and support of two of the founders of Chancellor Beacon, one of the first for-profit education management organizations in the country. This led him to Bruce Dobie, the cofounder of *The Nashville*

*Scene,* the city's alternative newsweekly, who would eventually become the chairman of LEAD's board of directors. He also spoke with and recruited Ralph Schulz, CEO of the Nashville Area Chamber of Commerce. It was not long until Kane began regularly visiting the living rooms of homes in the Belle Meade neighborhood, advocating for "at risk" students in one of the most established and wealthiest areas of the city. Tapping a source of dissatisfaction, Kane found many supporters who "had only been seen as a source of money [to MNPS] when they also wanted to find more hands-on ways to contribute. . . . But MNPS had been hesitant to get them involved in any such way." Kane's Belle Meade supporters would become a base of powerful partners in fighting off the political challenges during the chartering process.

Nashville's "upper class" was not the only group that became personally familiar with Jeremy Kane. A far greater challenge faced him in West Nashville, where he was commonly mistaken for—and treated as—a bill collector as he went door-to-door recruiting students. *The Tennessean,* Nashville's major newspaper, dedicated a story to one of his recruiting trips to a local barbecue restaurant, noting the incongruity in the regular clientele and Stanford graduate in a "starched white shirt."[8]

In Kane's opinion, the community was initially very distrustful of the "ugly white guy in a suit"; however, through hundreds of conversations in homes and on doorsteps, he became known throughout the informal information networks so important in communities of poverty. He recounts an instance in which he introduced himself to a visibly distrustful person, only to have an unrelated bystander say to the individual, "I checked him out; he's good." However, more than simply "selling" the LEAD concept, Kane organized community focus groups to discuss what they wanted in a new school. Fortunately, the views expressed—longer hours, better access to teachers, and better nutrition—aligned perfectly with what LEAD's application proposed. After developing a strong charter application and building a coalition of politically connected idealists, West Nashville community leaders, potential school parents, and the city's elite, Jeremy Kane was ready to submit his application to the MNPS school board.

**CRISIS DESCRIPTION**
From his experience at the Charter School Resource Center, Kane knew that the charter school application process was arduous—an application lacking

a rigorous and substantial managerial and instructional strategy was unlikely to be approved. Downloading Tennessee's official application from the state's website, Kane completed it, substantially expanding upon required elements. Ultimately, LEAD's application was 267 pages long and encompassed the school's vision, academic structure, community assets, and short- and long-term goals. Despite the strength of LEAD's conceptual model, the research-validated instructional strategies adopted, clearly available resources, and the fact that the school would be operated by the past executive director of the state's charter school association (and thus hardly a neophyte to charter schools and their challenges), Kane still expected a protracted challenge from the MNPS school board. "I knew our plan had to be academically sound, or [an MNPS associate superintendent] would tear us to shreds."

MNPS was regarded as ambivalent—at best—about charter schooling, and Kane did not anticipate the charter being approved on its initial submission—no MNPS charter petitioner had ever been approved on its initial application. However, Tennessee's charter school law requires public school district boards of education to provide, in writing, "specific objective reasons" for the denial, then allowing petitioners fifteen days to remedy the deficiencies and resubmit.[9] Previously, when the MNPS board of education rejected charters, their rejection letter accompanied a detailed list of items to be revised for resubmission.

Kane was therefore shocked when the first LEAD application was rejected *without* an invitation to resubmit, containing a single assertion that the application was "incomplete." The board identified a single deficiency in LEAD's 267-page application—"the absence of Section 18"—a brief form requiring a charter petitioner to describe its "types and amounts of insurance coverage."[10] Kane characterizes Section 18 as a procedural requirement and a problem Kane could have remedied very quickly—LEAD had procured necessary insurance. Particularly distressing to Kane was the sole reason Section 18 was not included in LEAD's application—the section did not appear on the state's model charter application template posted on the Tennessee State Department of Education website.

Regardless of the ease with which the defect could have been remedied, the result was "crushing" to LEAD's stakeholders. While LEAD could include the document and submit a "new" charter application, it would delay *initial* consideration for another year instead of the fifteen-day window allowed under state law. Unlike prior petitioners whose applications contained significant substantive defects, LEAD seemingly would not be given the opportunity to correct the easily fixable identification of its insurance provider.

Kane immediately ascribed the MNPS board's motives to politics and turned to his network of politically connected supporters. He hoped to bring political pressure on the MNPS board to reconsider. Unfortunately, the problem devolved further into what Kane considered a bureaucratic morass, now requiring a legal, rather than a political, solution.

The issue turned on a "gray area" in Tennessee law: could a public school district *wholly* reject charter applications on the basis of incompleteness and make a petitioner begin the process anew, or was the omission of a required document merely a type of "deficiency" that a district had to identify and allow a petitioner to correct? MNPS's opinion was the former—the Tennessee State Board of Education's was the latter. Ultimately, LEAD's application became mired in a debate between "one lawyer [MNPS] hashing things out with another [State Board of Education] lawyer." As the lawyers debated, Kane felt powerless to affect the outcome—the broad network of community and political support he spent months building was useless in this arena. Fortunately, the lawyers ultimately concluded that a missing "Section 18" form was no grounds for outright and irremediable dismissal; rather, it had to be part of a broader list of issues that needed to be fixed for resubmission. This challenge was one of the most difficult for Kane, as he discovered he was powerless to affect it—he had to accept that he "had no control over the outcome."

With this victory, MNPS was legally required to review and discuss LEAD's application in its entirety. Through informal connections to the MNPS board of education, Kane learned that the district was not providing public notice of the charter petition review committee meetings in which LEAD's application would be discussed; to the contrary, the superintendent characterized them as closed to the public.[11] Given his prior experience, Kane believed that public scrutiny was essential to this process.

Convinced that LEAD's instructional model and business plan could readily withstand any review—no matter how severe—he was concerned that politics would again threaten to derail LEAD's application. Having become more familiar with the "process" during the board's previous challenge, Kane now employed his own legal strategy, utilizing Tennessee's open meetings law to compel the district to have the meetings in public. Eventually, MNPS was forced to recognize that the meetings should be advertised and open to the public.

With the charter review committee meetings scheduled, Kane describes this part of the application process as an "iron butt" phase. He sat for ten hours listening to the committee discuss various "concerns" with LEAD's application. While he had to maintain silence, the time spent listening to these discussions was extremely important in knowing what to expect in a subsequent five-hour interview he would have with the school board regarding LEAD's application.

Observing the nuanced politics between committee members, political rivalries began to emerge and Kane came to see the board as an aggregation of individuals with varying views on charter schools rather than a monolithic entity opposed to charters. Although MNPS received two charter applications in addition to LEAD's, Kane was the only applicant to take advantage of the opportunity to glean the board members' individual political leanings and alter his presentation accordingly. Kane attributes the fact that LEAD's application was ultimately successful—and the other two ultimately were not—in no small part to the time he spent "studying" the board.

The MNPS review committee identified fifty deficiencies in LEAD's application, with many as trivial as the replacement of a colon with a semi-colon. As the recommendations did not substantively alter LEAD's mission or instructional program, Kane adopted recommended changes and submitted to a five-hour interview with the board. Kane invited community members and the parents of prospective students to also attend, and Kane observes that they filled the room in a show of support.

The preparatory work completed while compiling the application and sitting through ten hours of committee meetings allowed Kane to successfully defend LEAD's instructional and operational model. He also described the curricular model and strategies for special education students. Kane describes the discussion as "outlasting" the school board. He also addressed board members' specific and individual concerns that had been articulated during the review committee meetings. One of Kane's fellow LEAD charter petitioners was concerned Kane was overwhelming the board with information and suggested he "hush up a bit." Kane responded by stating that he wanted to stay until the board literally had no further questions.

With the successful passage of the charter application, Kane now faced a new set of demands. He had to open a school, hire staff, recruit students, and find capital resources within a nine-month period. Noting that the best way to hire a good faculty was to hire someone else's, Kane "trolled" through school websites, e-mailing job announcements to teachers whose teaching skills and methodologies seemed to align with LEAD's instructional program. He shocked a newspaper contact by requesting that they print his personal phone number in a story about recruiting teachers, resisting her suggestion that "people just don't do that." Kane similarly continued to aggressively recruit students, despite having already received close to one hundred applications for LEAD's initial semester.

The most significant start-up challenge faced by LEAD, however, was not students, staff, or fundraising. Kane's second crisis—and the one he believes came closest to derailing LEAD—was scrambling to find a building in which to house the school.

Kane knew that nationally one of the most significant challenges charter petitioners face is obtaining an adequate school facility without having school facility funding.[12] However, LEAD's charter school application proposed what was appeared to be a "win-win" leasing arrangement with MNPS. MNPS had 288 empty classrooms—including in schools located in the area of the city that LEAD desired to serve.[13] To make use of this space, LEAD proposed in its charter application,

> LEAD would simply like the district to know that should reorganization of schools occur, shifting vacancies that would create space in an MNPS facility, LEAD would very seriously consider relocating in such space. LEAD will be raising and spending resources for capital development with or without such opportunities, but the school would also be happy to see MNPS reap the benefits of that spending.[14]

Even with MNPS's agnosticism to charters, Kane believed an opportunity to use underutilized space to generate funds and serve "at risk" students would be too good to resist. It therefore, came as a surprise when the district evidenced little interest in leasing LEAD an unused school facility. In February 2007, MNPS offered Kane a single subset of classrooms in a building in which the other MNPS middle school charter school was already operating. Kane regarded this as a non-offer. First, the building was dilapidated and LEAD would have to use its facility funds to improve an MNPS facility, but more troubling was MNPS's attempts to ensure LEAD would fail. Kane knew that if LEAD chose to occupy this building, it would be placed in direct competition for students with the other charter middle school already operating in the facility.

Moreover, LEAD would not be serving the specific West Nashville community from which Kane had already recruited students and demonstrated significant parental support—recruitment would have to begin anew, after Kane took a significant loss in credibility. With these probable effects—of which Kane believes MNPS's administration was well aware—the facility offer was a non-offer at best, and at worst, a "Trojan Horse" resulting in the failure of LEAD or the MNPS KIPP school.

The district's failure to be cooperative was a continuation of its earlier, obstructive actions to LEAD's charter application. Kane sensed that this would be an opportune time to make use of media contacts, believing the transparency of the tactic would not sit well with the public. In an interview with a local newspaper, LEAD's board chair posed the question, "Why would a school system, one, forgo revenue and, two, forgo maximum utilization of their capital assets?" This prompted one MNPS board of education member to publicly rebuke the district's administration and propose making "good-faith efforts" toward working with charter schools as an expectation of the MNPS superintendent.[15]

LEAD's fallback plan was breaking ground on a school on land that had been previously leased; however, this would require raising $1.5 million in thirty days. Kane believed that "no one expected us to succeed" in reaching this goal. Fortunately, through heavy and strategic media coverage of the dilemma, LEAD's challenge caught the attention of the parish priest of St. Vincent De Paul School. At the time, St. Vincent De Paul was facing declining enrollment, and the administration had recently decided to cut grades 6–8 from their program. This vacated the school's top floor, which they then offered to lease to LEAD. This was similar to the arrangement that LEAD had wanted with MNPS. In contrast to MNPS's response, St. Vincent De Paul leapt at the opportunity to utilize their empty space.

The land crisis could have been an overwhelming situation for LEAD and Jeremy Kane, as raising $1.5 million within thirty days, even with help from prosperous supporters, was going to be a monumental task. In the end, St. Vincent De Paul provided a workable solution that allowed LEAD to focus on the immediate priorities of hiring staff and recruiting students. It was again the informal network, community contacts, and astute planning that made St. Vincent administrators aware of LEAD's needs and provided Jeremy a solution to his crisis of capital resources.

## CRISIS ANALYSIS

Despite more than a year of preparation, the assistance of Vanderbilt University faculty, and experience as the executive director of Tennessee's charter school association, Kane still faced two External-Predictable crises before LEAD opened its doors—both of which were of such a significant threat that either would have prevented LEAD's opening. Both crises share a common genesis—and one experienced by many charter school petitioners—a public school district's utilization of bureaucratic, procedural barriers to prevent implementation of an innovative educational method designed to serve students failing in "traditional" schools.

Applying the crisis typology proposed in this work, the crises experienced during LEAD's development were predictable. While the precise nature of the bureaucratic barriers erected was open to speculation, Kane was—or should have been—aware that MNPS would attempt to slow or thwart the charter process. The LEAD Academy case study naturally contrasts with the story of Franklin Career Academy (FCA) profiled in chapter 11. FCA was the first charter school in New Hampshire and was the test subject for state and district charter policies. With New Hampshire Department of Education's failing to implement policy changes to force districts to provide basic per pupil allocations to charter schools, FCA lived with fiscal uncertainty throughout its life span. Eventually, with no stable, long-term source of funding, the school was forced to close.

Unlike FCA, Kane had seen the types of obstacles utilized by districts to block charter applicants. As the executive director of Tennessee's Charter School Resource Center, Jeremy witnessed KIPP Academy Nashville—an MNPS charter middle school that had opened in the 2005–2006 school year—struggle through the charter application process, scramble to find a school building, and publicly clash with the district over an order to transfer students out midyear.[16] He wrote his application and prepared his supporters to expect a long fight with the district administration. Moreover, public school districts nationally have a well-established pattern of using bureaucratic hurdles to slow or stop charter petitions. In his article "Games Charter Opponents Play," Joe Williams identifies a national trend among school districts to attempt to thwart charter petitions with "bureaucratic sand" thrown in petitioners' proverbial faces. As with LEAD's experience, Williams contends these tactics seldom address the substantive aspects of a charter application—such as the strengths or weaknesses of its instructional model—focusing instead on erecting procedural and bureaucratic barriers designed to frustrate and dishearten often eager charter petitioners.[17]

The LEAD crises are categorized as External owing to their source beyond the walls (in this case, proverbial) of LEAD. The source of the crisis was the attitude of MNPS toward charter public schools. Given the external status of resistance, there was little Kane or the other LEAD petitioners could do to handle the crisis genesis—Kane could not make the MNPS board see that the exclusion of a single, readily available document was not a sufficient basis for a total rejection of a 267-page charter application—particularly when the document was not required by the state's application process.

The intractability of the administration's attitude was even more evident in the refusal to lease unused school space to LEAD in the area of the city in which LEAD already had substantial community support, providing instead space in which LEAD would have to serve a population already served by two other charter schools. In both of these External-Predictable crises, the preparation and efforts made by Jeremy helped overcome these obstacles and guide the embryonic school community to a successful school opening in the fall of 2007.

## CRISIS TREATMENT

I think that people have to stop being so afraid of taking risks . . . it's a gamble . . . and we have to go into it with that attitude, that here are two students [being interviewed with me], that if we wouldn't have risked, the statistics would have been against them.

—*Jeremy Kane*

In their quest to open a charter school in MNPS, Jeremy Kane and the LEAD school community overcame two significant crises. Their experiences offer the following "rules of engagement" not only for starting a charter school, but for guiding any school through a tempestuous political environment.

**Build a Broad and Diverse Base of Support**

Different groups of supporters were useful in overcoming different challenges faced by LEAD. Parents and grassroots organizers provided a visible and vocal group in attendance at important school board meetings, members of the business community provided key contacts and school board allies, and Nashville's elite provided financial and political support during the start-up period. Additionally, Jeremy built a relationship with the local press and utilized them to his advantage, printing stories that advocated for LEAD's application approval. Each group of LEAD supporters provided assistance at crucial moments during the struggle to open the school.

**Expect a Fight**

Jeremy Kane has met charter school hopefuls who believe that merely the desire to do what is best for students is adequate in gaining approval, but his experiences as the executive director of the Tennessee Charter School Resource Center taught him that charter schools are "assaulted" on a daily basis (hence, the title of this chapter). Districts in New York, Ohio, and New Jersey have strategically utilized zoning laws to prevent charter schools from opening in promising locations. Such actions motivated California voters to pass Proposition 39, which requires districts to offer unused capital resources to charter schools.[18]

Seeing these trends—and how KIPP Academy was treated by the district administration—Jeremy Kane was well prepared with solid educational research, broad political support, and supportive public opinion. Jeremy's background in politics informed his strategy for fighting the bureaucratic obstacles he encountered; these obstacles should be expected and prepared for by all prudent charter school applicants.

**Know Your Core Values, and Do Not Compromise Them; Compromise on Anything Else**

Through the development of LEAD's charter application, Jeremy reviewed a sizable amount of educational research. From this background, he knew what components of LEAD's model were essential and which were more minor. School board members and the district administration were uncomfortable with the grades 5–12 structure of LEAD, but the middle school through high school model was a key component of LEAD's focus on college attendance. He insisted on its inclusion. Alternatively, Jeremy Kane opened LEAD with half of the student body he had originally planned, because the size of the class was something he was willing to compromise for his larger goal.

### The Devil Is in the Details

LEAD's 267-page application was, at first, missing four pages that had the potential to torpedo the school's entire application. Although Section 18's absence was due to an incomplete application posted to the state's website, the successful resolution of the crisis depended on two lawyers' interpretation of a statute—and LEAD was fortunate that this interpretation came in their favor. Jeremy admits in an introspective leadership profile, "If [I am] going to trip up it will be over a period at the end of a sentence." When preparing to face an administrative battle, getting the small details correct can be just as important as one's larger messages.

### CONCLUSION

On July 31, 2007, LEAD opened its doors to one hundred new fifth and sixth graders. The first year's test scores show extremely high value-added scores in reading/language arts and social studies, and average results in mathematics and science. During the second year (the 2008–2009 school year), LEAD has grown to include a seventh grade, and the academy continues its mission to do "whatever it takes" to educate its students. The charter school continues to struggle over its long-term facilities question, as they hope to eventually grow into their own school building. The school's existence, and survival through two significant crises during its start-up, is testament to the persistence and passion of Jeremy Kane and the LEAD community.

### REFLECTIVE QUESTIONS

#### Reflection on the Reading

1. MNPS is presented as acting too restrictively toward LEAD and other charter schools seeking establishment in the district. Why do districts sometimes feel threatened by charter schools? How might these be valid

concerns from a district perspective? Given these issues, what role might a charter school fill in a large, urban district?

2. In what ways did each of the following stakeholder groups (parents, district bureaucracy, school board, state bureaucracy, business community) assist LEAD's application process? In what ways did they hinder the process?

3. Describe the disadvantages and advantages of being the principal of a charter school compared to leading a traditional school.

4. How did Jeremy Kane's relationship with Nashville's media help LEAD's application? Name some elements that would need to be present in order for media pressure to be effective on district officials and school board members.

**Application to Theory**

5. What do you think were the three most important "preparation and primary prevention" steps taken by Jeremy Kane that contributed to his success?

6. The crisis for LEAD Academy was an External-Predictable one. How might Jeremy Kane's experience have differed had he been the first charter school seeking establishment in MNPS? How did he benefit from the experiences of previous aspiring charter school leaders?

**Application on the Job**

7. How broad and diverse a base of support does your school have in its community? Do you have well-developed relationships throughout varied interest groups, including parents, community leaders, the press, and local philanthropists?

8. Do you recognize when to shelve your altruistic motivations to focus on the pragmatic discussions of resolving conflict and overcoming bureaucratic obstacles? Do you arrive at these conflicts armed with rigorous educational research and theory?

9. How do you currently prioritize which political battles to tackle and from which to refrain? Do you tackle the "loudest" ones instead of the most important?

# "You're Not Going to Need That Money This Year, Right?"

## How Franklin Career Academy Operated Without Promised State Funding

**OVERVIEW**

When Alfred Shanker conceptualized the American "charter school" in 1988, he envisaged introducing innovation and entrepreneurship to public education, offering an alternative to educate students failed by "traditional" educational institutions.[1] William Grimm and the Franklin Career Academy (FCA)—New Hampshire's first charter school—appeared to epitomize Shanker's vision. A graduate of the United States Naval Academy and a successful bond trader and investor returning to Franklin after a career in America's financial centers, Grimm saw a need for an alternative education program to, in the words of FCA's charter, provide "an innovative choice charter high school for predominantly at-risk . . . students." Believing that "our results . . . [would] argue for continuation of the school," Grimm and FCA's faculty, parents, and students soon discovered the truth in Stanford professors David Cuban and Larry Tyack's conclusion that "education reforms are intrinsically political."[2] After opening in 2004, FCA was constantly beset by varying crises, reaching a critical mass in 2008, at which point FCA and its stakeholders could no longer resist. Despite demonstrably achieving its academic goals at a cost of approximately 60 percent of New Hampshire's average, FCA finally closed its doors four years after opening.

The lessons of FCA are many, and it would be relatively easy to characterize FCA's closure as a "failure" by a school leader to effectively prepare for, recognize, and address a crisis. However, analysis of the case compels a different outcome—it was only through Grimm's responses to what was essentially a perpetual state of crisis that FCA did not succumb sooner.

## CASE NARRATIVE

Our basic thought was—and it turned out to be incorrect, at least temporarily—if (a) we can do a real good job and show that we were helping kids who needed help—we tested them three times a year in core subjects as well as reading to monitor progress—and if we could show we were doing a really good job, and if (b) we do it for about two-thirds the average cost of public education in New Hampshire, we thought that would be enough it. Apparently not, would be my assessment.

—*William Grimm, chair, Franklin Career Academy*

Franklin, New Hampshire, is a picturesque town of approximately 8,700 people located in Merrimack County, in the south-central area of the state. Prior to 2004, it was perhaps most noted for being the birthplace of nineteenth-century United States Senator Daniel Webster. However, that year, events began that would propel sleepy Franklin into a national spotlight—and the national debate on the "charter schools" movement.

Although considered "poor" by New Hampshire standards (in 2004, the New Hampshire Department of Education ranked it in the lowest quintile of property wealth), relative to many of the other schools and communities profiled in this work, Franklin appears affluent.[3] In 2000, average household income was $41,689, and fewer than 9 percent of all residents lived below the federally established poverty level. Emerging as a "bedroom" community for the state capital in Concord in the late 1990s, by 2006, 65 percent of all Franklin residents commuted from Franklin to another community for work.[4] Typical of the area, Franklin is not ethnically diverse—over 97 percent of the population is white—and the vast majority of the town's children live in two-parent homes.

Franklin's third-largest employer—employing approximately 260 residents (approximately 14 percent of the noncommuter population)—is School Administrative Unit 18, the local school district ("District").[5] The district's three elementary schools, middle school, and high school serve a K–12 student population of approximately 1,408 students. However, in 2001, Franklin earned the dubious distinction of having New Hampshire's highest drop-out rate—approximately 50 percent of the students beginning high school in Franklin did not complete it. "When half the kids who start high school drop out before graduation and have some of the lowest achievement scores in the state, it's pretty clear you have a problem," observes Grimm.

A native of the nearby community of Exeter, New Hampshire, William Grimm was characterized by the *Concord Monitor* as the "ultimate product of public education."[6] Graduating from Exeter High School, he was selected to attend the U.S. Naval Academy at Annapolis. Upon completion, he served six years in the U.S. Navy, subsequently earning a master's degree from the University of Southern California's school of business and beginning a career as an investment banker and bond trader.

After a successful career in Chicago, Los Angeles, and on Wall Street, Grimm returned home to New Hampshire in the late 1990s. Locating in Franklin, Grimm became involved in the community, in which the drop-out problem was a source of considerable concern. However, it was not until 1999 that another Annapolis graduate—then-presidential candidate John McCain—urged him to get "personally involved" in solving the problem by taking an active role in local education. "Probably the best thing he told me was to never quit when it gets difficult. And boy, did it get difficult," Grimm laughs. Grimm subsequently ran for the local school board in Franklin and was elected chairman.

In 2001, as federal money became available for charter schools, he began to explore the idea of establishing a school in Franklin specifically targeting students who were "at risk" of dropping out of school. "We were not only looking at 'poor' kids, but kids who were capable of getting 'As' but who were getting 'Cs' because they were disengaged." Focusing on individualized instruction and high accountability—what would eventually evolve into an "individual development plan" for every student at FCA—"I saw this as an opportunity to get some significant federal money to help us with this situation."

> I actually thought—and most of us thought this would be a positive thing for the community, not even so much to get outside of the established process, but to provide a specialized education for some kids, to see if it would help them. We thought public school choice would help everybody.

Grimm brought the idea to his fellow board members and did not face express opposition. "A few [of the eight other board members] supported it, and the others didn't say anything against it, so we brought the idea to the [Franklin] city council," which had to approve local charter school applications under New Hampshire law. "The council agreed that they would consider the application, so we started planning."

Grimm and several other individuals interested in the charter school petition began to develop a charter school petition. "We had a strong charter board, but we also put together a pretty remarkable and active senior advisory board," Grimm notes, including two university presidents, the president of a regional hospital, the president of the Franklin Business Development Corp., and a retired rear admiral with a doctorate in education who was previously provost of the United States Naval War College. "These were all successful people committed to improving education."

While developing FCA, Grimm and the other petitioners visited a number of schools in the New England area that were successful with "at risk" student populations. When visiting a school in Providence, Rhode Island, that would largely serve as the model for FCA, he invited the local school district superintendent along. "We were very open about what we wanted to do." Grimm and others secured two federal grants totaling approximately $660,000. These were restricted funds, intended for planning and initial equipping of the charter school—and importantly—were not supposed to be used for operational purposes.

Working with the New Hampshire Center for School Reform in late 2002 and early 2003—approximately six months after securing the federal planning grant and contemporaneously with receiving the first disbursement of federal "start-up" money—the charter petitioners presented the proposed school plan to the Franklin City Council. Grimm received his introduction to politics in education when the council refused to even read—much less consider—the charter petition:

> [The City Council] wouldn't even look at the application—they were certainly serious about that. If they weren't going to look at the application, that's a "no" right there. They didn't articulate any reason they wouldn't look at it—they said they were not sure that the state would pay the difference and they were concerned that if Franklin kids went to the charter school, the district would lose the state funding as the money would follow the kids. . . . That was true, but a very

specious argument. They had about a 50 percent cumulative drop-out rate at the time [the students FCA targeted], and they [already] lost money for those kids.

Grimm, who was still on the Franklin school board, wondered why the council reversed its earlier guarantee to consider the petition after many months of planning and preparation. "We subsequently discovered that two members of the local board of education communicated with the City Council, encouraging them to refuse the petition. We would have never known it, except a member of the City Council e-mailed one of the [school] board members, thanking them for 'the information' about the charter petition, and it got forwarded around, ending up in my e-mail."

Grimm was displeased by what he considered the "unethical" efforts of board members operating "behind the scenes" and depriving the public the opportunity for discussion and "individual board members misrepresenting the board's 'official' opinion about the charter—we had not discussed it at the board level." He requested the local board censure those members involved. When they refused, Grimm resigned from the Franklin school board.

However, Grimm persisted with the idea of the charter school. Building on his experience while serving on Governor-Elect Craig Benson's transition team in 2002, Grimm knew Benson, a Republican, was a staunch supporter of school improvement efforts. "New Hampshire had a charter school law on the books [since 1995], but never had a charter school." In 2003, the New Hampshire Department of Education adopted a regulation permitting the state to directly approve charter schools, bypassing the local approval process. The state-approved charter schools would be funded by the state's contribution to local districts, which would be transferred to the charter schools. "Of course," recalls Grimm, who worked on the initiative, "we knew that it could be a problem to have the money passing through the local school districts and not directly to the schools . . . that's a prescription for disaster, because once the money was in their accounts, they would think and feel it was theirs . . . but that's the way it was."

Proceeding under the new regulation, Grimm and the other FCA charter petitioners submitted their proposal directly to the State of New Hampshire, and, in August 2003, received authorization to proceed with Franklin Career Academy as a state-sponsored charter school. FCA was to begin operations during the 2004–2005 school year, serving grades 7–12, becoming New

Hampshire's first charter school.* Grimm was selected to serve as chairman of the FCA's operating board. "We had significant interest in enrollment. We began with about forty students and about that same number on a waiting list during our first year. We expected to have around $7,200 per student total in year one for operational expenses"—which included a discretionary grant from the governor's office. While Governor Benson's appropriation was a single-year commitment, both Grimm and Governor Benson believed the New Hampshire legislature would approve additional funding for the operation of state charter schools. "We were still thinking that if the state was going to approve two state-sponsored charter schools a year, then the legislature would fund them. . . . We assumed that they [the New Hampshire Department of Education, which approved the charters] would at least . . . request reasonable funding for the new schools."

Despite the initial resistance of some local school board members, the school district's administration did not actively oppose the charter school petition. "Money was a huge issue. . . . The local superintendent's primary concern was that the charter school would not impact local school funding, which, given that the money was supposed to follow the kids, didn't seem to be a problem." While funding was "always" a concern, Grimm and the charter board believed they had sufficient funds to start operations:

> We still had one year of our federal grant—$315,000—and had to use that money primarily for educational supports—so we were well-supplied. We also had a one-time $165,000 appropriation for operational funding for one year only [that] Governor Benson obtained for us and the state's second charter school. But we were going to be operating on the state funds generated for each student—around $3,400 [$3,340]. With the governor's appropriation, this made about $7,200 per student in 2004. The state and local government would be spending around $10,000 for the other students in Franklin during the same period.

Grimm soon learned that his assumption—that "the system" would support an innovative educational system producing better results for less money—was erroneous.

---

*After approving FCA's petition, the New Hampshire State Board of Education granted an additional five charter petitions for the 2004–2005 school year.

## CRISIS DESCRIPTION

We were at the opening ceremony August 24, 2004, which was really nice. The governor was there and spoke, as well as Nick Donahue, the state commissioner of education. Parents, kids, community leaders, everything. I will never forget this. During the reception ceremony, I asked the commissioner about how the state funds were going to flow through the local district, and he asked me, "You're not going to need that money this year, right?" I didn't know what to think. I went to get the local superintendent, because I wanted him to hear this at the same time I did.

—*William Grimm*

"The problem was—and I cannot believe nobody saw this coming—under the state charter school law, every student was supposed to receive the 'minimum' state funding"—the amount the New Hampshire legislature was required to pay under its obligation to provide for a free and adequate public education—"which most local districts supplemented with local tax money."* However, the commissioner explained to Grimm, while New Hampshire appropriates state funding on a per pupil basis, it is on a two-year delay. "He told us that the money that they [the Franklin school district] are getting [in 2004] is based on the[ir] enrollment [in 2002.]" As a result, under the commissioner's interpretation, any FCA students transferring from Franklin or other schools would not generate state funding until 2006. Grimm noted that under such an interpretation, no charter school could possibly succeed. "We were already going to educate kids for about 60 percent of the cost." Grimm did not see how FCA could operate without *any* state funds. Grimm wonders, "I don't know if that was an intentional [tactic] by somebody someplace to scuttle the charter schools, but . . . it was going to have that effect."

A solution would have to lie beyond the local system. "It was obvious they weren't going to voluntarily give us the money." Although Grimm characterizes the position of the Franklin board as understandable, "it [was] legitimate for the local school board to think that money is owed to them—and I agree

---

*In a report published in December of that year, the New Hampshire Center for Public Policy Studies determined that all New Hampshire districts spent "much more" than the state appropriation, noting specifically that, during the 2002–2003 school year, Franklin spent $5,399 per elementary school student.

with them on that point—that was money that was based on the head count from two years ago"—the state's charter law created an exception to that funding mechanism. "The state law was pretty clear that the money was supposed to follow the kids during the year of enrollment."

While the Franklin district administration professed support for a "state solution," the solution never manifested. "I asked [the local superintendent] to accompany me to speak with the [state] commissioner about this—along with two commercial bankers who had offered to help. The superintendent did not have the time to attend any of the four meetings we held." Given the Franklin board's early opposition to using local funds to support the charter school, it was unlikely that a funding solution could be reached with the local board. "To be totally honest, I don't know if we even considered [directly] asking them for the money."

Instead, Grimm turned to the state. "At the opening ceremony, [Governor Benson] told me that the system was 'not supposed to work that way,' and he would try to have the state fix it. . . . We hoped the Governor would impose a solution, frankly." Unfortunately for FCA, Grimm soon discovered it was a problem beyond the governor's unilateral authority to solve, and it would take more broad-based political consensus—including those who were opposed to the very concept of charter schools. "It would definitely take legislative action and cooperation with the New Hampshire Department of Education." Grimm was immediately concerned by the potential politicalization of the problem. "This gave a cause celeb to those people opposing charter schools, letting them say, 'see—they really are taking money from the public schools.' It was very bad."

Despite financial instability, FCA began the year using its operational grant from the governor's office. The federal grant allowed funds to be spent for school supplies, and this freed FCA to use its state grant for temporary operations; however, the governor's grant could only support operations through March—at the latest. Grimm was assured by the New Hampshire Department of Education that they were working on a solution. "Every time I called them—which was pretty frequent, starting that August [2004]—I was assured, 'We're working on it.' So I figured we would have a solution before the money ran out." Grimm continued to hope that the school's academic success would vindicate any efforts made to fund the school.

FCA began the year with approximately thirty-eight students, adding two more during the year. While FCA attracted the at-risk students Grimm initially targeted, state law forbade FCA from declining admission to any New

Hampshire student if space was available. "The only requirements were that the student or parents be a New Hampshire resident, and that [he or she] have transportation to the school. If those two requirements were met, we had to admit the student." As a result, approximately one-third of the students admitted would fall into the definition of "at risk," with the remaining two-thirds equally divided between previously home-schooled students and students to whose parents FCA's individualized instruction appealed:

> We always knew it wouldn't just be at-risk students—we couldn't set that as an admission requirement, and when the petition was being put together, we knew parents of other types of students were interested. . . . But it gave the charter school's opponents another weapon, alleging that we weren't serving the students we were "supposed" to serve. Well, we were "supposed" to serve everybody, under state law.

As instruction began, the individual development plans, high accountability, and parental and community involvement began to produce expected academic results. "We had small class sizes because we had three teachers and, oh, forty kids. But we also had a lot of volunteers—including board members and parents—working in the school." Volunteers also came forward as students expressed interest in learning in particular areas. Upon several students wanting to learn martial arts, a parent volunteer taught a tae kwon do class. Students desiring to work in intern programs were offered opportunities in local businesses—"we had a student who was interested in becoming a doctor, so the local hospital offered to allow him to go on rounds with the doctors."

Grimm observes that with teaching interventions targeted to specific student learning deficiencies, performance increased dramatically—on nationally normed assessments, some FCA students increased performance by several grade levels in a single year. Parents were very pleased with their students' progress. A New Hampshire Public Radio story in 2005 detailed significant parental support for the charter school and its programs and concern for their children's futures if they had to return to the schools in which they were not succeeding before coming to FCA.[7]

As the 2004–2005 school year continued, funding issues persisted. The crisis put a personal strain on Grimm and the other FCA board members. "While most [school] boards meet once a month, we were meeting at least every two weeks—and sometimes more often. . . . I must have driven to Concord—the state capital—twenty times, talking to the department of education and legislators." Grimm and other board members continued to pressure the New Hampshire Department of Education for a solution—one either permitting the school to use its federal grant for operational purposes, or compel students' "sending" districts to forward the state funds the individual students were supposed to generate, which other local boards of education had agreed to do for three of the state's charter schools. "We're working on it—we're working on it," was the constant reply, according to Grimm. While Grimm does not believe the issue directly impacted the school's instructional program—"we didn't have to cancel any programs"—he notes the issue was stressful for teachers, parents, and students. "Because we decided early on that we were going to be transparent about everything and keep the parents and teachers apprised" of what was happening in the school's governance, "they knew the challenge we faced with funding, and knew that unless a solution was found, we could not complete the year."

As the year progressed, it became apparent that the New Hampshire Department of Education was unable or unwilling to compel the Franklin Board of Education to send the state aid that was supposed to follow each FCA student. Agreeing that transferring state funds was required by law, the department of education issued nonbinding "advisories" encouraging local boards to "borrow" the state aid owed the charter schools or issue tax anticipation notes. The Franklin Board of Education declined to follow the advisory.

Grimm and the other board members increasingly saw the only potential for completing the year was obtaining permission to spend federal grant money for operational purposes. Grimm requested the New Hampshire Department of Education—which oversaw the federal grant—for authority to do precisely this. "We were repeatedly told that they asked the United States Department of Education permission to do so, and it was denied." In February 2005, the desperation of the situation led Grimm and others "who had some connections in Washington" to directly ask the U.S. Department of Education if using the grant money for operational purposes was permissible:

> We were told, yes, under some circumstances, but the New Hampshire Department of Education would have to approve our request because they were the body administering the federal grant. Well, we let them know that this is not

what we were being told by the New Hampshire Department of Education, and we were basically told that they would take care of it. The next day, we get a phone call from the [New Hampshire] Department of Education saying, "We've solved your problem for you!" We could use our federal funds for 2004–2005 for operational purposes, and that let us complete the year. But it didn't solve the ongoing funding problem.

In April 2005, the situation with the Franklin school board deteriorated to the point that the board unanimously approved a letter asking the New Hampshire State Board of Education to revoke the charter of FCA. The letter noted the financial stability of the charter school was in considerable doubt, and openly questioned whether parents were aware of the school's instability. Grimm laughs, "It was true that we were not financially solvent—but they didn't volunteer it was their fault."

Commenting on the Franklin Board of Education's request in an interview with New Hampshire Public Radio, New Hampshire State Board of Education chairman Dave Reudig contended that when the FCA's charter was approved by the state board, it was not given sufficient scrutiny.[8] Reudig alleged that he, as state board chairman, was "never aware" that FCA was counting on direct state aid to fund the charter school. Grimm was incredulous, noting both the unlikelihood of the New Hampshire Department of Education's believing the charter schools could operate for two years without operational funding, and, more specifically, observing that, in spring 2003, then–New Hampshire Commissioner of Education Donahue signed an assurance that the State of New Hampshire would be responsible for funding the charter schools. Donahue's assurance was included in a grant application seeking a portion of $7.2 million in federal funding for charter schools—a portion of which the state received—that guaranteed, upon expiration of the federal start-up money, that the state would provide for the "continued operation" of the schools.[9] "Nobody at the state or local board level wanted to pay for it, that's the bottom line," opines Grimm.

Without a funding solution in place at the end of the 2004–2005 school year, in late May 2005, Grimm and the FCA's board of directors announced the charter school would be unable to open in September 2005. However, the efforts of Grimm and other petitioners that spring paid off—New Hampshire state legislators "found" eight hundred thousand dollars "that was not specifically appropriated" in the department of education's budget and directed that it be spent to provide $6,500 per pupil in total state support for New Hampshire's charter school students during the 2005–2006 school year. "But the budget was not signed until the end of June, and"—in Grimm's estimation—"the [New Hampshire] Department of Education held up the funding for another month. We didn't know if and how we would be funded until July 22." More troubling to Grimm, however, was the fact that this was—again—a one-time appropriation, and it did not solve the ongoing problem with charter school funding.

> We waited until July 22, but with no [long-term] state aid guaranteed, we could not, in good faith, operate the school. We knew from numerous trips to [the state legislature] that a solution could be forthcoming, but again, in good faith, it was not stable.

In addition to the school's closing and students having to return to their sending schools, FCA was unable to use its remaining federal charter school grant appropriation—approximately $283,000. "We hoped that we might be able to use it if a solution to funding could be found during that year, and we were able to re-open during the 2006–2007 school year," Grimm recalls.

## CRISIS ANALYSIS

I cannot believe nobody saw this coming. . . . I don't know if that was an intentional [tactic] by somebody someplace to scuttle the charter schools, but. . . . it was going to have that effect.

—*William Grimm*

The events surrounding the creation and first year of Franklin Career Academy typify a school crisis—particularly its multidimensional nature, self-perpetuation, and progressive deepening in intensity and effect. Any number of issues in this case study could constitute a *crisis*, as the term is used in this book, including—by definition—a serious and ongoing threat to the school's ability to exist. Applying the modified typology of crisis proposed in this work (see chapter 1), FCA's crises seemingly defy or embrace all quartiles, varying from Internal-Predictable (forecast of interrupted education because of lack of continuous funding) to External-Unpredictable (varying and contrary governmental positions as to whose responsibility it is to fund charter schools).

However, deeper examination of the case suggests the typology of the crisis—at least from the perspective of William Grimm and the FCA—is an External-Predictable crisis. The crisis resulted from a lack of strategic forecasting by policymakers in New Hampshire desirous of state-sponsored charter schools. Most importantly, perhaps, this included a failure to anticipate the challenges facing charter petitioners—even those as educated and successful in highly regulated industries as William Grimm—when facing a powerful and entrenched bureaucracy, political resistance, and what David Tyack and Larry Cuban characterize as public education's almost unique ability to resist change.[10]

The state's lack of forecasting is particularly interesting given what Joe Williams characterizes as the well-documented and "blatantly political" opposition charter school petitioners faced nationally between 1996 and 2006—due, in part, to the decision by many states, including New Hampshire, to permit the authorization of charters at the state level.[11] As a result, the New Hampshire state charter schools legislation created educational "reform" without an appreciation of existing governance and regulatory structures in public education, requiring supports to evolve on an ad hoc basis, reacting to specific challenges and obstacles.

Grimm—who, after four years, remains somewhat dubious that the bureaucratic barriers encountered were unintentional—notes, in retrospect, that any effective intervention would have had to occur prior to the charter petition being filed. "I was on the education transition team [in 2002] that worked to permit state charters, and I do not recall anyone from the department of education telling me about the two-year delay in state funding until the opening day ceremony. I mean, it's a little hard to accept that this was an oversight." Further reflecting, Grimm notes lessons he learned from twenty years of business—"I know it's hard to change, and people tend to resist change"—but this was particularly true with the education establishment:

> I didn't think it was going to be easy, but the charter school was not an idea just to have a charter school. It seemed to be a very good way to improve public education in certain areas for certain students. . . . In retrospect . . . I have a much greater appreciation for how hard it is and how long it takes to change a culture.

## CRISIS TREATMENT

On August 24, 2004, after being told that the New Hampshire State Department of Education did not foresee providing the state funding upon which FCA would rely for operations, William Grimm, the board, faculty, parents, and students of FCA had little choice but to react to the crisis before them. As Grimm notes, "The only alternative was to close the school."

The crisis response model suggests that successful crisis response requires immediate decision-making and quick and decisive leadership. Preparation for this response requires anticipating and planning for crisis situations prior to onset, as well as developing leadership dispositions upon which a leader can almost instinctually rely at the onset of crisis. Extending Principal Anna Switzer's observation about a school in crisis, a leader in crisis can only be the leader he or she was the day before the crisis.

Grimm's response epitomizes this. Despite the passage of nearly three decades since his training at Annapolis, Grimm instinctually relied on training intended to develop naval officers as "critical thinkers and creative decision-makers with a bias for action." After the state commissioner's announcement, Grimm immediately gathered political decision makers available at the opening ceremony whom he forecast playing an important role in addressing the crisis—the governor, the state commissioner of education, and the local school superintendent, securing assurances from the governor that "we [the state] would take care of it." This permitted him to allay immediate concerns of parents, faculty, and students that could have easily resulted in the "compilation of panic, defeatism, and melodrama" often accompanying crises, and overshadowed the opening of the school. Grimm's response exemplifies the importance of communicating with those directly impacted by the crisis. Additionally, his response spoke directly to "psychological concerns and fears of those involved."

However, Grimm knew he could not blindly trust the governor's office to solve all of the problems, and he considered the challenges facing FCA. These included:

1. A lack of sustainable funding and lack of agreement regarding the method in which FCA would be funded
2. Parents, faculty, and students who were aware the school could close, and a community expecting demonstrably improved academic performance from students despite this

3. A relatively hostile local school system unlikely to send state aid intended for FCA students without the direct intervention of a body with the legal authority to compel them to do so

4. A highly bureaucratic state agency authorizing the charter school that was now providing contradictory information regarding continuing funding while occupying the primary structural position in which the problem would be "solved" under the existing system

5. A reason to openly question the motives of a number of individuals within and without the New Hampshire Department of Education, who ostensibly supported FCA

Grimm knew that addressing these challenges would require "a tremendous amount of [FCA] board focus" while enduring a "tremendous amount of uncertainty." FCA's board moved to contain speculation resulting from uncertainty by committing to "transparency" regarding financial and operational developments. They assured faculty, parents, and students that FCA planned to offer all scheduled programs, and they were committed to keeping all stakeholders apprised of both the efforts the charter school was making in securing funding, *as well as setbacks.* "When we told them about problems and challenges, we also told them what we were doing about it. Obviously everyone knew we were trying to get this fixed." This minimized speculation that might have resulted from uncertainty,[12] thus increasing trust in the school's leadership while minimizing potential impact on instruction. Grimm recalls,

> We [took the] approach that the operation of the school is to be totally open to parents and staff—but we didn't know how tough that would be until we started. It was difficult to consider and react to a situation, then make sure everyone was aware of it. But any parents would tell you that while they weren't happy with the situation, they were informed about what the issues were, what we were doing, and how we were going to address it.

Grimm and the FCA board maintained this level of communication with parents—and particularly staff—throughout the school year. It became particularly important in spring 2005, when it appeared New Hampshire's charter structure would not change to provide sustainable funding. As a result, "[faculty and staff] knew what the situation was and what it had been.

We kept them advised all along, and when the financial uncertainty led them to interviewing for other jobs, we told them we understood that they would have to do what they deemed prudent. We understood and I did write strong letters of recommendation."

After committing to transparency in communication and governance, Grimm and the board then realistically forecast what would happen if they did not receive the state appropriation on which they were depending or any other state aid. "We knew we didn't have the money to complete the year—our best estimate was that we could operate until March." The board also saw the probable results of this closure—students scrambling to enroll mid-semester in "new" schools, and FCA teachers unlikely to find jobs three-quarters of the way through a school year. This forecasting framed the board's options, ultimately resulting in the board's knowing that overcoming the crisis would require proactive governance during the 2004 school year: "We didn't want to close the school, anyway . . . [but] we felt that we could not, in good conscience, allow the students and staff to be affected without trying everything we could."

Grimm and the FCA board also strategically identified the source of the crisis—the failure of the State of New Hampshire to appropriate adequate funding—and focused their response on that source. The board knew funding was unlikely to come from the source to which the New Hampshire Department of Education suggested they look—the Franklin school board—and decided not to spend time and resources pursuing it from the local board. "It would have been pointless to ask the [Franklin Board of Education] for money. Their entire opposition to the charter school was always about money." Instead, Grimm focused on obtaining funding from the state, which previously committed to funding the state-sponsored charter schools.

Grimm and the board's decision to primarily pursue funding from the state instead of the Franklin board was sound, and it ensured that re-sources—including time—were not spent in a broad-based response unlikely to produce results. As noted above, the source of FCA's crisis was inadequate forecasting and planning by the State of New Hampshire, and not the Franklin Board of Education's declination to provide state funds it earned two years earlier under the state's funding formula and had already budgeted for the 2004–2005 school year. It would be unlikely that the Franklin Board of Education—which had already begun the school year and was operating on its fiscal

year 2005 budget—could have financially sustained the $77,000 shortfall re-
sulting from transferring this money to FCA. It was even less viable politically,
given the Franklin board's very public opposition to using local funds for the
charter school. By focusing instead on the State of New Hampshire, Grimm
and the board chose an opponent both publicly committed to financially
supporting the charter school and capable of more realistically providing the
support. Perhaps most importantly, they focused on the entity whose actions
precipitated the crisis.

However, perhaps the greatest lesson FCA offers is the need to "close the
crisis circle." Grimm's correct identification of the precipitating event of the
crisis—lack of a *sustainable* funding mechanism for charter schools in New
Hampshire—informed his response to it. Despite the New Hampshire Legislature providing state aid on a one-time basis, Grimm and the FCA board determined that without a realistic funding mechanism, "we knew we couldn't
prudently open a school." Until the precipitating event was addressed, the
crisis would be self-perpetuating and would eventually exhaust the ability of
FCA and its supporters to "manage."

## CONCLUSION

FCA closed in May 2004. However, with student performance results vin-
dicating the academic model of the school, Grimm continued to lobby for
changes in New Hampshire's method of funding charter schools. In addition to the "special" appropriation from the legislature, in fall 2005, the New
Hampshire Commissioner of Education informed local school districts from
which students were enrolling in charter schools that they could either pass
the minimum state aid generated by those students to the charter schools or
the state would withhold that same amount of money from their budgets. In
Grimm's estimation, this would not solve the larger issue—he was convinced
that local districts could not be trusted to transfer funds in a timely fashion,
and he continued to work for direct state funding of state-sponsored charter
schools. In spring 2006, the New Hampshire Legislature amended the state
funding law, permitting state aid to go directly to the state-sponsored charter
schools.

As a result, FCA reopened for the 2006–2007 school year with approximately forty students. However, the United States Department of Education
did not reward the FCA board's decision not to spend the remaining $283,000

of its federal start-up money during the 2005–2006 school year. The department stated that this money was no longer available to FCA—although it was committed to the school's "third year" of operation. Without the federal start-up grant or funding from the State of New Hampshire, Grimm knew that it would be increasingly difficult to educate students with one-third to one-half of the student spending in comparable "traditional" public schools. Financial uncertainty continued to plague FCA, and Grimm continued to advocate at the state level for increased funding for state-supported charter schools while resisting local efforts to close the school. In March 2006, a member of the Franklin City Council contacted the New Hampshire Governor's Office, requesting the governor use his authority to grant the Franklin Board of Education's April 2005 request to close FCA.

Limping through the 2006–2007 school year with the state's emergency, one-time appropriation, Grimm and the FCA board narrowly decided to re-open for the 2007–2008 school year; however, FCA was about to require a new level of personal sacrifice by Grimm. The school could not sustain an administrator's salary, and Grimm resigned from his bond trading job to serve as the school's head. "It was not what you would call a financially motivated decision," laughs Grimm. The continuing and pervasive financial uncertainty—as well as the danger of the school closing in mid-year—dramatically lowered student enrollment for the 2007–2008 school year. By March 2008, thirty students remained enrolled in FCA, each generating just $3,800 in state aid. The previous year (2006–2007, the last year for which state data is available) the average New Hampshire high school student generated $11,983.99 in state, local, and federal funds.[13]

Although national testing continued to vindicate FCA's instructional method—according to Grimm, the "average" FCA student gained two years of academic achievement in 2007–2008, with 50–75 percent of all students increasing scores in language arts, math, reading, and science—the school needed approximately $8,000 annually, or approximately 70 percent of the $11,000 in funding provided for the "average" New Hampshire public school student, to sustain programs and operations. In spring 2008, efforts by Grimm and others resulted in the New Hampshire Legislature's dramatically increasing state aid to the state-sponsored charter schools. On June 4, 2008, the legislature passed House Bill 1642, providing the state-chartered schools $5,000 in state aid for the 2008–2009 school year. It was bittersweet for Grimm as—the previous day—the FCA board voted to again close the school's doors. "It was too little, too late."

## REFLECTIVE QUESTIONS

### Reflecting on the Reading

1. FCA was a tremendously promising educational model that—ultimately— failed owing to political factors. Who was at fault for FCA's failure, and why?
2. At FCA, William Grimm made extensive use of a "guiding coalition," on whom he relied for advice during the funding crisis. Is it likely Grimm's response to the crisis would have been as focused without this level of support? Does reliance on such a coalition come at the cost of rapid response? Why or why not?

### Application to Theory

3. Strategic forecasting is an important element of both crisis avoidance and crisis response. Grimm made extensive use of forecasting in identifying the probable consequences of the initial funding crisis—a March 2005 closure—and the most likely source of continued funding—the State of New Hampshire. In a crisis situation, how likely is it that you would have the information necessary to focus a response, preventing dissipation of resources and loss of time?

### Application on the Job

4. How familiar are you with funding sources for each of your school's programs that you consider "critical"? Is this funding guaranteed, contingent, or appropriated on an annual basis? How would the loss of funding for one of these programs affect your school?
5. Assume that the political hierarchy in your school district was adversarial to your school's vision or goals. Could (or would) you attempt to go around it for your school's students, faculty, and other stakeholders? To whom would you go and how would you proceed? If not, why not?

# 12

# "You Begin to Make Progress After Three Years, and, All of a Sudden, That Is Taken Away from You."

## *How Woodland Elementary School Survived a Rezoning of 95 Percent of Its Students and Parents*

### OVERVIEW

We were on our way—we were going to do some great things—the culture of the school was changing, and the community bought to what we were doing. And I think the perception was beginning to change about the school. So we were chugging along, getting there, picking up speed, and then we hit a wall.

—*Dr. Noris Price, principal, Woodland Elementary School*

The story of Woodland Elementary School in Sandy Springs, Georgia, is one familiar to many school leaders—a political decision by the school board "rezoned" a school's attendance area, resulting in a significant shift in the student population. However, the relatively common challenge occasioned by rezoning and Woodland's experience diverge markedly. At Woodland, the rezoning occurred after three years of major school-level reform focused on academic excellence and building a "neighborhood school." The rezoning resulted in 95 percent of the student population moving to a new school and a loss of approximately one-half of the faculty and staff. Dr. Noris Price, Woodland's principal, characterizes the transformation as so systemic that, after the rezoning, "[we had] a building and teachers, but [we] really didn't have a school community, because our students and parents—and many of our staff—have now been shifted entirely to a new school."

Woodland offers school leaders an opportunity to consider how challenges—no matter how great—can be overcome by a school leader who uses crisis as a catalyst for a positive change.

## CASE NARRATIVE

I became the principal in August 1997. The first challenge [was that] the community was changing—many more minority students were coming to the school, and there was a negative perception in the community about what that meant for the school, [and] concerns about how "my" child's education will be impacted by interacting with children from a very different background than their own.

—*Dr. Noris Price*

Woodland Elementary School is located in Sandy Springs, Georgia, one of metropolitan Atlanta's residential communities. A picture of suburban affluence, Sandy Springs is home to several "Fortune 500" companies (including United Parcel Service and Newell Rubbermaid), as well as several large research hospitals.[1] Sixty-five percent of all Sandy Springs residents have a bachelor's or higher college degree, with approximately 23 percent of adult residents possessing a graduate or professional degree.[2]

Of these residents, 80 percent are employed in "white collar" industry, with an average household income approximately 100 percent higher than the state's average ($132,209 to $66,521 in 2007).[3] In 2007, more than 20 percent (20.7%) of all Sandy Springs households earned more than $200,000, while less than 1 percent (0.06%) used food stamps.[4] In 2000 (the year of the crisis considered in this case study), the median home value in Sandy Springs was $311,898—almost five times the state average ($70,700).

Fulton County—in which Sandy Springs is located—is ethnically diverse. In 2000, approximately 48 percent of the county's residents identified themselves as "white," while 44 percent identified themselves as "black."[5] Sandy Springs stands in stark contrast; in 2000, 78 percent of Sandy Springs resi-

WOODLAND ELEMENTARY SCHOOL

dents were white (non-Hispanic), with black residents constituting 12 percent of the population.

Dr. Noris Price came to Fulton County in August 1997. "I was not the principal they were expecting in Sandy Springs," she laughs.

> First of all, I'm an ESOL [English for Speakers of Other Languages] student. I came to the United States from the Dominican Republic when I was ten years old. I grew up in the south Bronx. I struggled in school—not knowing English and learning it as I went along—and that's what motivated me to get into education. I went to college [only] because I had a counselor who cared enough to help me navigate the college process.

Returning to New York City, Price first taught in a Catholic school in upper Manhattan and then the New York City public schools. For three years, Price taught in a school that was "99 percent free and reduced-price meals, 99 percent minority." After working in New York City for six years, Price and her husband relocated to Alexandria, Virginia. "That was a shock. I went from a high poverty school to a very upper-middle-class community in Fairfax County—99 percent Caucasian. The only three people of color in the school were the assistant principal, a custodian, and me [laughs]."

While a teacher in Fairfax County, Price was encouraged by her principal to pursue school administration. "I had not seriously considered leadership before, [but] he saw something in me, and encouraged me to get my administrative certificate." After obtaining her leadership certification, Price spent two years as an assistant principal and five as a principal in the Fairfax County School District.

In 1996, Price's husband took a job in Atlanta. Price, however, was very happy professionally in Fairfax County. "We tried the commuter-marriage for a year before deciding that it wasn't for us." At the conclusion of the 1996–1997 school year, Price contacted her former supervisor in Fairfax County—Dr. Steven Dolinger—who was superintendent of schools in Fulton County, Georgia. "He told me to 'come on down'—he had a principal position for me." After being approved by an interview panel, in August 1997, Price was hired as principal of Woodland Elementary School.

Initially, Dr. Price was curious as to why Dr. Dolinger placed her at Woodland—an elementary school in one of the least ethnically diverse and wealthiest communities in Georgia. While Price worked with affluent students in Fairfax County, she primarily considered her "calling" as working with a diverse student body, especially disadvantaged students—"students who were in the position I was in when I came to the United States." Dr. Price recalls,

> Sandy Springs is a very affluent community . . . very highly educated, and so I had no clue why Dr. Dolinger would put me there—that was not my background. I quickly learned that I was needed there. The school was going through a transition. There was "white flight" taking place at the school. The community was changing, and, coming in, I had the challenge of trying to convince people that having minority students in the school did not mean a less quality education. And it did not mean lower expectations.

Price was quickly disabused of her assumptions of suburban privilege at Woodland. In the mid-1990s, Sandy Springs experienced its first significant construction of relatively low-rent apartment buildings, permitting economically disadvantaged individuals and families to move to a neighborhood that had been long gentrified by high housing prices. While Sandy Springs had always had a number of rental units (approximately 30 percent in 1990), the demographic composition of apartment residents began to change from single "twenty-somethings" to ethnic and linguistic minority families with school-age children.

This resulted in an influx of minority students in Sandy Springs public schools. Although Sandy Springs remained disproportionately populated by affluent Caucasians, the elementary school population implied a different future for the community. Additionally, in order to make the school's population more reflective of the county's diversity, the school district implemented a "Majority to Minority Program," transporting students from the south end of the county—students who were predominantly black and economically disadvantaged—to Woodland. By 1997, Woodland's student population was approximately 50 percent minority (predominantly African American), with approximately 21 percent of the students qualifying for free or reduced-price meals.

This diversity was not universally welcome within Sandy Springs. Woodland was not a school accustomed to change. Price's predecessor was principal for approximately a decade, and the school had a "very experienced" faculty— "twenty-, twenty-five-, or thirty-year veterans." Both the teachers and the community were "in shock" from the racial and economic transformation of Woodland. The new students brought instructional challenges to teachers long accustomed to teaching middle- and upper-middle-class white students:

You [begin] to hear these comments . . . these students are not the same as the ones we used to teach. These students are not as motivated as the ones we used to teach. These parents are not as involved as the ones we used to have. Terms that very much had undertones of class and race.

Immediately, Price noted that minority students were disproportionately performing at a lower level than their Caucasian peers. "We started disaggregating data for minority students—and you have to bear in mind that this was years before No Child Left Behind." Her initial review of student performance data showed that while the school's "gifted" students were performing at a comparable level to their peers in local private and neighboring, but less diverse, public schools, this achievement was not shared by other students—Woodland's average scores for minority students on standardized tests were in the bottom quartile of the state's elementary schools: "I remember looking at that data, and the students that were black or Hispanic or ESOL were not performing well at all in comparison to their white peers." It appeared to Price that there was an expectation among the faculty that these students would or could not achieve. "[Many teachers] were not really focusing on educating all of the students, and particularly minority students." Demonstrative to Price of this lack of equal expectations was the school's gifted program:

The [gifted] students did not represent the population of the school. All the students in the program were Caucasian. You're talking about kindergarten through fifth grade [seven hundred students] . . . [and] there wasn't a single gifted minority kid in this school?

Upon Price's hiring, she was informed that one the district's goals was to increase community involvement and engagement in the school. Price knew that to build a true "neighborhood" school, she would have to change faculty and community perceptions about minority students. Beginning her work with Woodland's teachers, she first focused on changing paradigms about the education of "minority" children:

We had to help the teachers who had not dealt with [minority students] before, and explain that it did not mean a less-quality education or low expectations. [We had to] provid[e] professional development to help them understand how to work with a diverse student population.

A committed data user, Price believed that teachers were simply unaware of the achievement gap—"I thought I would get, 'Wow! We didn't realize that, what do we need to do, everyone is going to rally around and we were going to go to work.'" Price did not get the reaction she expected:

> In a meeting where I shared the data and started talking about the achievement gap, and you would have thought I dropped a bomb in that cafeteria. It was like they had never heard such a thing, and many of the staff members indicated they were offended that I would share this data and talk about an achievement gap. . . . They viewed it as an insult. Some of them even perceived it as I was accusing them of being racist.

Price knew that the teachers' paradigm had to shift, and the school had an immediate mission—to focus on increasing the academic performance of historically underperforming students while convincing the Woodland community that the inclusion and focus on these students would not adversely affect the performance of their traditionally high-performing peers.

To achieve this goal, Price initiated neighborhood outreach programs to both affluent parents and those of historically underperforming students—"everything was on the table." Price built faculty and community teams to implement both in-school and out-of-school programs that were research-based and focused on increasing academic performance among minority students. To change teachers' preconceptions about minority student achievement, Price provided professional development demonstrating high academic achievement by lower socioeconomic status and minority students.

To reach affluent Caucasian parents, Price employed a twofold approach. First, she realized that these parents were ones that would be receptive to data and research, and she demonstrated that poor minority students could coexist in schools with higher-performing middle-class students without a deterioration in student performance—"and we could show that our highest-achieving kids scored comparably to kids in local, elite private schools." Second, she invited parents to become more involved in the school, becoming emotionally invested in the achievement of all students.

Contemporaneously, Price reached out to the parents of economically disadvantaged Hispanic and African American students. "We had to change our perception of parent involvement—it doesn't mean just coming to class and volunteering—I can be involved if I turn off the TV and make sure my kid does his homework and comes to school on time." Price moved PTA meetings to evenings so all parents could participate—not just affluent suburban mothers.

Going into the community and homes, Price convinced parents that their child's achievement was greatly dependent upon their engagement. "She was everywhere," one parent recalls. "Very highly visible. You saw her all the time in the community. And she was always smiling and positive. I started smiling as soon as I saw her."

Not everyone shared Price's commitment. Between 1997 and 2000, approximately 20 percent of the faculty retired or resigned—a higher than average turnover rate for Woodland. Price views the departures with optimism: "It was not a mass exodus, but it was enough to give me the flexibility to hire some people who understood the mission and the expectation. It was an opportunity to bring new blood and hire new people."

Importantly, however, the students stopped leaving. By spring 2000, Woodland had a student enrollment 30 percent greater than its building capacity (500 versus 850). Additionally, as community engagement increased and teachers implemented new instructional strategies, test scores increased. That same fall, Woodland's test scores had increased almost an entire quartile. "We were well on our way."

## CRISIS DESCRIPTION

And then we had a great school, three years later, making great strides, and [the district] said, you are going to lose a large percentage of your kids. I didn't realize [the numbers] they were talking about at the time. I think at the last count it was . . . 95 percent of [our] students shifted to the "new" school, and we ended up getting kids from three other area schools. . . . You begin to make progress after three years, and, all of a sudden, that is taken away from you. So we were starting over again at square one.

—*Dr. Noris Price*

Since fall 1999, Price and the Woodland parents and faculty knew that the school was a prime candidate to have its student attendance area redrawn. Fulton County was building a new elementary school in Sandy Springs, ostensibly to relieve overcrowding at Woodland and other elementary schools. This was welcome news to Price and Woodland parents and faculty. Wooldland was making extensive use of "learning cottages"—a euphemism for temporary classrooms—and these were inconsistent with the newly increased expectations of the school by parents, faculty, and the community. "[Woodland] had a capacity of five hundred kids, and we had 850. We needed relief. So we knew [redistricting] was coming, and it was going to bring some relief, and we were excited about that."

Through the fall of 1999, Price and Woodland faculty and parents believed a minor rezoning would occur, essentially taking students from several overcrowded elementary schools and populating the new elementary school. However, the school district proposed a number of plans—including one that would shift virtually every attendance zone in Sandy Springs. "The board [of education] had three redistricting plans they were discussing. While we didn't know which plan they would choose—and would not until the night the board voted—we knew which plan was the worst [laughs]—but we viewed it as unlikely that the board would choose that plan."

Although Price did not know what would happen with the rezoning, she was relatively certain of her own plans. She was interested in the principalship of the new elementary school. Price recalls,

> When the school was being built, I knew that's where I wanted to go . . . . I'[d] always wanted [to open a new school], and I looked forward to it—to build a school from the ground up. It has no culture, and you are creating that culture. I was very excited about that.

Price did not discuss her plans with Woodland's parents and faculty; however, many suspected that her record of success at Woodland made her the natural candidate to open the new school. "We were terrified that we would lose Dr. Price to the new school—she had done so much for our school, and we didn't see anyone else being able to lead like she had," recalls one teacher.

As the fall semester of 1999 progressed, the redistricting process began with community meetings and discussions. The process quickly became highly politicized and devolved into a rancorous debate about "those apartment kids." Price recalls,

> It was awful, just awful. It pitted subdivisions against subdivisions, school communities against school communities. . . . It became racially divisive, socioeco-

nomically divisive. Those meeting were unbelievable. [I] heard things [I] never believed [I] would hear—racial undertones like you would not imagine. There was even a lawsuit that came out of the process.

At the end of the process, the Fulton County Board of Education decided on a plan that would shift the attendance zones of multiple schools—the "worst" plan. "We knew the full impact in January–February [2000], when they drew the lines and shared the map with the community. When they redrew the lines, they didn't just do it for Woodland—they did it for all the schools in Sandy Springs." Price characterizes the result as a "domino effect," moving 95 percent of Woodland's students to a new school, reducing the school's population to approximately five hundred, and populating Woodland with students from three different elementary schools, plus the 5 percent of Woodland's remaining students. "It was the worst-case scenario. We were going to lose 95 percent of our students, [and] approximately half of our faculty."

The news was devastating to Woodland's faculty and parents. They were upset by the board's decision, and many faculty members were openly questioning whether they would remain at Woodland. "There was a great deal of uncertainty regarding the students we would be receiving. . . . We had approximately fifty students out of 850 who were remaining with the school." Some families elected to enroll their children in private schools, and Woodland lost approximately twenty-five teachers and staff. Price's concept of a community school and culture ended. "We had to start all over again."

The transition brought additional challenges to a school working to overcome a perception that it did not represent the community it served. In a community that was approximately 75 percent middle-class Caucasian, Woodland's new student population was extremely diverse. Drawing the attendance lines around Woodland to incorporate most of the multifamily dwellings enrolling students in public schools, Woodland moved from a school that was approximately 50 percent minority to a school in which minority students composed approximately 70 percent of the enrollment by fall 2000. Additionally, while Woodland's student population would drop from 850 to five hundred, its number of students from lower-SES families would dramatically increase—approximately 35 percent of Woodland's new students qualified for free or reduced-price meals.

Finally, with Woodland's reduced student numbers, the school was designated as one of the county's "special education center" schools for students with exceptionalities, in which the district concentrated students with a specific learning disability in a particular school. Woodland was designated as a special education center school for students with moderate to severe mental disabilities and behavior disorders, which resulted in students with disabilities from multiple schools in the county being sent to Woodland. Given these changes, convincing families to remain at Woodland would be, in Price's estimation, "a hard sale."

It was not, however, a sale Price had to make. As the board considered the new attendance zones, it was also considering principal assignments for the 2000–2001 school year. Price had requested a transfer and was recommended to lead the new elementary school. Despite her interest, Price immediately knew she should not leave Woodland. The night before the board was to vote on her transfer, Price called the assistant superintendent, informing him she was going to stay at Woodland. "He came the next day to talk to me. He kept asking, 'Are you sure you want to do this?' And I said, I'm sure—I can't do this to the school. And I pulled my name out of the running." Price explains her decision:

> When I saw what was going to happen to Woodland, after I worked so hard with the staff for three years and the parent community, I could not walk away from it. I knew that once I walked away, not only were the students going to leave, but the teachers who were committed to the vision we developed for Woodland were going to leave, and the school would be devastated. I decided not to open the new school and stay at Woodland and see it through this very difficult transition.

Despite her superintendent's concern, Price remained at Woodland. "I couldn't leave the other half of my staff there, knowing what was coming. My school [Woodland] was facing a crisis—I needed to be there."

## CRISIS ANALYSIS

The crisis for me was the fact that I had to create basically a new school in an existing building without most of the existing staff. We ha[d] to convince families that we were a viable option to educate their children.

—*Dr. Noris Price*

The events creating a crisis at Woodland Elementary School in spring 2000 epitomize the definition of a crisis proposed in this work—a threat to a school's foundational practices. Between 1997 and 2000, Woodland significantly revisited and redefined its foundational values and mores, becoming a school noted for being racially and socioeconomically integrated while maintaining high academic standards for all children. Importantly, Woodland had a culture of including and involving parents and its surrounding community, meeting Fulton County's goal for the school to be a true "neighborhood" school. In a single board of education meeting, all this was challenged—the school population was no longer representative of the historic community it served, and its new "community" was limited largely to a series of low-income apartment buildings.

The facts of the case compel a classification of Woodland's crisis as External-Predictable. As Price readily admits, the crisis was not an immediate onset—after the Fulton County Board of Education redefined its attendance zone in January/February 2000, Woodland's administration, faculty, and parents had approximately six months to prepare for its influx of new students and parents in August 2000. As the case demonstrates, Price made the most of this time to prepare. She knew that an unsuccessful crisis response during the six-month interval could have created an environment of organizational malaise—a looming crisis that stakeholders felt powerless to avert and that could lead to an erosion of teachers and parents who had other professional opportunities and school attendance options, respectively.

As Price observes, this devastating response was precisely what she feared occurring, and justified her plunging her school into frenetic activity in preparation during the six-month period—"we couldn't sit around and feel sorry for ourselves." Although six months would pass prior to the rezoning occurring, Price knew that if she did not move immediately to address the crisis and get teachers and parents to view it as an "opportunity," the situation could easily devolve into an unproductive one. Within the same week the board's decision was announced, Price had the faculty and parent groups working on the "new" Woodland—"I kept them busy."

As noted in earlier chapters of this work and in literature on crisis response, identifying the external or internal source of a crisis is a significant step in crisis prevention. As Norman Augustine, the former chief executive officer of Martin Marietta and an expert in crisis management, suggests, one of the best ways to avoid a crisis is to consider everything that "could cause

trouble" as well as the challenges that could result, and the "cost of prevention."[6] This is particularly true for crises having an *internal* source, over which
school leaders can expect to have far greater control.

However, the source of this crisis is externally evident—the Fulton County
Board of Education imposed the school's new attendance zone with what was
perceived as little consideration for the Woodland community. As a result,
the source of the crisis is external to the school itself and there was little Price
could have done to prevent the crisis. While it could certainly be argued that
*internal* factors—such as the school's overcrowding—played a significant role
in the board's decision to rezone Woodland, and rezoning would have been
far less likely had Price taken steps to ensure that the school was not overcrowded, this is highly speculative.

## CRISIS TREATMENT

We saw this as we could throw a pity party and feel sorry for ourselves
. . . instead, we saw it as an opportunity for us to do something
different—to meet the needs of the students we were going to get.

—*Dr. Noris Price*

In February 2000, Price faced a situation in which it would have been relatively
easy (and completely understandable) for a leader to proverbially lose heart.
The "neighborhood" school culture of Woodland—built through significant
effort over a three-year period—would be completely transformed when the
school's attendance area was rezoned and 95 percent of existing students and
parents would attend another school. The incoming students were from three
other elementary schools, lacking a cohesive culture or parental commitment,
and—with a relatively lower socioeconomic status and increasing numbers of
English language learners and students with moderate or severe intellectual
disabilities—represented a significantly greater educational challenge.

Exacerbating the crisis, half of Woodland's faculty—who, after three
years, were very invested in Woodland and committed to its institutional
culture—would be forced to leave due to the school's "resizing" (moving
from 840 students to just over five hundred). "It would have destroyed the
place had Dr. Price gone, too, and we were very worried about that," recalls
a Woodland teacher.

Price knew that she had to transform the reassignment of students to an opportunity to build upon Woodland's emerging culture—one focused on increasing the achievement of every child. She reframed the crisis and kept her stakeholders focused—and quite busy—planning for the new year, preventing dwelling on the potential negative consequences of the move. "We're going to be a very different place, and we have to do things differently. We knew the schools the students were coming from . . . [and] business as usual could not be the name of the game. We couldn't wait until the students arrived to do something."

Price turned to her Parent-Teacher Association Local School Advisory Council and school leadership team. Despite the fact that virtually all of the parents' children were leaving Woodland, the Local School Advisory Council remained committed to the continuing growth and success of Woodland. The Local School Advisory Council, Price, teachers, and support staff identified a primary challenge as building culture and cohesion among parents and students coming from three different elementary schools. "The interesting thing about it is they wanted to figure out a way that we could bring everyone together—the parents did—that would unify us and make us one happy family."

Price also began to visit community gatherings and events in the attendance zones from which Woodland's new students would come, promoting their children being moved to Woodland as a good opportunity. "Many of them had never heard of Woodland, and many of them were concerned about their children going to a new school—which is understandable."

> During that spring, I had to go to the schools, had community meetings, and try to convince families that they were going to have a good school, and their kids were going to be OK. I had to do a lot of [public relations] work to convince people that we were a good school.

Price invited incoming parents to participate in the dialogue about the "new" Woodland, and a number accepted her invitation. Empanelling groups of teachers and parents, Price held a number of meetings at which all—including parents and teachers who would be moving away—were welcomed to suggest possibilities for Woodland's growth and improvement. "Woodland was constantly 'buzzing' with ideas and energy about next year—working groups were always suggesting new ideas for 'next' year. There was no time to dwell on the negative side of what was happening."

By keeping stakeholders focused on the solution to the crisis and not the crisis itself, Price prevented a negative stigma from engulfing the discussion of rezoning. In Price's estimation, it would have been very easy for Woodland to sink into a "winners and losers" mindset—with the losers decidedly being those families and faculty remaining at Woodland.

Instead, Price redirected emotion positively, and importantly, never let any parents or students see her as anything other than entirely optimistic and excited about the prospects for the new school. "Change is hard, but it can also be very energizing," she notes. "The important thing when you're in charge is to always be optimistic, not just appear optimistic—people can pick up on it if it's not authentic—[and] you'll slip." Noting that she could not "underestimate" the importance of this step, Price observes, "When we got our teachers and parents involved and motivated, there was little room for negativity."

Price also notes the role teams played in maintaining a positive environment and generating energy and ideas for the transformation. She goes as far as to attribute much of the intellectual genesis for the new school's instructional programs to teacher and parent teams—"most of the good ideas were theirs . . . I was [just] the head cheerleader." Parents and teachers disagree. "We could have never done it without Dr. Price," one teacher observes.

By creating teams to respond to the crisis, stakeholders obtained considerable "buy-in" to the solution, and were not left waiting for the administration to come up with a solution they could review—and question. Moreover, the teams served as an effective bulwark to prevent stakeholders from responding selfishly to the crisis—"it's hard to put your own interests and agenda first when you are on a mixed parent/teacher/community team."

In the weeks following the board's decision, the discussion evolved from one focusing on structures—such as having a uniform policy—to more substantive unifying elements. The Local School Advisory Council wanted Woodland to be known for high academic achievement and high parental involvement from the Sandy Springs community. Price and the council began to look at practices that increased parental involvement—including *mandating* involvement, as some magnet and charter schools had done. "This led to looking at schools with high parental involvement and uniform policies, and in the process of visiting schools, we looked at theme schools."

During this period, Price had an important meeting with an associate superintendent. Having visited a number of theme schools, Woodland's parents and faculty were interested in the possibility of converting Woodland into a theme or magnet school. Price outlined their suggestions to the associate superintendent, who suggested that Price and her faculty and parents consider "converting" Woodland into a charter school. Noting that both state and federal financial incentives existed for starting charter schools, he suggested, "If you are looking at doing things differently, you should look at charter schools."

With support from Fulton County, Price and her team began to explore the charter school option. "We knew that we would have far more options as a charter school, and that was empowering." Price again assembled parents and teachers, holding an all-day exercise in Woodland's library. Placing the parents and teachers into teams, Price offered parents and teachers the opportunity to design the school they would want Woodland to be ideally—"If we could create the ideal school, what would that look like? To brainstorm that, with no barriers, forget about the finances, just what would the ideal school be like? That is a powerful exercise. What would it look like?"

The teams took half a day to identify the attributes of the school they wanted. "We made it clear that everything was on the table—all ideas were welcome." Having looked at the theme schools previously, parents and teachers were familiar with a number of items they wanted—students who are problem solvers and critical thinkers, all teachers using problem-based "gifted" teaching strategies, and significant parental involvement in the school and learning process. "That afternoon, we put the rules back in place and said, 'Now, how many of these items can we get within our budget.' By the end of the day, we could realistically adopt 80 percent of the items on our 'ideal' list."

Price refined the new Woodland model through numerous meetings with parents and teachers. Communication was essential to building stakeholder investment. "We did surveys with parents, surveys with teachers, open forums taking parents through the school development process. I had over twenty meetings within a period of three to four months. I had breakfast meetings, lunch meetings, dinner meetings, any opportunity possible." Price's goal was not entirely to secure philosophical buy-in to the process. Under Georgia law, 51 percent of the parents of the *incoming* students and teachers would have to vote to approve Woodland's "conversion" to a charter school. Naturally, Price set her goal far beyond this:

> To me, that was not sufficient—51 percent was not a mandate. And that is not even 51 percent of all parents and teachers—it's 51 percent of the people who show up at a called meeting. My goal was 75 percent of all faculty and parents wanting to go forward with the charter school, and unless 75 percent agreed, we were not going to move forward with the charter process.

To reach her target participation goal, Price took different tactics for her two audiences. To convince parents of the importance of converting Woodland to a charter school, she focused on the goals of high expectations for all students and increased student achievement. "We specifically identified and explained the commitment it required from teachers and parents." However, the area of most significant parental concern had nothing to do with academics—"it was uniforms." This surprised Price, but she knew that the parents and faculty focus groups identified uniforms as a key component of unifying students and parents from Woodland's three "feeder" schools. "Parents were concerned that their children could not express their individuality with uniforms," Price recalls.

To respond to this concern, Price provided information on other schools that had been successful in implementing uniforms, noting specifically how much money and time uniforms saved parents. "We educated where we could, but in the end, we always let parents know [state law allowed] families to 'opt out' of a charter school if they were not happy with it, and choose another public school."

The challenge from faculty had nothing to do with uniforms or individual expression: "For teachers, it was about 'is it going to be more work?'" Price responded candidly. Given that Woodland would be revising its entire instructional methodology to integrate "gifted" teaching strategies for all children (such as problem-based learning), "the answer [was] yes—if you do thing[s] differently it is always going to be more work. So initially, yes, we will have to work harder." However, once teachers became convinced that these strategies would significantly strengthen instruction—and "we were capable of doing them"—teachers supported the conversion. "They did ask for—and we received—a commitment that we would have a teacher planning day once a month, so teachers could work in teams on integrating new instructional strategies." Additionally, as with parents, Price made sure teachers knew they had the option to transfer to another school if they did not want to go through the charter process.

By making sure parents and teachers who were reluctant to embrace the conversion knew they had the option to leave, Price implemented a key component of change leadership. As Harvard professor John Kotter—a leading international authority on change—noted in *Leading Change*, it is important to either obtain commitment from stakeholders for your change process or, when possible, remove them.[7] By offering parents and teachers an opportunity to leave, she provided her supporters with a significant weapon against opposition that became unreasoning (such as a teacher opposing the charter simply because of the increased work expectations)—the teacher did not have to stay. "We didn't want anyone here who did not want to be here," she recalls. "The change would be hard enough without that." Additionally, any departures allowed Price the opportunity to fill a vacancy with an employee fully committed to the goals of the "new" Woodland.

Price also publicized her high goal to key members of her guiding coalition. By establishing a very high rate for buy-in and participation, she ensured that her "leaders" would not flag in their efforts to obtain consensus to convert to a charter school—"the goal kept everyone working, meeting, all the time. When you're meeting with parents and teachers multiple times a week, you reach the point that you just want to rest! With our goal, we couldn't do that." Their efforts paid dividends. At the vote considering whether to convert Woodland to a charter school, Price not only exceeded the state's goal of 51 percent of all parents and teachers who attend a "called" meeting, but her own goal of obtaining commitment from 75 percent of all parents and teachers:

> We ended up with 95–96 percent of all parents in support of the charter, and 89 percent of our staff. So way above that benchmark I set. And again, these were new people. So you have to get the buy-in and have a grasp of what we were proposing. I don't know how I survived it, but it happened.

## CONCLUSION

In 2003, Woodland was recognized as a Georgia School of Excellence and received the Parental Involvement School of Excellence Award from the National

Parent-Teacher Association. Woodland also received the Outstanding PTA and Outstanding Principal Award from the Georgia PTA. Additionally, Woodland received its first Title I Distinguished School Award—an award it continues to win annually.

Test scores and student performance at the new Woodland soared. By 2006—when Price left to accept an associate superintendency in Clarke County, Georgia (home of the University of Georgia)—Woodland's test scores, where 70 percent of students were meeting or exceeding state-established standards in 2003, increased to over 90 percent of students' meeting or exceeding state standards. Additionally, Woodland's voluntary student population—set at 450 in 2000—exploded. By 2008, Woodland enrolled more than one thousand students.

Most importantly to Dr. Price, however, was that Woodland's growth continued after her departure: "It shows it wasn't just me, but a *true* team effort" (original emphasis). While parents and teachers miss the iconic principal, Woodland continues to grow in her absence. "I'm so proud of what they are doing," she observes.

The story of Woodland Elementary School—and Dr. Noris Price—readily demonstrates the role a crisis can play in generating a better school environment. Like a forest fire clearing choking underbrush, a school crisis can focus resources and commitment, providing an urgent problem—and opportunity for evaluation and growth.

## REFLECTIVE QUESTIONS

### Reflections on the Reading

1. Place yourself in Dr. Price's position in spring 2000—you have spent three years building a strong coalition of parents and teachers and have taken great strides toward becoming a "neighborhood" school. You then learn that 95 percent of your students have been rezoned to another school and you will lose half your faculty. How would you address this crisis in your school?

2. Continuing to place yourself in Dr. Price's position, would you have accepted the transfer to head the "new" elementary school? Why or why not? How would you have distinguished between your duty—if any—to the 95 percent of students who were transferring versus the 5 percent remaining at Woodland?

**Application to Theory**

3. Woodland provides an example of a Predictable crisis—Price and her stakeholders were aware that school zoning would occur, and they knew that possible effects included a "worst-case" scenario. How important were her actions in anticipating the crisis and forecasting its probable consequences to its successful resolution?

4. The crisis at Woodland was precipitated by actions of the Fulton County Board of Education—a body tasked with making educational decisions in the "best interests" of students. How could, if at all, Price have intervened with the board earlier to prevent the crisis resulting from the board's decision to rezone Woodland?

**Application on the Job**

5. Do your parents and teachers consider themselves to be as unified a "team" as was Dr. Price's team at Woodland? If not, what lessons could you take from Woodland's example to build a unified team, effectively creating a unified front to assist you in handling crises?

6. One of the lessons for school leaders from this work is the importance of flexibility when facing crises. How did Noris Price employ flexibility to overcome the crisis and—ultimately—increase achievement at Woodland through this crisis?

# "It Was like a Steamroller. We Sort of Saw Things Coming and We Couldn't Prevent . . . It."

## *How John Dewey High School Fought to Uphold Its Identity Despite the Threats of District Policy*

**OVERVIEW**

Principal Barry Fried is a veteran school administrator of nearly two decades and a steadfast school leader during a time when the core being of his school—John Dewey High School—has become increasingly stressed. Since the turn of the twenty-first century, his high school has faced undue pressure of high-stakes accountability measures and other district policies that have taken shape in New York City (NYC). For several years, John Dewey High School has been—more or less—an innocent bystander in a collision between failing neighborhood schools and transfer policies in NYC. Now it finds itself in a state of crisis with great unease about its future vitality—an existence very foreign to the high school with a long-standing tradition of excellence in teaching and learning.

## CASE NARRATIVE

Things had been pretty stable. Dewey has been an educational hotbed
of innovative learning because the program has been based on student
choice. Think of it as a precollegiate campus.

—*Barry Fried, principal of John Dewey High School*

Nestled in the heart of Brooklyn, New York, John Dewey High School is—in
many ways—like many other urban high schools across the country. It serves
a large student body—consistently more than three thousand students over
each of the past three school years—many of whom are economically disadvantaged, minorities, or from newly immigrated families to the United States.
And, the high school consistently serves between 36 and 40 percent students
on federally subsidized lunch.[1]

Simultaneously, and perhaps unexpectedly, John Dewey High School has
developed a reputation as one of the nation's premier high schools, with a
unique, college-oriented learning program; highly professionalized teaching
staff; and intellectually driven student body. The school was recently ranked
by *U.S. News & World Report* as being among the top 505 high schools nationally and, with a few exceptions, traditionally performs well on the New York
State Accountability System.

John Dewey High School has also maintained relatively low drop-out and
high college attendance rates. It has had an annual drop-out rate of less than
5 percent from the 2004–2005 school year through the 2006–2007 school
year (the last year results are available), with over three-quarters of the student body planning to attend a college program after high school.[2] Principal
Fried both recognizes these accomplishments and continues to work toward
improvement.

The high school provides students with a great deal of choice in the content
and pace of their educational program. While students do not have complete
authority over which courses they take, the high school does encourage self-
paced curriculum, allowing particularly ambitious students to even graduate
early. The school also provides a resource center with one-on-one instruction
for students with peer or teacher tutoring, along with an extended-day program that pays teachers to remain on site an additional hour each day to assist
students in their coursework. As Principal Fried asserts, John Dewey High

School is a "precollegiate campus," where there is much focus on independent learning time and significant responsibility on students to pursue a rigorous and satisfying program of study.

This intellectual and creative freedom partnered with an emphasis on self-motivated learning is facilitated by the organizational structure at John Dewey High School. The school is not on a semester schedule, but changes programs of study four times each school year. Coursework in each quarter (i.e., cycle) is primarily determined by student and teacher interest in fields of study. The teaching faculty consists of approximately 160 teachers and is organized by departments, with noncore areas organized in an interdisciplinary fashion. Each department is supervised by an assistant principal, which allows the school's principal, Barry Fried, to focus his efforts primarily on the bigger mission and strategic planning for the school.

Since the 2001–2002 school year, Barry Fried has proudly served as principal at John Dewey High School. With twenty-seven years of experience in the field of education, seventeen of which have been spent in leadership positions, he believes that the school's culture and organization has fostered positive relationships between administrators, teachers, and students, making the school—as he describes it—"an educational hotbed of innovative learning."

He has also witnessed how the school's efforts to maintain this tradition have come under mounting duress owing to recent accountability measures and policy initiatives emanating from the state and city education systems. These stresses have slowly built from being an inconvenience to becoming a full-fledged crisis, which continues to threaten the unique learning environment at John Dewey High School.

## CRISIS DESCRIPTION

During the past several school years, the New York State Education Department (NYSED) and New York City Department of Education (NYCDOE) have implemented a series of initiatives, particularly school restructuring and rezoning efforts. These have had considerable impacts on John Dewey High School. At the turn of the twenty-first century, NYSED's accountability system, inspired by the No Child Left Behind Act, became an impetus for a number of public school closings in NYC. Students at perpetually under-performing and dangerous schools were given the right to transfer schools, and successful schools such as John Dewey High School were required to accept them.

Oftentimes, the under-performing schools underwent small school conversions. A common scenario would be that a high school, which usually served an incoming class of one thousand students, would be divided into several small schools, each serving no more than 108 incoming students. Consequently, there were always approximately one hundred original students without a place in the newly restructured school. By the 2005–2006 school year, there were nearly five thousand students without their home school to attend throughout the district. Principal Fried attributes this policy to the first "wave of overcrowding at the school; here's an extra twenty students, fifty students, hundred students" that John Dewey High School had no choice but to incorporate into its student body.

NYCDOE also restructured the zoning policy of its public schools, with additional consequence for John Dewey High School. Prior to 2003, NYCDOE operated grade-level districts (i.e., K–8, high school), and John Dewey High School was part of the Brooklyn High School District. Under this structure, students were zoned for a local high school but could apply for attendance at a specialty high school elsewhere in the city. In 2003, NYCDOE restructured its schools, forming ten regions with schools grouped by geographic location, each containing elementary, junior high, and high schools.

More significantly, NYCDOE converted to a system of school choice. That is, there were no zoned schools, and student attendance was determined by a match between students' choice in schools and schools' preference for students. NYCDOE created the Office of Student Enrollment and Planning Operations (OSEPO) to monitor this matching system, but problems arose when students did not make enough school choices or made uninformed decisions about schools, which essentially left those students without a school match. OSEPO pooled these unassigned students and, according to Principal Fried, almost arbitrarily placed them in schools without much consideration for the appropriate match between a student's learning needs and a school's programming.

Over a compressed time period, John Dewey High School faced an influx of students from failing schools and those that had no other match within NYC public schools. The high school experienced overcrowding and a new profile of students: those that were not at John Dewey High School for the intellectual rigor and freedom it provides but rather were there through arbitrary assignment by the OSEPO. These strains, labeled "collateral damage" in a recent report by the Center for New York City Affairs,[3] began with the conversion of under-performing schools into small learning communities, but were more manageable before the 2003 zoning policy changes—known as regionalization—of the NYC public school system.

As Principal Fried candidly explains, "Up until the regionalization, we still had mechanisms to control it [i.e., the influx of less responsible, unmotivated students]." The school would hold a conference with students and parents and simply told them that they could go back to their zoned high school if they did not wish to comply with the learning culture at John Dewey High School.

The regionalization and abandonment of zoned schools stripped the school of that alternative. With a significant number of John Dewey's student body now determined at will by OSEPO, coupled with the entry of students from neighboring failing schools, Principal Fried and his teachers now encountered many more students with known attendance problems and records of low academic performance—an ill-suited student profile for the educational expectations and programming at John Dewey High School.

Principal Fried readily admits that the unique teaching and learning environment at John Dewey High School likely made the ramifications of accountability measures and rezoning policies even more difficult to bear. The pedagogical ideologies of many long-committed teachers were shaken by the realities of the new type of student flooding into the school. Students were coming from environments in which less self-control, less academic press, and less respect were common.

Knowing that this change in the student population was coming did not prevent its burden on the school's operation. "It was like a steamroller. We sort of saw things coming and we couldn't prevent some of it," says Principal Fried when describing the culminating impact of converging external pressures. The administration at John Dewey High School continuously examined achievement and other schooling records of incoming students to ensure that the school would not be blind to their needs. This practice continued once students were attending the high school. Administrators analyzed academic performance indicators, attendance patterns, and disciplinary records acknowledging that the changing nature of students would require adjustments in the school's approach to managing its student body.

While working to better handle these new students, they were simultaneously trying to maintain the unique culture of teaching and learning for the school's own "salvation." This fragile balance cracked in the fall of 2005, when, without any forewarning by the district office, nearly two hundred incoming students showed up at John Dewey High School for the first day of class.

Due to the district's student assignment policy and OSEPO's seemingly arbitrary placements, Principal Fried had become accustomed to the arrival of ten or so students at the start of each school year. As he describes, "That was normal and we knew how to handle that situation," but two hundred! The school's faculty did not have a clue that this was coming, since OSEPO had not communicated with them. Fried explains further: "We didn't have enough staff, we didn't have curricular programs for students, and we didn't know their needs."

John Dewey High School was already at capacity for the 2005–2006 school year, and the traditional organization of learning at the school was certainly not conducive to hundreds of unplanned students. An important ingredient of the self-paced, independent curricula at John Dewey High School was that approximately seven hundred students per period lacked assigned physical space. These students were expected to use their open period responsibly to either utilize the resource centers or eat at the cafeteria.

The new two hundred students—placed at Dewey by chance more than choice—were not equipped for this new level of autonomy, and discipline issues rose significantly. Principal Fried and his teachers "felt suffocated" and realized that all the lessons learned from past accountability measures and rezoning shifts in NYC could not prevent this new state of crisis at John Dewey High School.

Unfortunately, "this was just the first crest" of disarray at John Dewey High School, according to Principal Fried. Many internal and external strains catapulted the school into an unfamiliar and chaotic existence. First, an increase in weapons found within NYC public high schools during that time period resulted in weapons detection teams conducting full-fledged, random weapons scanning at all high schools throughout each school year. On one such day, a weapon was recovered from a student outside John Dewey High School's building. While the gun was unloaded and nonoperating, it was reported by the news media and resulted in more frequent weapons scanning onsite. According to Fried, "this brought out a lot of fears in people. They would say, 'This is not the Dewey that we used to have.'"

John Dewey High School did not find much-needed assistance from the NYCDOE—a problem more fully explored in the next section. As the city shifted to a regionalized school organization model, many staff nearing retirement age left the district, leaving few key decision makers with institutional knowledge and high school–related experience. This lack of expertise came at a very inopportune time for John Dewey High School, a time in which Principal Fried and his teachers would have truly benefited from district assistance. Essentially, the school had to depend on its own resources.

Looking back on the culmination of unfortunate events, Principal Fried explains that "there is nothing that is actually a pin-point event [that led the school into a state of crisis]. It is convoluted and very complex." What was clear, however, was the cynicism so prevalent and disheartening within the school community. The mentality of fear and uncertainty at the high school seemed piercing. Fried laments, "We were always looking over our shoulders."

### CRISIS ANALYSIS

The crisis at John Dewey High School certainly embodies the three core features of a crisis. The upheaval of the school's tradition of teaching and learning certainly struck at the core of the high school's being. The focus on student responsibility for learning and academic rigor both fell prey to the pressures introduced by the new influx of students.

This crisis was the end result of years of complex, mounting consequences from the district's accountability measures and rezoning policies. Principal Fried himself described the crisis's emergence as "convoluted and very complex." The strains and unintended consequences from NYCDOE policies slowly chiseled away at the school's well-being until it rendered it helpless in the fall of 2005. And, when faced with two hundred unexpected students that infamous day, Principal Fried and his teachers were forced into the urgency of crisis decision-making.

The two-dimensional typology previously introduced in chapter 1 illuminates some of the complexity endemic to the nature of any crisis (see figure 1.1, page 11). Recall that the first dimension classifies the "center of gravity" of the crisis. Clearly, the primary source of the crisis at John Dewey High School is the burdensome pressure placed upon the school by the *external* policies of NYCDOE: the small-school conversion initiative and the shift in zoning policies, which created a regionalization of schools and systemwide student choice.

The other dimension of the crisis typology specifies the predictability of a crisis onset, which is less clear at John Dewey High School, as would be expected from a "convoluted and very complex" crisis. Principal Fried compared the onset of the crisis to a "steamroller," because the school's leadership could see the consequences of district policies coming, but they could not prevent those ramifications altogether. John Dewey High School had braced itself for problems, frequently examining academic records and other data on incoming students to become better acquainted with their unique needs. The school, however, was completely blindsided by and unprepared for the influx of two hundred additional students in fall 2005. Despite this element of surprise, these events—in the aggregate—more closely resemble a Predictable crisis.

At John Dewey High School, it is clear that both external and internal factors contributed to the uprising of the crisis and facilitated its stronghold at the school. The NYCDOE district office was devoid of much high school expertise among high-ranking officials, leaving leaders at John Dewey High School to primarily fend for themselves at a time when extra support and guidance would have been invaluable and perhaps provide greater resolve against the district policies that threatened the culture of the school. Additionally, transparent and reciprocal lines of communication between OSEPO and John Dewey High School were lacking, contributing to the utter shock of two hundred additional students in the fall of 2005.

Truly, the relations between NYCDOE and John Dewey High School exemplify the "fragmented, complex, multi-layered educational policy system" described so frequently by scholars.[4] The loose coupling and poor communication between the high school and district office allowed NYCDOE to misunderstand (or remain ignorant of) the reality within which John Dewey High School operated, leaving a great deal of the school's well-being to chance.

Principal Fried admitted that the long-entrenched ideologies of teaching and learning at John Dewey High School made the disruptions to the school's tradition all the more difficult to bear. Teachers who had, for years, embraced the rigor and unique learning opportunities at the high school found it difficult to adapt to the needs and demands forced upon them by the new type of student flooding through the school doors. The diversifying learning needs and societal realities—such as increased incidents of violence—that became more prominent at the school over the years truly overwhelmed many of these adults.

## CRISIS TREATMENT

With the new state of crisis at John Dewey High School, Principal Fried had no choice but to respond to the unfortunate and unfamiliar reality. He sensed the urgency of fear and cynicism inundating his school's culture, particularly among the teaching faculty. Without hesitance, he took numerous steps to counteract the crisis encroaching upon the tradition of excellence, academic rigor, and pride at John Dewey High School. However, Principal Fried soon realized that even the best formulated strategies could not prevent the crisis; rather, he had to assume the role of leading the school through this rocky time instead of around it.

Prior to the disastrous influx of two hundred students in the fall of 2005, Principal Fried was of the mind-set that preparation for the new type of student coming to John Dewey High School would allow the school to partially maintain its tradition of teaching and learning, while simultaneously meeting the needs and demands of new students. This belief was deeply shaken at the start of the 2005–2006 school year, when many at the high school realized that much of John Dewey High School's trademark values and programs would fall victim to the inundation of hundreds of "mismatched" students.

From this crisis emerged three primary issues for Principal Fried to tackle. How to reorganize the school's strategies for teaching? How to uphold the school's good reputation in the community? And, finally, and most challenging, how to mend the mounting culture of cynicism and disbelief now so prevalent at John Dewey High School, especially among his teachers? He realized that getting control of the logistical challenges presented by so many new and unplanned students would begin to address the latter issues of school reputation and cynicism. Principal Fried bluntly states, "It was like triage; what can we do to stop the bleeding?"

First, Principal Fried knew that the school's approach to teaching had to adapt to the new makeup of students. With the staff's consultation, he reorganized the school's long-standing nine-week course schedule for the 2008–2009 school year. As described earlier, coursework at the school was traditionally organized in nine-week cycles. Every nine weeks, students changed courses, and new course offerings were often determined by the learning and teaching interests of students and teachers, respectively. Recognizing that many of the new students needed more structure, Principal Fried decided to couple nine-week courses into "bands" whereby students stayed with the same teacher for the equivalent of a semester term. While the two courses were still treated as distinct, it certainly decreased the amount of free choice present in the old model.

Continuous review of student achievement data—including results from state assessments, placement and diagnostic exams for incoming freshmen, classroom assessments, and student portfolios—revealed that there was now a much greater demand for coursework emphasizing "the basics." This, again, presented Principal Fried with two conflicting realities: many students needed more basic skills, but teachers had always prided themselves in providing enrichment and innovative courses at the school.

He explains that, despite the opposition of many teachers, he "had to take care of the needs of existing students, which compromised some high-end electives." Some students needed a skills-building science class before going immediately into a high-level science course, while many also needed a two-year math basics program to scaffold necessary skills for advanced math concepts. Principal Fried had to increase literacy sections from two to six, which also "chews up [teaching] resources." Essentially, using more teachers for core classes sacrificed the human resources available to instruct advanced coursework and diminished the professional opportunities traditionally enjoyed by many of the teachers.

Other modifications were made at John Dewey High School to meet student needs. Principal Fried recognized that many incoming students required additional interventions to prevent their dropping out. Principal Fried created student-teacher committees and used community-based organizations to steer the more problematic students back on track, while always keeping his primary goal at the forefront of his mind—"how to bring these students more into the traditional Dewey program, while still giving them necessary support."

Doing so was exceptionally difficult. Seeing that many discipline problems resided with freshmen, he cut down on their independent study time because they were not using it constructively. Fried also pulled on teachers to provide extra learning time for this at-risk student population, and he knew he had to encourage the most experienced teachers to do so. As Fried asserts, "We couldn't just put the greenest teacher in front of those challenging students." But those more experienced teachers often put up a great deal of resistance. They were accustomed to more fulfilling professional assignments and were disheartened by the lack of motivation and level of disrespect shown by many of these students.

To cope with these internal strains, Principal Fried had to rely extensively on his own resources and networks, given the lack of high school expertise within the NYCDOE district office. He convened his own meetings with principals from other high schools in the district to gather feedback from his colleagues, discuss strategies to lead John Dewey High School through its difficulties, and further professional learning opportunities for himself.

Principal Fried also sought out professional learning opportunities for his teachers and staff. He sent teachers to professional development sessions and brought in outside experts to provide training on matters such as conflict resolution and classroom management. He convened meetings between teachers and students to open up lines of communication among stakeholders at the school. In fact, he provided numerous opportunities for stakeholder dialogue, including town-hall forums paired with mailings and phone messages to parents. The school also benefited from a scaled-up gang prevention program to assist with students either affiliated with gangs or at risk of affiliation.

All of these strategic moves were an attempt to address the needs of students and bolster teachers' ability to deal with them, but Principal Fried still had an immense challenge of salvaging the school's reputation. This challenge was twofold: he had to maintain a positive image with the media and somehow chip away at the culture of cynicism becoming so ingrained at John Dewey High School.

During these difficult years, Principal Fried found that many disgruntled employees vented their frustrations through the media, as if they had their own personal agenda. There were several instances in which inaccurate stories leaked to the press, and reporters—hungry for a good story—did not bother to check other sources to confirm the stories.

For example, when the scanning team discovered the unloaded, inoperable weapon off-site around the high school, the media simply reported it as a weapon found at John Dewey High School. At these times, Principal Fried found himself primarily engaging in damage control. He did, however, eventually build up good relationships with the local media through proactively showcasing special school events and inviting reporters on-site to view the positive efforts underway at the school.

Perhaps the biggest task was to reverse the extent of the "suffocating" cynicism so abundant at John Dewey High School, especially among teachers. It became very easy for people to play the blame game, "pointing fingers at everyone except themselves," explains Principal Fried. He accepted that it was natural for people to be fearful in uncertain times, but he also knew that those mind-sets had to be healed. In response, Fried faced this obstacle head-on as the school's leader. He states,

> I am the responsible person. I have to answer to everything and I have to lead through example. It is important for staff to see we still have a mission at John Dewey High School. If I lose my composure, what kind of example do I set?

Principal Fried firmly believes that the school, and in particular the adults in the school, have one of two choices as they move forward: "We can wallow in the crisis or we can move forward and fight the same common cause." Fried has chosen the latter and intends to lead that charge through his own example and action. What has made this increasingly difficult has been the fragile state within which the high school continues to exist. Each time Principal Fried feels as if the school is making progress, another glitch arises and the strength of the crisis rears its head again. He states,

> As we started to move forward, it just took one incident—a small or large one—to undermine everything. Everything was fragile. It kept taking the wind out of us.

One recent "glitch" was a lockdown in the school during the spring of 2008. A weapon was reported by a student to a teacher, and within ten minutes, the entire building was locked down. While it was not implemented perfectly, everyone was safe and the school was even given a nod of appreciation from the local New York police department. Of course, some just took this as another sign of problems plaguing John Dewey High School, but Principal Fried views it as a glimmer of hope and evidence of the resilience taking shape at the school.

## CONCLUSION

As John Dewey High School moves forward, Principal Fried acknowledges that the state of crisis is certainly not behind them. In fact, when asked at what stage of the crisis the school is in, he explains the following:

> We're sitting on the hump. We should have enough impetus to move us forward. There are always detractors, and it's a matter of fending them off and getting people to ride with us in the right direction. In order to move forward, we have to at least fight the same battle; that in itself is a challenge.

The school remains in a very fragile state as it still learns to cope with the new reality of its existence. Principal Fried attests that OSEPO and John Dewey High School are finding a slightly better equilibrium, as OSEPO has begun to understand that student placement decisions must take into consideration schools' cultures.

This is not to say that the concerns are resolved; rather, many of the student challenges persist, employee and community faith in the school remain shaky, but the school community—and particularly its leader, Principal Fried—continue to fight for the survival of John Dewey High School. Principal Fried compares the next steps as being "like a game of pick-up sticks. Very gingerly, you have to maneuver." Through it all, he diligently maintains his resolve and continues to find the right balance between meeting the new needs of students and maintaining the integrity of the school's program as much as possible. Perhaps his biggest remaining challenge is bestowing his teachers with that same determination.

To carry his school over this hump, Principal Fried believes that "first and foremost, there needs to be a reestablishment of trust because, in a crisis, that is one of the foundation blocks that is shaken." Students need to be reminded that the teachers and school leaders are there for them, and parents need to be reassured that the school is a safe and positive learning environment for their children. Teachers need to keep working together and accept that it takes time to heal, but they must continue the fight. And, new strategies and resources for teaching and learning need to be continuously evaluated to examine their efficacy and productivity.

Principal Fried holds the responsibility of creating a culture of mutual respect in which the school's stakeholders continue to learn from one another.

He needs to create a sense of empowerment among his teachers, students, and the greater community in order to move the school back to its long-standing tradition of excellence and passion for learning. As he explains, in a time of crisis a leader need not be reactionary but should gather information and work with people.

I need to be composed and collected at all times—at least publicly. When you gauge a leader, it's how they respond to a crisis. Followers take that lead from me.

—*Barry Fried, principal of John Dewey High School*

## REFLECTIVE QUESTIONS

### Reflection on the Reading

1. One of the trademarks of John Dewey High School was its unique culture of student learning. However, it was this culture that made adaptation to new district policy so challenging. Do you believe that building such a unique culture is worthwhile given the potential for those challenging side effects?

2. Principal Fried made numerous efforts to modify teaching and curricular programs to the needs of the new students as an immediate response to the crisis. Do you believe this was the right choice, or should he—and the teaching staff—have required more adaptation by the new students to fit into the school's existing culture of learning?

### Application to Theory

3. The authors categorize the crisis at John Dewey High School as being an External-Predictable crisis, but they recognize that the influx of two hundred students in 2005 had an element of unpredictability due to strained communication lines between the high school and district office, particularly OSEPO (in charge of student placement decisions). Do you think Principal Fried could have done anything differently to improve those communication lines prior to the onset of two hundred unannounced students in 2005?

4. The model of crisis leadership discussed in chapter 1 explains how critical a strong school culture is as a primary prevention to the onset of crises.

However, in this case study, the strength of the school culture at John Dewey became an obstacle to overcome. How do you account for that apparent oddity?

## Application on the Job

5. How would you react to a large influx of unexpected and/or ill-suited students at your school? What resources would you rely on to meet these students' needs? What priorities would you set?
6. How would you go about gathering resources to aid in reforming your school's instructional program, assuming you had limited resources from your district office?
7. How would you bolster the morale and commitment of families, students, and teachers at a school inundated by cynicism and tentative about the school's future success?
8. Have you built relationships with local media so that they report on the many good things that occur at your school?

# Six Principles for Leading Schools During Crisis

This book illustrates the danger and opportunity inherent in crises through the investigation of twelve school leaders. Applying their experiences to current, research-based theories of crisis management, this book explored what, specifically, is a *school* crisis, and how it differs from crises in other structures and environments. Specifically, we wondered how does a *school* crisis emerge? How are leaders involved in various stages of its evolution? What contextual factors contribute to the onset and impact of a school crisis? Finally—and perhaps most fundamentally—how should a school leader identify and respond to a crisis? Chapter 1 developed a theory on the life cycle of crises in schools and the ways in which leaders need to be engaged during their evolution. The twelve case studies then allowed for the application of this theory to school leadership during crisis.

At the nexus of crisis management theory and the experiences of our profiled principals are broad lessons applicable to current school leaders. Supplementing this concluding chapter (which attempts to distill these lessons) is an "appendix/self-audit," providing leaders the opportunity to evaluate how prepared their schools are to handle crisis experiences.

## REVISITING CRISES IN SCHOOLS

Returning to chapter 1, we suggest that a school crisis is distinguishable by several common features. First, it is an event—or series of events—threatening a school's core functions or foundational practices. While some school leaders will characterize every *problem* as a *crisis* (ranging perhaps, from a losing football season to resignation of a popular teacher), few such events will meet this definition.

Instead, a crisis is more than a significant challenge or problem—it is an event that endangers a school's ability to serve its primary purpose: the delivery of effective teaching and learning. Some crises, such as the attack of September 11 or the devastating storms of Hurricane Katrina, occur suddenly, without warning. Others evolve more incrementally, such as "punitive" accountability measures, shifting student needs, or a debilitating education bureaucracy highly resistant to a school's needs. Regardless of whether its onset is evolutionary or immediate, regardless of whether it results from choices or omissions by school leaders, crises share the commonality that they threaten the ability of the school to viably continue the status quo.

The experiences of the school leaders detailed in the previous twelve chapters readily demonstrate that crises are as unique as the schools in which they occur. Perhaps the only universal aspect of crises across school contexts is the significant consequences of failing to address one. Although it may initially seem to be an academic exercise, successful crisis management requires a leader to identify the origin of the *true* crisis to tailor his or her response accordingly; otherwise, that leader's response may only address a symptom of the crisis.

While each school leader in this book faced a crisis presenting an obvious (but distinct) threat, crises can be grouped along two axes, based on the center of gravity of each crisis (whether its genesis was primarily one of forces internal or external to the school community) and how well its onset could be anticipated (i.e., how predictable it was). The crisis in Bailey, Colorado—a drifter's seemingly random selection of a classroom to hold hostage—defied forecasting (Unpredictable crisis). By contrast, in Chicago, Dr. Sallie Pinkston could predict that reforms would exacerbate a teacher retention problem (Predictable crisis).

Along the theory's other axis, the staff at H.W. Smith were challenged by an immigrant group internal to the school community (Internal crisis), while the pupil assignment modifications that swamped John Dewey High

School originated in district policy, external to the school community (External crisis).

Below is table 1.2, replicated from page 10 in order to review how each of the twelve school crises falls within this two-dimensional typology (i.e., external or internal source; predictable or unpredictable in its origin). The selected cases reflect more External than Internal crises, and more Predictable than Unpredictable crises. Perhaps this is appropriate given the environment within which schools exist—the school environment is highly regulated, organizationally interdependent, and positioned in a complex web of external factors and stakeholders (e.g., federal, state, and district policy; community needs; economic and other market forces).[1] As most school leaders can attest, schools are organizationally designed to manage processes and systemic functions. External threats to these processes are more likely to escalate beyond a principal's ability to contain consequences, thereby erupting into a crisis. Even if the threat is predictable, the bureaucracy of education does not readily enable a rapid response to unique school-level needs.

Through the study of these twelve case studies, we identified the most effective crisis responses. We now suggest a core set of dispositions and actions that all school leaders should strive to develop in order to recognize, manage, and resolve a pending crisis.

**Table 1.2. Twelve Case Studies: Leading Schools During Crisis**

|  | PREDICTABLE | UNPREDICTABLE |
|---|---|---|
| **INTERNAL** | *Internal-Predictable Crises*<br><br>Chapter 7: Permanent Teacher Turnover | *Internal-Unpredictable Crises*<br><br>Chapter 5: Systemic Grade Fraud<br>Chapter 6: Challenges of an ELL Population |
| **EXTERNAL** | *External-Predictable Crises*<br><br>Chapter 8: Accountability (NCLB)<br>Chapter 9: Demographic Transition<br>Chapter 10: Charter School Start-Up<br>Chapter 11: Charter School Finances<br>Chapter 12: Elementary School Zoning Changes<br>Chapter 13: High School Zoning Changes | *External-Unpredictable Crises*<br><br>Chapter 2: School at Ground Zero, 9/11<br>Chapter 3: High School after Hurricane Katrina<br>Chapter 4: School Violence |

## PRINCIPLES FOR SCHOOL LEADERS IN TIMES OF CRISIS

It is apparent from the previous twelve chapters that there are few commonalities in the manifestation of school crisis—both the effects and duration of the crisis are highly dependent upon the source of the crisis and the context in which it occurs. Consider the experience of Bryan Krause at Platte Canyon High School, whose crisis incident (school invasion and shooting) was over in a single day. Contrast that with the experience of Barry Fried at John Dewey High School, who continues to struggle with the district's ad hoc and unpredictable zoning procedures three years after his crisis's origin. A similar comparison could be made between virtually every other crisis in the book.

However, in analyzing the responses of these school leaders, commonalities clearly emerge when detailing effective responses to crises. For example, both Krause and Fried—as different as their crises were—used transparent communication with stakeholders as an integral component of their crisis response. Similar patterns emerge across other case studies, and these can be summarized in the following six principles, described in more depth throughout this chapter:

Principle 1: Respond to a Crisis Before It Becomes One

Principle 2: Identify Truly Immediate Priorities

Principle 3: Let Time, Efforts, and Resources Flow in Proportion to Your Prioritization

Principle 4: Communicate, Communicate, Communicate

Principle 5: Be Flexible

Principle 6: Do Not Personally Succumb to the Crisis

### Principle 1: Respond to a Crisis Before It Becomes One

Edward Devlin, a disaster recovery planning consultant, observes that "preventing a crisis is the least costly and the simplest way to control [one]."[2] While such advice may seem obvious and simplistic, it is, in fact, anything but. As has been noted across crises in this work, crises are frequently born out of unclear circumstances and can appear to be immediate in their onset. Many times, however, the source of the crisis has been immediately below the surface, visible to a discerning eye. While Unpredictable crises are, by their very definition, difficult to anticipate, even Predictable crises—such as threatened restructuring of a low-performing school—contain significant ambiguity.

The crisis responses detailed in this book repeatedly demonstrate that a cohesive school culture committed to continuation and recovery greatly contributes to a school surviving a crisis. Schools—as highly regulated and regimented organizations—are challenged by unpredictable inputs. However, where leaders have built trusting relationships and resilient cultures prior to the crisis, a school's response will be more flexible and it will recover from a crisis more quickly. Additionally, as Marco Franco of Sobrante Park Elementary School would readily attest, these relationships are only beneficial if they have been built *prior* to a crisis occurring—the middle of a crisis is a difficult time to build trust and instill resiliency.

Principal Switzer at NYC Public School 234 summarizes this reality in observing, "You can only be the school on the day of the crisis that you were the day before the crisis." She elaborates that the collaborative nature of professional work within the school, the ability of stakeholders to communicate with one another, and the mutual respect that school community members held for one another were essential elements in her school's ability to overcome the devastating effects of September 11. These strengths facilitated quick and cohesive action in the immediate moments of the terror attack and allowed for the continuation of the school's identity in the midst of the chaotic rebuilding of NYC's public school system.

Similarly, H.W. Smith's long history of successfully absorbing immigrant groups into the Syracuse school system created a strong culture of support and acceptance that is assisting the school as it struggles with the challenging Bantu ethnic group. Building a supportive culture was a priority for Principal Eugene following Hurricane Katrina, as she realized the importance it would play for retaining high-quality teachers during a truly unstable time in the life of G.W. Carver High School.

In all of these examples, a strong, collegial culture committed to school sustainability was a critical point during the crisis onset and responses. Conversely, the dysfunctional culture ingrained in Greenacre High School allowed unethical grade fabrication practices to persist despite repeated and systemic attempts to change the school's culture. This negative culture eventually threatened the integrity of the district's many other accomplishments, creating a crisis when brought to light. This subculture at Greenacre High School grew to involve approximately one-quarter of the high school's teachers and essentially precluded the school from developing a counter-culture focusing on student achievement and true academic gains. If, as Principal Price observes, a school's culture is a reflection of the school's principal, then it is inescapable that Principal Roberts bears considerable responsibility for continuing Greenacre's culture—and, as a result, its vulnerability to crisis.

**Principle 2: Identify Truly Immediate Priorities**

The second common lesson from the experiences of our twelve school leaders is that, in the immediate moments of a crisis, a leader is faced with a multiplicity of demands and concerns, all of which seem urgent and compelling. In order to develop an effective and strategic response, a school leader must first identify *the most immediate priorities*, and then distinguish how they can be accomplished through short-term objectives and long-term goals. A principal can, as a start, identify Maslowian necessities, such as ensuring the physical and emotional safety of community members.

For example, when faced with the physical threat of an armed intruder in a classroom, the initial response of Principal Krause at Platte Canyon High School was to order a school lockdown, limiting the intruder's threat to the larger school community. Krause subsequently turned his attention to the students in the classroom with the gunman. In Unpredictable crises—which Platte Canyon exemplifies—these short-term goals function most effectively when they are established prior to the onset of crisis. Krause knew precisely what to do when a student reported seeing a "stranger with a gun" in one of his classrooms, and it resulted in the rapid response to which evaluating authorities attribute containment of the crisis's impact.

As Principals Krause, Switzer, and Eugene observe, the onset of an Unpredictable crisis—whether a school shooting, terrorist attack, or weather catastrophe—does not provide much time for reflective thought. These sorts of crises benefit from disaster preparedness training prior to the crisis event, allowing the school leader and community to focus on execution, not scrambling.

In Predictable crises, school leaders have the luxury of more reflective thought. The unfortunate trade-off is that Predictable crises are typically more complex and less obviously compelling to affected stakeholders, requiring incremental action, evaluation, and response to achieve long-term goals. This does not mean that the principal should focus any less on identifying and addressing immediate priorities—only that it becomes more challenging. At Woodland Elementary School, after learning that the school would lose 95 percent of its supportive parents and half its teachers, Noris Price immediately focused on reframing the devastating news of restructuring into a positive opportunity for change. As Price noted, if stakeholders dwelled on the "bad" news, it would become dynamic and the situation might have quickly become irretrievable.

Almost immediately after the district's decision on rezoning was announced, Dr. Price forecast potential problems and tailored her response to minimizing the threat of the crisis on the emotional well-being of her community. Within the same week of the rezoning decision, Dr. Price redirected faculty and parent groups toward work on the "new" Woodland. By keeping them focused on long-term goals, she not only addressed the short-term objective of avoiding a demoralized community, but she also fostered buy-in for long-term recovery. Price's practice of establishing benchmarks for "short-term wins" and celebrating early successes toward a longer-term goal is a research-validated staple of transformational leadership and organizational change.[3]

It is equally apparent that responding to immediate priorities cannot guarantee long-term success if it does not address the root cause of the crisis (as opposed to its symptoms) or if it derails support for long-term goals. Principal Pinkston at Chicago's Johnson Elementary ultimately wanted to address the chronic turnover of teachers and end the resulting poor student performance at her school, but she recognized that she could not "come in and [make] . . . drastic changes right away." Instead, Principal Pinkston initially embarked on incremental change, a practice validated in leadership theory.[4] She used her first years to incorporate small-scale initiatives to essentially identify the strong teachers and lay the groundwork for a renewed school culture before implementing stronger measures in subsequent years.

Similarly, the primary dilemma for Franklin Career Academy was the lack of long-term guaranteed funding. Principal Grimm did find resourceful ways to extend short-term funding streams—such as with his federal charter school grant—but ultimately could not resolve the core crisis of securing a steady, long-term funding stream for the school's ongoing operation. Forecasting that it would be virtually impossible to resolve the long-range problem of sustainable funding for the charter school, Grimm and the other directors made the reluctant decision that the school could no longer continue operations.

### Principle 3: Let Time, Efforts, and Resources Flow in Proportion to Your Prioritization

After identifying priorities in a time of crisis and the short-term objectives and long-term goals for attaining them, a leader must focus time, effort, and resources appropriately toward achieving those goals. As the economist Charles Benson observed, the scarcest resource in a school is time—and this is particularly true during a crisis.[5] Virtually every choice a leader makes comes at the expense of something else, and while appropriate prioritization may seem obvious in hindsight, times of crisis are filled with distractions and conflicting demands from multiple stakeholders. This is particularly true in the field of education, which contains a high level of interpersonal interdependencies in daily operation.[6]

Reflecting on data suggesting that discipline was distracting teachers from instruction at G.W. Carver High School, Principal Eugene and her assistant principal assumed more discipline responsibilities—even issues that would normally be handled within the classroom. Although some critics would assume that more responsibility should have been left to teachers, the dynamics of her teaching staff and instructional needs of students suggested another course should be taken. By strategically focusing the administration on discipline, it freed teachers to address instruction and demonstrated administrative support for a key area of teacher concern.

Jeremy Kane, founder of LEAD Academy, admitted that, in hindsight, he wished he had selected his battles more diplomatically rather than overextending himself. Primarily, he realized that not all conflicts with the school board or district administration were paramount to accomplishing his end goal. Perhaps, taking on peripheral battles did more to exacerbate existing tensions more than necessary.

Leaders should also monitor the allocation of time, effort, and resources expended, ensuring that these resources could not be better spent on another facet of the crisis. In doing so, leaders may wish to make use of data and evidence whenever possible. Crises are notoriously a time of high emotion and waning clear-headed reflection, so objective evidence becomes even more important to guide decision-making. Data-driven decisions enable a leader to validate the need for a particular crisis response, monitor its effectiveness, and determine a better course of action if a response is not accomplishing its intended goals. Essentially, using tangible evidence makes the case for a crisis response—and all the time, effort, and resources it demands—stronger. It also eases the implementation of a crisis response by bolstering stakeholder buy-in during a transitional time in the life of a school.[7]

For example, the continuous review of student achievement data—including results from state assessments, placement and diagnostic exams, classroom assessments, and student portfolios—revealed that there was a much greater demand for coursework emphasizing "the basics" at John Dewey High School following the unplanned mass influx of students. Despite the opposition of many teachers, he explained, "I had to take care of the needs of existing students, which compromised some high-end electives." He was only able to convince teachers of this reality—who believed a revised curriculum was unnecessary—through a detailed presentation of these data.

### Principle 4: Communicate, Communicate, Communicate

Numerous school leaders attributed success in crisis to the frequent and strategic communication in which they engaged with a broad base of stakeholders, as it facilitated priority-setting, evidence-gathering to devise and monitor a crisis response, and consensus-building among stakeholders in urgent times. Frequent and strategic communication also provides leaders with tools that are particularly advantageous in times of crisis.

First, it allows leaders to maintain quality control over the flow of information within and outside a school. This type of control is paramount in urgent times when deciphering rumors from reality can become exceedingly difficult and essential for the survival of a school community. Superintendent Richardson was very candid in sharing information about the grade-changing incidents in Greenacre. As soon as she had evidence to support her assertions, she communicated honestly and quickly with the public. She simultaneously explained the isolated breaches and reassured the community of the integrity of other district accomplishments. In this manner, she was able to prevent the spreading of exaggerated stories and uphold the district's overall reputation.

Frequent and strategic communication with a broad base of stakeholders also gives a leader the opportunity to communicate why a crisis response is necessary. Stakeholders are more likely to cooperate if they understand the rationale for particular parameters. Principal Franco provides two examples. First, he tried to ensure that his school community understood why he was embarking on reform efforts at Sobrante Park Elementary. As he said, "The key to doing that [suspending the school's bilingual program] successfully was that the audience must understand the reason for the change . . . if they don't see why you are doing this, it's hard to convince people." Second, he discussed the accountability process bluntly, saying "the answer is with us," as he gauged teachers' commitment to the reform effort.

During crisis events, stakeholders are frequently suspicious of information they receive, and they often question whether the individual conveying the message has a "hidden agenda." This makes it important for leaders to ensure that their messages are—or appear—objective, and, when possible, they use trusted external sources. In Greenacre, Dr. Richardson immediately knew that the public would mistrust the high school's standardized test scores after the discovery of school-level grade fraud. Consequently, she self-reported the district to its state department of education, immediately triggering the same audit to which the school would have been subjected if reported by a third party. As a result, she quickly (1) discovered that the school's standardized testing data was sound and (2) conveyed to stakeholders that "[she] was not trying to hide something."

Finally, school leaders can stay apprised of political agendas by engaging in frequent communication with a broad base of stakeholders. Jeremy Kane built a diverse and broad communication network in the Nashville community in order to gauge strengths and weaknesses and garner support for his embryonic school. By nurturing this network—which spanned from the poor of West Nashville to the power-wielding business community—he better understood the needs of West Nashville, the dynamics of the school board, and the potential roadblocks from district administration.

### Principle 5: Be Flexible

Leading a school through a time of crisis requires not only particular actions, but embracing certain leadership dispositions. Virtually every school leader featured in this book revealed the importance of being flexible and resourceful in a crisis response. As Napoleon Bonaparte famously remarked, "No plan outlasts contact with the enemy," and even the best-laid plans of school leaders are likely to fragment during crisis. Even in a model school invasion response like Platte Canyon, with responses annually practiced and excellent communication and relationships with local law enforcement, neither the school nor law enforcement authorities predicted that parents—upon learning that there was a school shooting—would immediately drive to the school, clogging the two-lane dirt road used for school evacuation and having to, in some instances, be forcibly removed by emergency responders.

Resourcefulness and flexibility require thinking outside the box, being a good and clear-headed learner, and willfully assuming the tedious work that accompanies a crisis response. In critical times leaders are expected to do much with very little. It becomes necessary to think strategically, use creative means to secure resources, and rely on nontraditional people to fulfill nontraditional roles.

Principal Sutton and Mr. Nicotera used creative strategies to enhance the fiscal resources available to Manual High School. By leading a campaign to sign eligible students up for federally subsidized lunch, Mr. Nicotera secured a Title 1 school designation and additional district funds for the high school. In the moments following the terror attack at the World Trade Center, Principal Switzer immediately drew on committed school community members to fulfill exceptional roles in exceptional circumstances. The school's secretary pulled together makeshift emergency cards to find ways of contacting children's parents, while the school's occupational therapist took charge of tracking the outflow of students during the frenzied evacuation from the school building.

Being resourceful requires, quite simply, hard work. It is very unlikely a leader will successfully handle a crisis without a great deal of personal sacrifice. Principal Eugene lacked many basic tools upon the reopening of G.W. Carver High School, including a computerized class scheduling system and transcripts for many incoming students. Despite this, she proceeded to create student class schedules by hand. Additionally, she and her staff tracked down students' cumulative records from around the nation to ensure each student would receive necessary coursework for graduation.

In Greenacre High School, upon suspecting grade fraud by high school teachers, Dr. Richardson hand-checked the grades of all students in elementary, middle, and high schools. While tedious, this allowed her to understand the scope of the unethical practice and devise a targeted response. Finally, Jeremy Kane built a broad base of West Nashville supporters only by knocking on hundreds of doors and talking to hundreds of prospective parents.

Many leaders acknowledged the paradox that a school community had to work together in crisis recovery but ultimate responsibility for the school's fate fell on their own shoulders, and they did not shy away from this challenge. Principal Birnkrant observed, "The moment they walk into this building until the moment they leave, they're our kids." Leadership during crisis requires the correct combination of this high level of commitment, the ability to act upon this commitment (even through tasks that require a hard slog), and the flexibility to constantly respond to the conditions of the crisis.

### Principle 6: Do Not Personally Succumb to the Crisis

One of the most fundamental lessons from the principals studied in the book was the tremendous personal toll of the crisis. Many school leaders featured in this book—and particularly those in Predictable crises—willingly accepted the challenge of leading during crisis, knowing full well the personal sacrifice required. As Jeremy Kane put it, "No one's going to trust you until you have [your own] skin in the game." Similarly, Dr. Pinkston welcomed the principalship at Johnson Elementary, a school plagued by poor teaching and low student performance; Dr. Eugene knowingly returned to New Orleans to assume a hands-on role in the public schools' recovery from Hurricane Katrina.

Dr. Richardson noted that she repeatedly quoted Rudyard Kipling's poem *If*, and most particularly, "if you can keep your head when all about are losing theirs and blaming you." Dr. Pinkston led Johnson Elementary through two tumultuous years before compiling a suitable staff at Johnson Elementary. Bill Grimm ultimately resigned from his job as a broker when Franklin Career Academy could not afford to pay a principal's salary and assumed that job himself. "It was not exactly a financially lucrative move," he notes, laughing. Additionally, Grimm's home became the center of FCA's advocacy center, culminating in an inability for either Grimm or his wife—who assisted him—to "escape" from FCA.

Despite the personal toll of crises, it is imperative that leaders remain sufficiently detached to make rational decisions for the school. Principal Fried understood that a leader cannot personally succumb to the crisis, regardless of how personally demanding it is. "I need to be composed and collected at all times . . . when you gauge a leader, it's how they respond to a crisis. Followers take the lead from me." He held himself responsible for creating a culture at John Dewey High School that would persist despite the strains forced down upon them by the district's student placement policies and the closure of a neighboring school.

The crises profiled in this book personally impacted school leaders to varying degrees. Some principals were in extreme physical danger, a few had long careers ended, and others utilized the momentum of the successful resolution of their crisis to propel them toward greater opportunities. Each crisis, however, impacted leaders through differential physical and psychological stress. Beyond possible physical threats, the mental shadow from the ill-fated and stressful circumstances profiled in the case studies had a lasting impact on these educational leaders.

The authors attempted to probe the personal relationships and structures on which these leaders depended during their crises. Answers were as one would expect, with principals leaning on trusted staff members, family members, church, and close friends. The important commonality, however, is that these leaders had a support system to whom they could turn during rough times, and they had the self-awareness to know the limits of their caretaking ability. Burnout is endemic in most leadership positions, and there is no more crucial time to be wary of burnout than when the pressures are highest. An important aspect of leadership during crisis, then, is the self-awareness to know when you—the leader—need to remove yourself to regain energy and perspective.

This chapter now briefly turns to an examination of leadership principles that were primarily evident in specific types of crisis. First is an investigation into lessons learned that emerged predominantly in Internal rather than External crises. The chapter then turns to the wide-ranging lessons of Predictable and Unpredictable crises.

## PRINCIPLES FOR SCHOOL LEADERS IN INTERNAL OR EXTERNAL CRISES

In an Internal crisis, a school leader generally can anticipate the unintended consequences of a crisis response. This is more feasible than in an External crisis because school leaders are generally familiar with the dynamics of their schools and can better anticipate the impact of a crisis. For example, Dr. Pinkston knew that teacher attrition would be part of her long-term change effort at Johnson Elementary. Rather than seeing a short-term spike in turn-over as a sign of failure, she realized that it was simply a necessary step in discerning which teachers were willing to buy into her vision and which were not.

Leaders can also take the opportunity during an Internal crisis to prepare community members by explaining the expected bumps along the way and making clear that they are not a sign of failure, but simply part of the expected process. This can be comforting for a school community, particularly one facing an Internal-Unpredictable crisis, because it adds an element of certainty in quite uncertain times. For example, Principal Birnkrant keeps her staff constantly apprised of the current efforts of assimilating the Bantu community into H.W. Smith. Through regular staff meetings and communication with the local refugee center, they were able to brace themselves for the challenging road ahead.

In External crises, leaders spent more time explicitly addressing the crisis's long-term psychological impact on the school community. While the emotional well-being of stakeholders should be a priority for all leaders during any type of crisis, it is a particularly important issue in External crises because school stakeholders are more likely to perceive a lack of control over their situation. That is, their locus of control shifts, and their sense of security is shaken, as they become vulnerable to forces beyond their power.[8]

This need for psychological healing was particularly evident in External-Unpredictable crises—such as the events of September 11, Hurricane Katrina, and the shooting at Platte Canyon High School—when the onset of the crisis was entirely out of the school's control. In a more nuanced way, the experiences of John Dewey and Manual High Schools show similar threats to comfort, as district decisions—outside the school's immediate control—significantly impacted its culture.

## PRINCIPLES FOR SCHOOL LEADERS IN PREDICTABLE OR UNPREDICTABLE CRISES

In Predictable crises, a leader can minimize the extent to which a school's well-being is left to chance. While anticipating a crisis does not guarantee that its onset will be avoidable (indeed, this book argues very much to the contrary), it does grant a leader better preparation for the crisis response. For several years before fall 2005, John Dewey High School had been adapting its instructional strategies in response to the district's student placement policies. While the influx of two hundred unplanned students in the fall of 2005 heightened the sense of crisis for his staff, Principal Fried's prior efforts made the unfortunate situation less damaging. Similarly, through diligent planning and strategic networking, Jeremy Kane maintained the fate of LEAD Academy in his grips rather than leaving it in the hands of district administrators.

School leaders may also recognize that some district policies and expectations were often unsuited to address an Unpredictable crisis. School policies are developed to respond to problems, not crises, and existing school structures are often weighted in favor of "conservatism and inertia."[9] While many rules are not conventionally made with crisis-level circumstances in mind, school leaders had to be judicious and strategic in choosing which ones to break in an Unpredictable crisis. Ultimately, few principals allowed district or school policy to constrain their crisis response when the two conflicted.

Principal Birnkrant found that the policies governing students' grade placement at H.W. Smith did not align well with the school's need to serve immigrant students. She candidly explained, "We often find that we can't do what's best for kids because it doesn't fit the neat little chart." And during the turmoil of September 11, Principal Switzer willingly ignored the standard protocol for student pickup. "We broke all the rules—you have to think out of the box—there is no 'box.'" The very nature of Unpredictable crises means that leaders may need to blaze new trails and not simply rely on policies that are suited for less exceptional times.

## THE OPPORTUNITY IN SCHOOL CRISES

The emerging principles for leading schools during crisis put forth in this book provide current and forthcoming school leaders with a framework to fortify their own school's ability to prepare for and overcome a crisis. Overall, the stories of the twelve principals profiled offer insight for leaders to face in all types of crises, from those that seem completely out of their control (e.g., External-Unpredictable) to those that present greater opportunity for preparation and management (e.g., Internal-Predictable).

Perhaps the most poignant and promising lesson from all the crises featured in this book is that crises can be utilized as an impetus for much-needed change. It provides the sense of urgency necessary for organizational trans-formation.[10] Numerous school leaders—such as Principal Franco, Principal Fried, Principal Pinkston, and Principal Price—found hope in their dire situations by reframing their crisis as an opportunity for fundamental school improvement. This is perhaps the biggest lesson for successful school recovery: a leader can transform a school's fate by using crisis as the stimulus for a fresh start.

Such a step can be exceedingly difficult—but perhaps all the more important, given the education system's notorious resistance to change. Both Franklin Career Academy and Manual High School ultimately lost their fight against a system that was not amenable to their unique needs. John Dewey High School and H.W. Smith continue to struggle against the forces that threaten the unique culture of their schools. Hope can be found, however, in the telling of these stories transparently. The goal of this book then is to help pave the way for others facing crises to minimize damage and improve their chances of recovery.

# Appendix/Self-Audit
## A School Crisis Inventory

This book opens with a theoretical overview of existing crisis literature from a business and management perspective and then applies it to the context of K–12 American education. We then profile the onset of, leadership through, and recovery from crisis in twelve case studies. The book closes with a concluding chapter that integrates the theoretical and the practical into six key principles to be utilized by current and aspiring school leaders.

This appendix has a similar purpose as the reflective questions that close each case study in that it provides a more participatory experience for the reader; this exercise requires an investigation into your specific school's circumstances and the extent to which you are prepared to face crisis. We hope this inventory will assist you in both identifying and preparing for the most likely threats to the core mission of your school.

Our intent is that you utilize the appendix in collaboration with other members of your leadership team and school community. The following pages of this exercise are formatted so that you may photocopy the tables, allowing you and your staff to first complete the exercise independently before sharing as a group.* By comparing answers, you will either validate the perceived level of crisis preparation or create discussion to resolve disparities among your staff.

---

*It is the hope of the authors that school leaders utilize this appendix with their leadership teams, which may require you to make photocopies of it. Using fewer than five photocopies within your school appears to be consistent with the "fair use" provision of United States and International Copyright Law. We designed this appendix to be utilized among school leadership teams, and we encourage you to do so as long as no large-scale (greater than five) photocopying of this appendix occurs.

The exercise is split into the following six stages:

1. Defining the core values and foundational practices of your school
2. Identifying your vulnerabilities: Internal-Predictable crises
3. Identifying your vulnerabilities: External-Predictable crises
4. Planning for Internal-Predictable crises
5. Planning for External-Predictable crises
6. General school preparation for Unpredictable crises

### STEP 1: IDENTIFYING YOUR SCHOOL'S CORE VALUES AND FOUNDATIONAL PRACTICES

In order to meet the definition of crisis proposed in this book, a situation must threaten the foundational practices and core values of a school community. What are your school's core values? How would you describe your school's foundational practices? There are certainly values and practices shared by many schools; however, there are also qualities unique to each school's culture. The leader of one school may believe that a particularly close community is what makes his school unique, while a comprehensive high school might be particularly proud of its dual-enrollment program.

A school's core values make up the belief system that underlies the actions of school staff. Values are the primary assumption most stakeholders operate under. They can be unspoken or explicit and may be positive or negative. Some schools hold a core value of maintaining the status quo, even at the expense of student achievement. Readers may prefer to think of core values as the set of adjectives that best describe the essence of the school. A core value is valid only if the majority of the school's stakeholders would agree with its inclusion.

*List or describe your school's core values below.*

_____

_____

_____

_____

_____

_____

_____

A school's foundational practices are the structures and routines that allow the school to implement its core values. They may be common planning time among teachers, a high-quality induction program, or looping. What foundational practices do you have in place that allow your school to implement its core values?

*List or describe your school's foundational practices below.*

_____

_____

_____

_____

_____

_____

_____

_____

_____

### STEP 2: IDENTIFYING YOUR VULNERABILITIES: INTERNAL-PREDICTABLE CRISES

Now that you have identified your school community's core values and foundational practices, the second step is to identify the crises that will most likely threaten them. Use table A.1 to identify the *Internal* crises that might threaten your school. The right-hand column allows you to rate the likelihood of this crisis's occurring on a scale of 1 to 5. An example is provided for you. Remember that an Internal-Predictable crisis has its "center of gravity" within the immediate school community—said in another way, Internal crises arise from forces under a school leader's direct control.

The following questions, while not exhaustive, may help you brainstorm what internal threats your school faces.

- Does your school suffer from persistently low achievement? If calculated, does your school score low on value-added measures?
- Is there an agreed-upon system for evaluating staff performance? Is it utilized on a regular basis?
- Are there ways for teacher/parent/student concerns to be picked up on quickly by the administration?

- Does your faculty work cooperatively and collaboratively? Is there a relationship of mutual respect and trust between the faculty and administration?
- Is a high percentage of your faculty ready for retirement? Does the majority of your faculty primarily comprise new teachers with fewer than three years of experience? Is faculty turnover a threat to your school?
- Do any faculty members exhibit unstable behaviors? Do any show an inappropriate familiarity with students?
- Have any of your students shown a tendency toward—or propensity for— abnormal or excessive violence?
- Are the finances of the school and supporting organizations (PTA, for example) audited or under the control of more than one person?
- Are student grades and other graduation indicators audited or under the control of more than one person?

**Table A.1.  Internal Crises**

| Internal Threats | Probability Ranking* |
|---|---|
| Example: Grade-fixing by a teacher or counselor | 2 |
| #1 | |
| | |
| | |
| | |
| | |
| | |
| | |
| | |
| | |
| | |
| | |
| | |
| | |
| | |
| | |

*Probability Ranking: 1 = highly unlikely, 2 = somewhat unlikely, 3 = possible, 4 = likely, 5 = highly likely

### STEP 3: IDENTIFYING YOUR VULNERABILITIES: EXTERNAL-PREDICTABLE CRISES

Use table A.2 to identify the *External* crises that could threaten your school. The right-hand column allows you to rate the likelihood of the occurrence of this crisis on a scale of 1 to 5. An example is provided for you. Remember that an *External* crisis has its "center of gravity" outside the immediate school community—said in another way, External crises arise from forces not under a school leader's direct control.

The following questions may help you brainstorm what external threats your school faces; again, this list is not intended to be exhaustive.

- Does your school have a powerful and/or informed advocate within the district office or school board?
- Does the contract between the school board and the teachers' union expire in the near future?

Table A.2.  External Crises

| External Threats | Probability Ranking* |
| --- | --- |
| Example: Student reassignment plan to be implemented next year which will significantly modify my zoning area | 5 |
| #1 | |
| | |
| | |
| | |
| | |
| | |
| | |
| | |
| | |
| | |
| | |
| | |

*Probability Ranking: 1 = highly unlikely, 2 = somewhat unlikely, 3 = possible, 4 = likely, 5 = highly likely

- Is your school labeled as High Priority under No Child Left Behind? What punitive actions will occur if your school does not meet Adequate Yearly Progress this year? What about next year?
- How secure are the district's financial resources? For charter and private schools, how diversified are your funding sources?
- For charter schools, when is your charter up for renewal?
- Is your district's student assignment plan going to be modified in the near future?
- What natural disasters is your school community most susceptible to? Is your school geographically close to a place of great symbolic value?
- Is your school secure from unwanted visitors?
- How geographically close is your school to law enforcement or other emergency services? Do you know the leadership from the local police district and their procedures in the event of a violence event?

### STEP 4: PLANNING FOR PREDICTABLE INTERNAL CRISES

You have now identified your school community's core values and foundational practices, as well as the potential threats they might encounter. Table A.3 allows you to explore potential *Internal* crises through the four crisis response phases: (1) Early Warning Signs and Uptake, (2) School Preparation and Primary Prevention, (3) Damage Control and Secondary Prevention, and (4) Community Recovery and Learning. At the bottom of each cell, rate your school's current capacity to secure the necessary resources and implement the crisis response on a scale of None (Doesn't exist/no access) to 4 (Excellent). We have provided enough space to detail five Internal crises, but feel free to photocopy this table to use for additional crisis planning. An example is provided for you.

We recognize that this exercise may be difficult to complete for a highly unlikely or somewhat unlikely crisis. Nonetheless, the biggest danger is to be completely caught off-guard. Therefore, we encourage you to walk through as many of these phases for as many of the Internal crises as possible. It may be that you can only get as far as developing early warning signs and uptake strategies for more nuanced crises.

**Table A.3. Planning for Internal-Predictable Crises**

| Internal Crisis | Phase 1: Early Warning Signs and Uptake | Phase 2: School Preparation and Primary Prevention | Phase 3: Damage Control and Secondary Prevention | Phase 4: Community Recovery and Learning |
|---|---|---|---|---|
| **Example:** Grade-fixing by a teacher or counselor | 1) Auditing procedures<br>2) Students questionably passing? | 1) Communicate with district leadership<br>2) Review other potential fraud | 1) Communicate with parents<br>2) Legal action against teacher/counselor | 1) Review auditing procedures<br>2) Clearly communicate grading/graduation standards |
| Current Capacity | 0 1 2 [3] 4 | 0 1 2 3 [4] | 0 1 [2] 3 4 | [0] 1 2 3 4 |
| #1 | | | | |
| Current Capacity | 0 1 2 3 4 | 0 1 2 3 4 | 0 1 2 3 4 | 0 1 2 3 4 |
| #2 | | | | |
| Current Capacity | 0 1 2 3 4 | 0 1 2 3 4 | 0 1 2 3 4 | 0 1 2 3 4 |
| #3 | | | | |
| Current Capacity | 0 1 2 3 4 | 0 1 2 3 4 | 0 1 2 3 4 | 0 1 2 3 4 |
| #4 | | | | |
| Current Capacity | 0 1 2 3 4 | 0 1 2 3 4 | 0 1 2 3 4 | 0 1 2 3 4 |
| #5 | | | | |
| Current Capacity | 0 1 2 3 4 | 0 1 2 3 4 | 0 1 2 3 4 | 0 1 2 3 4 |

Current capacity: 0 = none; 1 = low; 2 = moderate; 3 = acceptable; 4 = excellent

**STEP 5: PLANNING FOR EXTERNAL-PREDICTABLE CRISES**

Table A.4 (located on page 261) allows you to explore each potential *External* crisis. In the bottom of the cell, rate your school's current capacity to secure the necessary resources and implement the crisis response from None (Doesn't exist/no access) to 4 (Excellent). An example is provided for you.

**STEP 6: GENERAL SCHOOL PREPARATION
FOR UNPREDICTABLE CRISES**

*Unpredictable* crises are, by their nature, threats for which a school cannot directly prepare. These are not accountability issues on a time line or a new student assignment plan to be implemented in August. Instead, these are crises that hit on a random Tuesday afternoon. Without the capacity to prepare for the precise threat, schools can only prepare for an *Unpredictable* crisis by building a strong school community. What basic steps could you take today that would prepare your school community to successfully deal with an *Unpredictable* crisis? Below are a series of questions designed to help school leaders discern the capacity of their general school preparation.

A. Internal Culture
   1. Do all school stakeholders know, understand, and emulate the school's core values?
   2. Are all students held to high expectations?
   3. Do all members of the school community feel empowered to contribute to the school's core values?
   4. Are you and your leadership team engaged in daily school life (i.e., accessible and frequently a physical presence in classrooms and the hallways), or do you spend the majority of the time in your office? More importantly, are you *viewed* as accessible by students and staff when they have concerns?
B. School Faculty
   1. How often, and in what ways, do teachers meet and communicate with each other?
   2. Do you have a stable teaching force/administrative team or is turnover high?

**Table A.4. Planning for External-Predictable Crises**

| External Crisis | Phase 1: Early Warning Signs and Uptake | Phase 2: School Preparation and Primary Prevention | Phase 3: Damage Control and Secondary Prevention | Phase 4: Community Recovery and Learning |
|---|---|---|---|---|
| **Example:** | | | | |
| New Student assignment | 1) School board discussion 2) Demographics of potential new incoming students | 1) Educate teachers on incoming students 2) Connect with new community resources 3) Contact students' previous school(s) | 1) Closely monitor adjustments of school staff teacher/counselor 2) Change to a more appropriate curriculum | 1) Form Parent Advisory Council to maintain community communication |
| Current Capacity | 0 1 2 3 [4] | 0 1 2 3 [4] | 0 1 2 [3] 4 | 0 [1] 2 3 4 |
| #1 | | | | |
| Current Capacity | 0 1 2 3 4 | 0 1 2 3 4 | 0 1 2 3 4 | 0 1 2 3 4 |
| #2 | | | | |
| Current Capacity | 0 1 2 3 4 | 0 1 2 3 4 | 0 1 2 3 4 | 0 1 2 3 4 |
| #3 | | | | |
| Current Capacity | 0 1 2 3 4 | 0 1 2 3 4 | 0 1 2 3 4 | 0 1 2 3 4 |
| #4 | | | | |
| Current Capacity | 0 1 2 3 4 | 0 1 2 3 4 | 0 1 2 3 4 | 0 1 2 3 4 |
| #5 | | | | |
| Current Capacity | 0 1 2 3 4 | 0 1 2 3 4 | 0 1 2 3 4 | 0 1 2 3 4 |

Current capacity: 0 = none; 1 = low; 2 = moderate; 3 = acceptable; 4 = excellent

3. How often, and in what ways, do teachers meet and communicate with the administration? How often, and in what ways, do teachers meet and communicate with each other? Around which issues?
4. What tasks, outside of teaching, are teachers involved in on a regular basis (e.g., peer evaluation, mentoring, providing training sessions)?
C. Families and the Community
   1. How often and in what ways are parents updated about school events/news?
   2. How often are parents invited to the school and for what types of events?
   3. Do you have an open-door policy with the families you serve? Is it utilized?
   4. How does the school communicate news/events with the larger neighborhood/area?
   5. Does the school have a connection to local businesses?
D. School Bureaucracy
   1. Is someone from the school in attendance at important school board and central office meetings?
   2. Does the school have a powerful advocate with the district office or school board?
E. General Crisis Preparation
   1. Does the school have an evacuation plan that is practiced at least three times per year?
   2. Do families know where to pick up their students in the event of an evacuation?
   3. Does the school have a lockdown plan that is practiced at least three times per year?
   4. Do you meet with local law enforcement and the fire department annually? Does your second-in-command?
   5. Is there a commonly known and accepted "chain of command" so that, in the event that a leader is incapacitated, the school does not face a leadership vacuum?
   6. Can the school's evacuation site adequately cope with a high volume of anxious parents?
   7. Are there preplanned counseling and mental health resources on which you can depend in the event of an emergency?

F. Communication
   1. Through which primary methods would you communicate with your
      school staff quickly in an emergency?
   2. What is the backup to this communication medium?
   3. Do you have an efficient way of communicating quickly with parents/
      guardians?
   4. Do you maintain accurate emergency cards? Are duplicates of these
      kept off-campus?
   5. Does your leadership team carry each other's phone numbers, those
      of the central office, and other emergency numbers on their person at
      all times?

# Endnotes

**PREFACE**

1. Rudolph, B., & Garcia, C. J. (1986, February 24). Coping with catastrophe. *Time, 127*(8), 53.

2. Frenz, H. (Ed.). (1969). *Nobel lectures 1901–1967.* Amsterdam: Elsevier Publishing Company.

**CHAPTER 1**

1. Small, W. J. (1991). Exxon Valdez: How to spend billions and still get a black eye. *Public Relations Review, 17*(1), 9–25; Pearson, C., & Mitroff, I. (1993). From crisis prone to crisis prepared: A framework for crisis management. *Academy of Management Executive, 7*(1), 48–59.

2. Pearson, C., & Clair, J. (1998). Reframing crisis management. *Academy of Management Review, 23*(1), 59–76.

3. Mitroff, I. (2004). *Crisis leadership: Planning for the unthinkable.* New York: John Wiley & Sons.

4. Pollard, D., & Hotho, S. (2006). Crises, scenarios, and the strategic management process. *Management Decision, 44*(6), 721–36; Snyder, P., Hall, M., Robertson, J., Jasinski, T., & Miller, J. S. (2006). Ethical responsibility: A strategic approach to organizational crisis. *Journal of Business Ethics, 63,* 371–83.

5. Pauchant, T., & Mitroff, I. (1992). Recent research in crisis management: A study of 24 authors' contributions from 1986 to 1991. *Industrial and Environmental Crisis Quarterly, 7*(1), 43–66.

6. Fearn-Banks, K. (1996). *Crisis communications: A casebook approach* (second ed.). Mahwah, NJ: Lawrence Erlbaum Associates.

7. Pearson, C., & Clair, J. (1998). Reframing crisis management. *Academy of Management Review, 23*(1), 59–76.

8. Snyder, P., Hall, M., Robertson, J., Jasinski, T., & Miller, J. S. (2006). Ethical responsibility: A strategic approach to organizational crisis. *Journal of Business Ethics, 63*, 371–83.

9. LaPorte, T. R. (2007). *The politics of crisis management: Public leadership under pressure* [Review of the book *The politics of crisis management*]. *International Public Management Journal, 10*(1), 111–17.

10. Smith, D. (2005). Business (not) as usual: Crisis management, service recovery and the vulnerability of organizations. *The Journal of Service Marketing, 19*(5), 309–20.

11. Hanusheck, E. (1997). Assessing the effects of school resources on student performance: An update. *Educational Evaluation and Policy Analysis, 19*(2), 141–64.

12. Smith, M. S., & O'Day, J. (1990). Systemic school reform. *Journal of Education Policy, 5*(5), 233–67.

13. Hill, P. (2003). What's wrong with public education governance in big cities and how should it be fixed? In W. L. Boyd & D. Miretzky (Eds.), *American educational governance on trial: Change and challenges, 102nd yearbook of the National Society for the Study of Education* (pp. 57–81). Chicago: University of Chicago Press; Hannaway, J. (2003). Accountability, assessment, and performance issues: We've come a long way . . . or have we? In W. L. Boyd and D. Miretzky (Eds.), *American educational governance on trial: Change and challenges, 102nd yearbook of the National Society for the Study of Education* (pp. 20–36). Chicago: University of Chicago Press.

14. VanGundy, A. (1979). *A model of crisis decision making in organizations.* Washington, DC: National Inst. of Education (DHEW).

15. Boyd, W. L., & Crowson, R. L. (1981). The changing conception and practice of educational administration. In D. C. Berliner (Ed.), *Review of Research in*

*Education* (Vol. 9, pp. 311–73). Washington, DC: American Educational Research Association.

16. Dillard, H. (1989). Winnetka: One year later. *Communique, 17*(8), 17–20; King, K. (2001). Developing a comprehensive school suicide prevention program. *Journal of School Health, 71*(4), 132–38; Klicker, R. L. (2000). *A student dies, a school mourns: Dealing with death and loss in the school community.* Philadelphia: Accelerated Development; MacNeil, G., & Stewart, C. (2000). Crisis intervention with school violence problems and volatile situations. In A. R. Roberts (Ed.), *Crisis intervention handbook: Assessment, treatment, and research* (pp. 229–49). New York: Oxford University Press; Sandall, N. (1986). Early intervention in a disaster: The Cokeville hostage/bombing crisis. *Communique, 15*(2), 1–2; Trump, K. S. (2000). *Classroom killers? Hallway hostages? How schools can prevent and manage school crises.* Thousand Oaks, CA: Corwin Press; Wanko, M. A. (2001). *Safe schools: Crisis prevention and response.* Lanham, MD: Rowman & Littlefield Education; Watson, R. J., Poda, J. H., Miller, C. T., Rice, E. S., & West, G. (1990). *Containing crisis: A guide to managing school emergencies.* Bloomington, IN: National Educational Service; Watson, R. J., & Watson, R. S. (2002). *The school as a safe haven.* Westport, CT: Bergin & Garvey.

17. Selznick, P. (1948). Foundations of the theory of organization. *American Sociological Review, 13*(1), 25–35.

18. Augustine, N. (2000). Managing the crisis you tried to prevent. In *Harvard Business Review on Crisis Management.* Cambridge, MA: Harvard Business School Press.

19. *Ibid.*; Hale, J. E., Hale, D. P., & Dulek, R. E. (2006). Decision process during crisis response: An exploratory investigation. *Journal of Managerial Issues, 18*(3), 301–20.

20. Simola, S. (2005). Concepts of care in organizational crisis prevention. *Journal of Business Ethics, 62,* 341–53.

21. *Ibid.*; Knox, K. S., & Roberts, A. R. (2005). Crisis intervention and crisis team models in schools. *Children & Schools, 27*(2), 93–100.

22. Zaleznik, A. (1977, May–June). Managers and leaders: Are they different? *Harvard Business Review,* 67–78.

23. Both the National Center for Crisis Management and a partnership between the U.S. Secret Service and U.S. Department of Education have produced handbooks

describing how to effectively create a threat assessment and response team for schools. See Fein, R., Vossekuil, B., Pollack, W. S., Borum, R., Modzeleski, W., & Reddy, M. (2004, July). *Threat assessment in schools: A guide to managing threatening situations and to creating safe school climates.* United States Secret Service and United States Department of Education, Washington, DC; and Lerner, M. D., Lindell, B., & Volpe, J. (2003). *A practical guide for crisis response in our schools* (fifth ed.). New York: American Academy of Experts in Traumatic Stress.

24. Simola, S. (2005). Concepts of care in organizational crisis prevention. *Journal of Business Ethics, 62,* 341–53.

25. Paraskevas, A. (2006). Crisis management or crisis response system? A complexity science approach to organizational crises. *Management Decision, 44*(7), 892–907.

26. Pollard, D., & Hotho, S. (2006). Crises, scenarios, and the strategic management process. *Management Decision, 44*(6), 721–36.

27. Mitroff, I. (1988). Crisis management: Cutting through the confusion. *Sloan Management Review, 29*(2), 15–20.

28. Boin, A., Hart, P., Stern, E., & Sundelius, B. (2005). *The politics of crisis management: Public leadership under pressure.* New York: Cambridge University Press.

29. Beck, L., & Foster, W. (1999). Administration and community: Considering challenges, exploring possibilities. In J. Murphy and K. Seashore Louis (Eds.), *Handbook of research on educational administration* (second ed., pp. 337–57). San Francisco: Jossey-Bass; Blau, P. M., & Scott, W. R. (1962). *Formal organizations: A comparative approach.* San Francisco: Chandler; Boyd, W. L. (2003). Public education's crisis of performance and legitimacy: Introduction and overview of the yearbook. In W. L. Boyd and D. Miretzky (Eds.), *American educational governance on trial: Change and challenges, 102nd yearbook of the National Society for the Study of Education* (pp. 1–19). Chicago: University of Chicago Press; Cook, S., & Yannow, D. (1993). Culture and organizational learning. *Journal of Management Inquiry, 2*(4), 373–90; Furman, G. C., & Starratt, R. J. (2002). Leadership for democratic community in schools. In J. Murphy (Ed.), *The educational leadership challenge: Redefining leadership for the 21st century, 101st yearbook of the National Society for the Study of Education* (pp. 105–33). Chicago: University of Chicago Press; Leithwood, K., Leonard, L., & Sharratt, L. (1998). Conditions fostering

organizational learning in schools. *Educational Administration Quarterly, 34*(2), 243–76; Lugg, C. A., Bulkley, K., Firestone, W. A., & Garner, C. W. (2002). The contextual terrain facing educational leaders. In J. Murphy (Ed.), *The educational leadership challenge: Redefining leadership for the 21st century, 101st yearbook of the National Society for the Study of Education* (pp. 20–41). Chicago: University of Chicago Press; Marks, H. M., & Louis, K. S. (1999). Teacher empowerment and the capacity for organizational learning. *Educational Administration Quarterly, 35*(Suppl.), 707–50; Schein, E. H. (1985). *Organizational culture and leadership.* San Francisco, CA: Jossey-Bass.

30. Lortie, D. (1975). *School-teacher: A sociological study.* Chicago: University of Chicago Press.

### CHAPTER 2

1. NCES Common Core of Data (CCD), Public Elementary/Secondary School Universe Survey, 1999–2000 v.1b, 2000–2001 v.1a, 2001–2002 v.1a, 2002–2003 v.1a, 2003–2004 v.1a.

2. The Broad Prize for Urban Education District Fact Sheet. Retrieved January 22, 2009, from www.broadprize.org/asset/1097-2007newyorkbrief.pdf.

3. Hamilton, Linnae (Producer, Director, Editor). (2007). *Our school* [DVD]. (Available from Mighty Media, Inc., 101 Wooster Street, New York City, New York 10012).

4. *Ibid.*

5. *Ibid.*

### CHAPTER 3

1. Maxwell, L. A. (2007, October 3). Up from the ruins: State and district leaders are fighting to rebuild and repair New Orleans' schools. *Education Week.* Retrieved November 4, 2008, from www.edweek.org/login.html?source=www.edweek.org/ew/articles/2007/10/03/06nolafacilities.h27.html&destination=www.edweek.org/ew/articles/2007/10/03/06nolafacilities.h27.html&levelId=2100.

2. Tough, P. (2008, August 17). A teachable moment. *The New York Times.* Retrieved September 17, 2008, from www.nytimes.com/2008/08/17/magazine/17NewOrleans-t.html.

3. Louisiana Department of Education. (2006, February). District composite report 2004–2005: Orleans Parish. Retrieved November 1, 2008, from www .louisianaschools.net/lde/pair/DCR0405/DCR036.pdf; Recovery School District legislatively required plan. (2006, June 7). Retrieved November 1, 2008, from www .louisianaschools.net/lde/uploads/8932.doc.

4. Louisiana Department of Education. (2006, February). District composite report 2004–2005: Orleans Parish. Retrieved November 1, 2008, from www .louisianaschools.net/lde/pair/DCR0405/DCR036.pdf; Tough, P. (2008, August 17). A teachable moment. *The New York Times.* Retrieved November 1, 2008, from www .nytimes.com/2008/08/17/magazine/17NewOrleans-t.html.

5. Louisiana Department of Education. (2006, February). District composite report 2004–2005: Orleans Parish. Retrieved November 1, 2008, from www .louisianaschools.net/lde/pair/DCR0405/DCR036.pdf.

6. Recovery School District legislatively required plan. (2006, June 7). Retrieved November 1, 2008, from www.louisianaschools.net/lde/uploads/8932.doc.

7. *Ibid.*

8. NOLA Public Schools. (2007, July). Frequently asked questions about the Recovery School District. Retrieved November 1, 2008, from www.louisianaschools .net/lde/uploads/8947.pdf.

9. Knabb, R. D., Rhome, J. R., & Brown, D. P. (2005, December 20). Tropical cyclone report: Hurricane Katrina. 23–30 August 2005. Updated August 10, 2006. National Hurricane Center. Retrieved November 4, 2008, from www.nhc.noaa .gov/pdf/TCR-AL122005_Katrina.pdf; Murphy, V. (2005, October 4). Fixing New Orleans' thin gray line. *BBC News.* Retrieved November 1, 2008, from news.bbc .co.uk/2/hi/americas/4307972.stm; Tidwell, M. (2006). *The ravaging tide: Strange weather, future Katrinas, and the coming death of America's coastal cities.* New York: Free Press.

10. Maxwell, L. A. (2008, June 4). As year ends, questions remain for New Orleans. *Education Week.* Retrieved November 4, 2008, from www.edweek.org/ login.html?source=www.edweek.org/ew/articles/2008/06/04/39nola_ep.h27 .html&destination=www.edweek.org/ew/articles/2008/06/04/39nola_ep.h27 .html&levelId=2100.

11. Tough, P. (2008, August 17). A teachable moment. *The New York Times.* Retrieved September 17, 2008, from www.nytimes.com/2008/08/17/magazine/ 17NewOrleans-t.html.

12. Robelen, E. W. (2007, November 14). New teachers are New Orleans norm: Hundreds of fresh recruits, many of them new to K–12 teaching, are filling public school classrooms across the city in Katrina's aftermath. *Education Week.* Retrieved November 4, 2008, from www.edweek.org/login.html?source=www.edweek.org/ew/articles/2007/11/14/12nolahuman.h27.html&destination=www.edweek.org/ew/articles/2007/11/14/12nola-human.h27.html&levelId=2100/.

13. *Ibid.*

14. Maxwell, L. A. (2008, April 8). Playing catch up: Plenty of academic programs, but uneven progress, mark New Orleans' recovery district. *Education Week.* Retrieved November 4, 2008, from www.edweek.org/ew/articles/2008/04/09/32nolainstruction_ep.h27.html.

15. Plyer, A. (2008, August 21). New data reveals 16 New Orleans neighborhoods have less than half their pre-Katrina households. Retrieved February 21, 2009, from gnocdc.s3.amazonaws.com/media/GNOCDCAug21-08.pdf.

**CHAPTER 4**

1. Colorado Department of Education Fall 2006 Pupil Membership by District, School, Grade, Race/Ethnicity, and Gender. Retrieved December 9, 2008, from www.cde.state.co.us/cdereval/download/PDF/2006PM/School/06SCHOOLREGGRADE.pdf.

2. Colorado Department of Education Fall 2006 K–12 Free and Reduced Lunch by District and School. Retrieved December 9, 2008, from www.cde.state.co.us/cdereval/download/PDF/2006PM/School/06K-12FREDCorrected.pdf.

3. Platte Canyon School District Annual Report to the Public December 1, 2007. Retrieved December 9, 2008, from www.plattecanyonschools.org/currentinfo/annual_report_2007.pdf.

4. Willett, A., & Huspeni, D. (2006). Gunman assaulted girls before killing himself. Retrieved December 10, 2008, from www.gazette.com/articles/morrison-10664-school-girls.html.

5. Sheriff: School shooter sent letter to say sorry. (2006). Retrieved December 10, 2008, from www.cnn.com/2006/US/09/29/school.shooting/index.html.

6. Willett, A., & Huspeni, D. (2006) Gunman assaulted girls before killing himself. Retrieved December 10, 2008, from www.gazette.com/articles/morrison-10664-school-girls.html.

7. Redlener, I., Grant, R., Abramson, D., & Johnson, D. (2008). *The 2008 American preparedness project: Why parents may not heed evacuation orders & what emergency planners, families and schools need to know.* New York: National Center for Disaster Preparedness.

8. Wong, M. (2004). Terrorism and disasters: Crisis recovery. Powerpoint retrieved December 10, 2008, from www.schenectady.k12.ny.us/SchoolClimateInitiatives/Recovery/wongterrorism.ppt.

## CHAPTER 5

1. Bracey, G. (2007, October). The first time "everything changed": The 17th Bracey Report on the Condition of Public Education. *Phi Delta Kappan, 89*(6), 119–36.

2. Smith, D. (2005). Business (not) as usual: Crisis management, service recovery and the vulnerability of organizations. *Journal of Services Marketing, 19*(5) 309–20.

3. Kotter, J. (1996). *Leading change.* Cambridge, MA: Harvard Business School Press; Kotter, J., & Cohen, D. (2002). *The heart of change.* Cambridge, MA: Harvard Business School Press.

4. Kouzes, J., & Posner, B. (2007). *The leadership challenge* (fourth ed.). Hoboken, NJ: Jossey-Bass; Kotter, J. (1996). *Leading change.* Cambridge, MA: Harvard Business School Press.

5. Kouzes, J., & Posner, B. (2007). *The leadership challenge* (fourth ed.). Hoboken, NJ: Jossey-Bass; Kotter, J. (1996). *Leading change.* Cambridge, MA: Harvard Business School Press.

6. Boyd. W. (July 1999). Environmental pressures, management imperatives, and competing paradigms in educational administration. *Educational Management & Administration, 27*(3), 283–97; Tyack, D., & Cuban, L. (1996). *Tinkering toward Utopia.* Cambridge, MA: Harvard University Press.

7. Kouzes, J., & Posner, B. (2007). *The leadership challenge* (fourth ed.). Hoboken, NJ: Jossey-Bass.

## CHAPTER 6

1. The NCES Common Core of Data (CCD), Public Elementary/Secondary School Universe Survey, Selected Years 1987–1988 through 2006–2007.

2. New York State Education Department. (2007). *The New York State school report card accountability and overview report, 2006–07*. Retrieved January 13, 2009, from www.nystart.gov/publicweb-rc/2007/01/AOR-2007-421800010031.pdf.

3. Birnkrant, S. (personal communication, June 18, 2008).

4. The NCES Common Core of Data (CCD), Local Education Agency Universe Survey, 2006–2007.

5. The New York State Office of the State Comptroller. (December, 2004). Population trends in New York State's cities. Retrieved August 23, 2009, from www .osc.state.ny.us/localgov/pubs/research/pop_trends.pdf.

6. The New York State School Report Card 2006–2007; turnover rate of all teachers is 4 percent, 5 percent, and 11 percent in 2004, 2005, and 2006, respectively.

7. For example, see the Pew Research Center for the People & the Press. (2006). No consensus on immigration problem or proposed fixes: America's immigration quandary. Retrieved January 13, 2009, from people-press.org/reports/pdf/274 .pdf; Where black and brown collide. (2007, August 4). *Economist, 384,* 34; Sieh, M. (2008, July 27). Breaking down the barriers. *Metro Voices.* Retrieved January 14, 2009, from blog.syracuse.com/metrovoices/2008/07/new_program_wants_to_build _bri.html.

8. Blalock, E. M. (2008). Camp intervention at H.W. Smith Elementary School. *Post-Standard Video Archives.* Retrieved January 13, 2009, from blog.syracuse .com/video/2008/07/_ellen_m_blalock_219.html; Students sweltering in the heat of 6/9/08. (2008, June 9). WSYR ABC 9 Syracuse. Retrieved January 13, 2009, from www.clipsyndicate.com/publish/video/618109/students_sweltering_in_the_heat_6 _9_08?wpid=1277.

9. Mariani, J. (2008, May 9). Syracuse student found to have TB. *The Post-Standard Daily Newspaper.* Retrieved February 15, 2009, from www.syracuse.com/ poststandard/stories/index.ssf?/base/news-14/1210323538227530.xml&coll=1.

10. Lehman, D. V., & Eno, O. (2002, February). The Somali Bantu: Their history and culture. *The Center for Applied Linguistics.* Retrieved January 30, 2009, from www.cal.org/co/bantu/sbintro.html.

11. Lehman, D. V., and Eno, O. (2002, February). The Somali Bantu: Their history and culture. *The Center for Applied Linguistics.* Retrieved January 30, 2009, from www.cal.org/co/bantu/sbcult.html.

12. New York State Education Department. (2007). *The New York State school report card accountability and overview report, 2006–07*. Retrieved January 13, 2009, from www.nystart.gov/publicweb-rc/2007/01/AOR-2007-421800010031.pdf.

13. Zehr, M. A. (2008, April 30). Schools brace for Bhutanese wave. *Education Week, 27*(35), 1, 14–15; Talk of the nation. (2004, February 5). Reconsidering No Child Left Behind. Retrieved January 13, 2009, from www.npr.org/templates/story/story.php?storyId=1644511.

14. Somalia's struggle for stability. (2008, August 25). *PBS: The Online NewsHour.* Retrieved January 24, 2009, from www.pbs.org/newshour/indepth_coverage/africa/somalia/timeline/.

15. Lehman, D. V., & Eno, O. (2002, February). The Somali Bantu: Their history and culture. *The Center for Applied Linguistics.* Retrieved January 30, 2009, from www.cal.org/CO/bantu/sbpeop.html.

16. Lehman, D. V., & Eno, O. (2002, February). The Somali Bantu: Their history and culture. *The Center for Applied Linguistics.* Retrieved January 30, 2009, from www.cal.org/co/bantu/sbhist.html.

17. Lehman, D. V., & Eno, O. (2002, February). The Somali Bantu: Their history and culture. *The Center for Applied Linguistics.* Retrieved January 30, 2009, from www.cal.org/co/bantu/sbintro.html.

18. Lehman, D. V., & Eno, O. (2002, February). The Somali Bantu: Their history and culture. *The Center for Applied Linguistics.* Retrieved January 30, 2009, from www.cal.org/CO/bantu/sbpeop.html.

## CHAPTER 7

1. Allensworth, E., Ponisciak, S., & Mazzeo, C. (2009, June). *The schools teachers leave: Teacher mobility in Chicago Public Schools.* Consortium on Chicago School Research at the University of Chicago's Urban Education Institute.

2. Illinois ACORN. (2005, February 14). Here one year, gone the next. Retrieved January 15, 2009, from www.acorn.org/fileadmin/ACORN_Reports/ACORN_turnover_study.pdf.

3. Allensworth, E., Ponisciak, S., & Mazzeo, C. (2009, June). *The schools teachers leave: Teacher mobility in Chicago Public Schools.* Consortium on Chicago School Research at the University of Chicago's Urban Education Institute.

4. Chicago Public Schools, Office of Research, Evaluation and Accountability. Retrieved December 7, 2008, from research.cps.k12.il.us/resweb/qt.

5. Chicago Public Schools, Office of Research, Evaluation and Accountability. Retrieved December 7, 2008, from www.cps.k12.il.us/AtAGlance.html.

6. Chicago Public Schools. *CEO's school report for the 2007–08 school year.* Retrieved November 18, 2008, from research.cps.k12.il.us.

7. Jewell, M. Ex-GE chief dishes out advice. (2006, October 14). *The Associated Press Financial Wire.* Retrieved January 25, 2009, from LexisNexis Academic database.

8. Ingersoll, Richard. (2001). Teacher turnover and teacher shortages: An organizational analysis. *American Educational Research Journal, 38*(3), 499–534.

9. Illinois ACORN. *Here one year, gone the next: Summarizing the teacher turnover data for 64 ACORN neighborhood schools, 2002–2003 to 2003–2004.* Retrieved January 22, 2009, from www.acorn.org/fileadmin/ACORN_Reports/ACORN _turnover_study.pdf.

10. Barnes, G., Crowe, E., & Schaefer, B. (2007). *The cost of teacher turnover in five school districts: A pilot study.* National Commission on Teaching and America's Future.

11. Luekens, M. T., Lyter, D. M, & Fox, E. E. (2004). *Teacher attrition and mobility: Results from the Teacher Follow-Up Survey, 2000–01.* (NCES 2004-301). Retrieved January 22, 2009, from nces.ed.gov/pubs2004/2004301.pdf.

12. The National Commission on Teaching and America's Future, cited in ACORN .org. *The costs of teacher turnover in ACORN neighborhood schools in Chicago.* Retrieved October 16, 2008, from www.acorn.org/index.php?id=321.

**CHAPTER 8**

1. Center on Education Policy. (2007). Beyond the mountains: An early look at restructuring results in California, 2007. Retrieved January 15, 2009, from www.cep-dc.org/document/docWindow.cfm?fuseaction=document.viewDocument&documentid =186&documentFormatId=3716.

2. *Ibid.*

3. Author's calculations based on data downloaded from the California Department of Education's DataQuest tool. Retrieved January 29, 2009, from dq.cde.ca.gov/ dataquest/dataquest.asp.

4. Teicher, S. A., & Arnoldy, B. (2007, March 1). Hard recovery for failed US schools. *The Christian Science Monitor*, 1.

5. Oakland Board of Education Resolution Requesting the State Superintendent of Public Instruction to Commence the Return of Governing Authority to the Oakland Board of Education by January 30, 2007. Retrieved January 15, 2009, from www .urbanstrategies.org/programs/schools/documents/ResolutionRequest_001.pdf.

6. Author's calculations based on data downloaded from the California Department of Education's DataQuest tool. Retrieved January 29, 2009, from dq.cde.ca.gov/dataquest/dataquest.asp.

7. Murphy, K. (2008, May 9). Another suspicious Sobrante Park fire. *The Education Report*. Retrieved January 15, 2009, from www.ibabuzz.com/ education/2008/05/09/another-suspicious-sobrante-park-fire/.

8. Author's calculations based on data downloaded from the California Department of Education's DataQuest tool. Retrieved January 29, 2009, from dq.cde.ca.gov/dataquest/dataquest.asp. In the 2002–2003 school year the State of California replaced the Stanford 9 with another assessment, making longitudinal comparison before and after this year difficult.

9. California Department of Education. NCLB Program Improvement School Requirements. Retrieved January 15, 2009, from www.cde.ca.gov/ta/ac/ti/nclbpireq .asp.

10. Center on Education Policy. (2007). *Beyond the mountains: An early look at restructuring results in California, 2007*. Retrieved January 15, 2009, from www.cepdc .org/document/docWindow.cfm?fuseaction=document.viewDocument&documentid =186&documentFormatId=3716.

11. NovoMetro.com. (2006, September 18). What to know what's really going on in Oakland Unified? Ask a teacher. Retrieved January 15, 2009, from novometro .wordpress.com/2006/09/18/want-to-know-whats-really-going-on-in-oakland -unified-ask-a-teacher/.

12. Herman, R., Dawson, P., Dee, T., Greene, J., Maynard, R., Redding, S., & Darwin, M. (2008). *Turning around chronically low-performing schools: A practice guide*. (NCEE #2008-4020). Washington, DC: National Center for Education Evaluation and Regional Assistance, Institute of Education Sciences, U.S. Department of Education. Retrieved February 24, 2009, from ies.ed.gov/ncee/wwc/ practiceguides.

## CHAPTER 9

1. Hendrie, C. (1998, June 17). A Denver high school reaches out to the neighborhood it lost to busing. *Education Week, 17*(40), 22–23.

2. Horn, C. L., & Kurlaender, M. (2006). *The end of Keyes: Resegregation trends and achievement in Denver Public Schools.* Cambridge, MA: The Civil Rights Project at Harvard University; *Keyes v. School District No. 1,* 413 U.S. 189 (1973). Retrieved November 25, 2008, from supreme.justia.com/us/413/189/.

3. The NCES Common Core of Data (CCD), Public Elementary/Secondary School Universe Survey, 1990–1991 and 1991–1992.

4. The NCES Common Core of Data (CCD), Public Elementary/Secondary School Universe Survey, 1990–1991 and 1991–1992; Nicotera, S. (personal communication, July 31, 2008).

5. Hendrie, C. (1998, June 17). A Denver high school reaches out to the neighborhood it lost to busing. *Education Week, 17*(40), 22–23.

6. Bush, G. W. (2004, October). The essential work of democracy. *Phi Delta Kappan, 86*(2), 114.

7. Hendrie, C. (1998, June 17). A Denver high school reaches out to the neighborhood it lost to busing. *Education Week, 17*(40), 22–23.

8. Frankenberg, E., & Lee, C. (2002, August). *Race in American public schools: Rapidly resegregating school districts.* Cambridge, MA: The Civil Rights Project, Harvard University. Retrieved November 25, 2008, from www.civilrightsproject.ucla.edu/research/deseg/Race_in_American_Public_Schools1.pdf; Orfield, G. (1999, Fall). The resegregation of our nation's schools: A troubling trend. *Civil Rights Journal, 4,* 8–12.

9. Frankenberg, E., & Lee, C. (2002, August). *Race in American public schools: Rapidly resegregating school districts.* Cambridge, MA: The Civil Rights Project, Harvard University. Retrieved November 25, 2008, from www.civilrightsproject.ucla.edu/research/deseg/Race_in_American_Public_Schools1.pdf.

10. Orfield, G. (1999, Fall). The resegregation of our nation's schools: A troubling trend. *Civil Rights Journal, 4,* 8–12.

11. *A proposal to accelerate the ongoing renewal of Manual High School: Small schools at Manual.* (2001, April). Retrieved November 2, 2008, from www.elpueblointegral.org/Small%Schools%Proposal%to%DPS.pdf.

12. *Ibid.*

13. *Ibid.*

14. Leithwood, K., Louis, K. S., Anderson, S., & Wahlstrom, K. (2004). *How leadership influences student achievement.* Center for Applied Research and Educational Improvement and Ontario Institute for Studies in Education.

15. Educational Leadership Policy Standards: ISLLC 2008. (2008). The Council of Chief State School Officers, Washington DC.

16. Viadero, D. (2006). Scholars test out new yardsticks of school poverty. *Education Week, 26*(11), 1–15.

17. Nicotera, S. (personal communication, July 31, 2008).

18. *A proposal to accelerate the ongoing renewal of Manual High School.* (2001, February). Retrieved November 2, 2008, from www.elpueblointegral.org/Small %Schools%Proposal.pdf.

19. *Ibid.*

20. Hendrie, C. (1998, June 17). A Denver high school reaches out to the neighborhood it lost to busing. *Education Week, 17*(40), 22–23.

21. Yettick, H. (2002, December 6). Stepping up to the plate. *Rocky Mountain News,* 2S.

22. Nicotera, S. (personal communication, July 31, 2008).

23. Lee, V., & Ready, D. (2006). *Schools within schools: Possibilities and pitfalls of high school reform.* Columbia University: Teachers College Press.

## CHAPTER 10

1. Allen, J., & Marcucio, A. (2005). *The simple guide to charter school laws: A progress report.* Washington, DC: The Center for Education Reform.

2. Garrigan, L. (2007, March 22). Best foes forever. *Nashville Scene.* Retrieved January 30, 2009, from www.nashvillescene.com/2007-03-22/news/best-foes -forever/; Charter schools have their place [Editorial]. (2007, June 21). *Nashville City Paper.* Retrieved January 29, 2009, from nashvillecitypaper.com/news .php?viewStory=56782.

3. Tennessee Department of Education. *Report card 2007.* Retrieved January 30, 2009, from edu.reportcard.state.tn.us/pls/apex/f?p=200:40:2446366489884001::NO.

4. Tennessee Department of Education. *Report card 2007.* Retrieved January 30, 2009, from edu.reportcard.state.tn.us/pls/apex/f?p=200:1:163081503399649::NO.

5. USDA Economic Research Service. *County-level unemployment and median household income for Tennessee.* Retrieved January 30, 2009, from www.ers.usda.gov/data/unemployment/RDList2.asp?ST=TN.

6. Garrigan, L. (2006, September 21). Pedro Garcia vs. a few good kids. *Nashville Scene.* Retrieved January 25, 2009, from blogs.nashvillescene.com/pitw/2006/09/pedro_garcia_vs_a_few_good_kid.php.

7. Sarrio, J. (2006, November 28). Denied once, charter schools will try again. *The Tennessean,* p. 1A.

8. Kerr, G. (2007, April 22). Charter school has big dreams. *The Tennessean,* p. 1B.

9. T.C.A. § 49-13-108.

10. State of Tennessee Department of Education. (2008). Application for Public Charter School Charter. Retrieved January 30, 2009, from www.tennessee.gov/education/fedprog/doc/fpchartschapp08.pdf.

11. Maynord, A. (2006, October 16). Charter school review meetings will be open. *Nashville City Paper.* Retrieved January 31, 2009, from www.nashvillecitypaper.com/news.php?viewStory=57784.

12. Williams, J. (2007). Games charter opponents play. *Education Next, 7*(1), 12–18.

13. Maynord, A. (2007, April 18). Charter school can't lease empty Metro classrooms. *Nashville City Paper.* Retrieved January 29, 2009, from nashvillecitypaper.com/news.php?viewStory=55723.

14. LEAD Charter Application, p. 146.

15. Garrigan, L. (2007, March 22). Best foes forever. *Nashville Scene.* Retrieved January 30, 2009, from www.nashvillescene.com/2007-03-22/news/best-foes-forever/; Maynord, Amanda. (Undated). Charter school issues grow as hope of leasing space dies. *Nashville City Paper.* Retrieved January 30, 2009, from www.nashvillecitypaper.com/news.php?viewStory=55881.

16. Garrigan, L. (2006, September 21). Pedro Garcia vs. a few good kids. *Nashville Scene.* Retrieved January 25, 2009, from blogs.nashvillescene.com/pitw/2006/09/pedro_garcia_vs_a_few_good_kid.php.

17. Williams, J. (2007). Games charter opponents play. *Education Next, 7*(1), 12–18.

18. *Ibid.*

**CHAPTER 11**

1. Kahlenberg, R. (2008, March 26). The charter school idea turns 20. *Education Week, 27*(29), 24.

2. Tyack, D., & Cuban, L. (1996). *Tinkering toward Utopia.* Cambridge, MA: Harvard University Press.

3. Minard, R., Jr. (2004, December). *Understanding state aid FY05 & FY06.* New Hampshire Center for Public Policy Studies.

4. Economic & Labor Market Information Bureau, NH Employment Security, 2008. Retrieved October 11, 2008, from www.nh.gov/nhes/elmi/htmlprofiles/franklin.html

5. *Ibid.*

6. Ober, Gail. (2008, March 9). Saving a school: Struggle to keep Franklin Academy alive continues. Retrieved October 11, 2008, from www.fosters.com/apps/pbcs.dll/article?AID=/20080309/GJNEWS02/508271782/0/CITNEWS.

7. Quinton, A. (2005, June 17). Franklin Charter School future uncertain. New Hampshire Public Radio. Retrieved October 11, 2008, from the New Hampshire Public Radio database, www.nhpr.org/node/9032.

8. Quinton, A. (2005, April 19). Franklin school board wants charter revoked. New Hampshire Public Radio. Retrieved October 11, 2008, from the New Hampshire Public Radio database, www.nhpr.org/node/8625.

9. See also Dornin, C. (2008, June 12). Charter school founder blames state for closing. *New Hampshire Business Review.*

10. Tyack, D., & Cuban, L. (1996). *Tinkering toward Utopia.* Cambridge, MA: Harvard University Press.

11. Williams, J. (2007). Games charter opponents play. *Education Next, 7*(1), 1.

12. Bennis, W., Goleman, D., & O'Toole, J. (2008). *Transparency.* Hoboken, NJ: Jossey-Bass.

13. New Hampshire Department of Education, Division of Program Support, Bureau of Data Management. (2008, April 4). *State average cost per pupil and total expenditures 2006–2007.* Retrieved January 14, 2009, from www.ed.state.nh.us/ education/data/financial.htm.


## CHAPTER 12

1. *Sandy Springs, Georgia.* Retrieved December 1, 2008, from en.wikipedia.org/wiki/ Sandy_Springs,_Georgia.

2. All data from United States Bureau of the Census and United States Department of Agriculture Economic Research Service.

3. U.S. Census Bureau. Retrieved December 1, 2008, from factfinder.census .gov/servlet/ADPTable?_bm=y&-qr_name=ACS_2007_1YR_G00_DP3&-geo _id=16000US1368516&-ds_name=ACS_2007_1YR_G00_&-_lang=en&-redoLog=false.

4. *Ibid.*

5. United States Census. (2000). *Fulton County, Georgia.* Retrieved December 1, 2008, from factfinder.census.gov/servlet/QTTable?_bm=n&_lang=en&qr _name=DEC_2000_SF1_U_DP1&ds_name=DEC_2000_SF1_U&geo _id=05000US13121.

6. Augustine, N. (2000). Managing the crisis you tried to prevent. In *Harvard business review on crisis management* (pp. 1–32). Cambridge, MA: Harvard Business School Press.

7. Kotter, J. (1996). *Leading change.* Cambridge, MA: Harvard Business School Press.


## CHAPTER 13

1. Fried, B. (personal communication, July 16, 2008).

2. The New York State Department of Education. (2008). *The New York state report card: Comprehensive information report 2006–07.* Retrieved November 1, 2008, from www.nystart.gov/publicweb-rc/2007/97/CIR-2007-332100011540.pdf.

3. Hemphill, C., & Nauer, K. (2009). The new marketplace: How small-school reforms and school choice have reshaped New York City's high schools. The Center for New York City Affairs. Retrieved June 17, 2009, from www.newschool.edu/ milano/nycaffairs/documents/TheNewMarketplace_Report.pdf.

4. Smith, M. S., & O'Day, J. (1990). Systemic school reform. *Journal of Education Policy*, 5(5), 233–67.

## CHAPTER 14

1. Smith, D. (2005). Business (not) as usual: Crisis management, service recovery and the vulnerability of organizations. *The Journal of Service Marketing*, 19(5), 309–20; Smith, M. S., & O'Day, J. (1990). Systemic school reform. *Journal of Education Policy*, 5(5), 233–67.

2. Devlin, E. (2006). *Crisis management planning and execution.* Boca Raton, FL: Auerbach Publications.

3. Kotter, J. P. (2006). *Leading change.* Cambridge, MA: Harvard Business School Press; Yukl, G. (1998). *Leadership in organizations* (fourth ed.). Upper Saddle River, NJ: Prentice Hall.

4. Burns, J. M. (1978). *Leadership.* New York: Harper & Row.

5. Lortie, D. (1975). *Schoolteacher* (second ed.). London: The University of Chicago Press.

6. Smith, M. S., & O'Day, J. (1990). Systemic school reform. *Journal of Education Policy*, 5(5), 233–67.

7. Trice, H. M., & Beyer, J. M. (1993). *The cultures of work organizations.* Englewood Cliffs, NJ: Prentice Hall.

8. Lefcourt, H. M. (1976). *Locus of control: Current trends in theory and research.* Hillsdale, NJ: John Wiley & Sons, Inc.

9. Zaleznik, A. (1977, May–June). Managers and leaders: Are they different? *New Hampshire Business Review*, www.nhbr.com/apps/pbcs.dll/article?AID=/20080620/ NEWS0102/442840919.

10. Kotter, J. P. (1996). *Leading change.* Cambridge, MA: Harvard Business School Press.

# About the Authors

**Matthew Pepper** currently works for the Metro-Nashville Public Schools as the coordinator of Research and Data Quality and is also on staff at the National Center on Performance Incentives at Peabody College. Dr. Pepper began his career in policy at the Tennessee Department of Education while simultaneously earning an Ed.D. in educational leadership and policy from Vanderbilt University (2007). He currently works on district data quality issues and a university-district research partnership.

**Tim London** has worked as a teacher and school administrator, both in the United States and abroad, as well as with the American Federation of Teachers and a nonprofit foundation providing educational opportunities to underserved families. Dr. London received his doctorate from Peabody College, Vanderbilt University, and is currently a teaching fellow in the School of Education at Queen's University Belfast, Northern Ireland, focusing on educational leadership. Prior to this, he was an assistant professor of educational leadership at Kennesaw State University in Georgia.

**Mike Dishman** is an associate professor of educational leadership at Kennesaw State University and an attorney whose practice has centered on the representation of public schools for more than a decade. A frequently requested speaker at state and national education conferences, Dr. Dishman writes on law, leadership, and policy in education. He is the coauthor of six books on school law and leadership. He holds a J.D. from the University of Mississippi (1996) and an Ed.D. in leadership and policy from Vanderbilt University (2007). He serves on the editorial board of the *Peabody Journal of Education,* and previously served as an assistant professor of education law and ethics at the University of Alaska (1998–2001).

**Jessica Lewis** is a research associate at the National Center on Performance Incentives (NCPI) located at Vanderbilt University's Peabody College and currently heads up NCPI's evaluations of performance incentive programs in Texas. She received her Ed.D. in educational leadership and policy from Peabody College, Vanderbilt University, and her research interests include identifying strategies to improve the quality of teaching in the public education system.

---

***The authors consider this book to be a work of joint scholarship.